MONUMENTAL DESIGNS

MONUMENTAL DESIGNS

INFRASTRUCTURE AND THE CULTURE OF THE TENNESSEE VALLEY AUTHORITY

TED ATKINSON

UNIVERSITY PRESS OF MISSISSIPPI / JACKSON

The University Press of Mississippi is the scholarly publishing agency of the Mississippi Institutions of Higher Learning: Alcorn State University, Delta State University, Jackson State University, Mississippi State University, Mississippi University for Women, Mississippi Valley State University, University of Mississippi, and University of Southern Mississippi.

www.upress.state.ms.us

The University Press of Mississippi is a member of the Association of University Presses.

Any discriminatory or derogatory language or hate speech regarding race, ethnicity, religion, sex, gender, class, national origin, age, or disability that has been retained or appears in elided form is in no way an endorsement of the use of such language outside a scholarly context.

Copyright © 2025 by University Press of Mississippi
All rights reserved
Manufactured in the United States of America
∞

Publisher: University Press of Mississippi, Jackson, USA
Authorised GPSR Safety Representative: Easy Access System Europe - Mustamäe tee 50, 10621 Tallinn, Estonia, gpsr.requests@easproject.com

Library of Congress Control Number: 2025022071
Hardback ISBN 978-1-4968-5924-2
Paperback ISBN 978-1-4968-5925-9
Epub single ISBN 978-1-4968-5926-6
Epub institutional ISBN 978-1-4968-5927-3
PDF single ISBN 978-1-4968-5928-0
PDF institutional ISBN 978-1-4968-5929-7

British Library Cataloging-in-Publication Data available

CONTENTS

ACKNOWLEDGMENTS VII

INTRODUCTION 3

CHAPTER 1. A Dam Site More Modern:
Developing TVA Monumentality in Visual Culture. 24

CHAPTER 2. Documentary Forms:
Infrastructural Inevitability in *The River* and
The Valley of the Tennessee 57

CHAPTER 3. *Power* to the People:
The Spectacular Drama of Rural Electrification 88

CHAPTER 4. Back to the Future:
Crosscurrents of Development in Elia Kazan's *Wild River* 119

CHAPTER 5. From *Flood* to *Long Man*:
The Rise of the TVA Novel. 150

CODA 179

NOTES 185

BIBLIOGRAPHY 209

INDEX 221

ACKNOWLEDGMENTS

SOMETIMES IT SEEMED LIKE BUILDING A HYDROELECTRIC DAM SINGLE-HANDEDLY WOULD have been easier than writing this book. It suffices to say that the seven years of research and writing were among the most challenging of my life, owing to circumstances ranging from the global to the familial. I am thankful to my family, chosen family, friends, and colleagues for their support during this period and always.

I am grateful to the Institute for the Humanities in the College of Arts and Sciences at Mississippi State University for awarding me a fellowship at the perfect time. The course release and financial support enabled me to finish a full draft much sooner than I would have otherwise. Dean Rick Travis's leadership and the administrative acumen of Dr. Julia Osman, the institute director, made the fellowship possible.

For sections of the first three chapters, I drew from "A Forward Glance: TVA Modernism and the Regional Designs of National Progress," my contribution to *Reassessing the 1930s South* (Louisiana State University Press, 2018). I am grateful to Sarah E. Gardner and Karen L. Cox for inviting me to participate and giving expert editorial guidance. Thanks to Katie Owens-Murphy for inviting me to deliver a lecture on TVA cultural production. Preparing to give the talk, sponsored by the University of North Alabama and the Florence-Lauderdale Public Library in Florence, Alabama, proved instrumental in formulating my ideas early on.

Working on this project with the University Press of Mississippi has been a rewarding experience. Craig Gill does an outstanding job steering the ship as director. Mary Heath and Shane Gong Stewart were encouraging and supportive editors on this project, and I appreciate their expert guidance. Pete Halverson's work in book design is impressive as always. I appreciate the time and talents of all the other UPM staff who worked on this project. Matthew Lambert and the anonymous reader gave me constructive feedback during the external review process, and the book turned out better as a result.

Hailey Reeder was my graduate assistant during the final stages of manuscript preparation. Thanks to Hailey's eagle eyes and quote-checking skills, I made corrections before it was too late.

I visited TVA facilities at Wilson Dam in Muscle Shoals, Alabama, in 2017 and appreciated officials taking time from their busy schedules to show me around and talk TVA history. In 2022, I visited Norris Dam in Norris, Tennessee, and toured the powerhouse. Patricia Bernard Ezzell, TVA Senior Specialist (History), Communications, was generous with her time and knowledge.

My mother—may she rest in peace—was a bookkeeper, and my father is an accountant. Thankfully, their preference for numbers did not prevent them from appreciating and indulging my love of words.

Writing a book can seem like solitary confinement, but I was lucky to have canine office mates—the best kind—to keep me company. Sarty and Meav were by my side until they crossed the Rainbow Bridge, and then came Archie and Ada, both stalwarts.

My husband Derek provided love, encouragement, and perspective as I worked on this book, as he does in life. I am thankful for that beyond measure.

MONUMENTAL DESIGNS

INTRODUCTION

ON MARCH 4, 1933, PRESIDENT FRANKLIN DELANO ROOSEVELT DELIVERED HIS FIRST inaugural address, echoing many of the themes he had used en route to a landslide victory over Herbert Hoover. Famously, Roosevelt declared that "the only thing we have to fear is fear itself—nameless, unreasoning, unjustified terror which paralyzes needed efforts to convert retreat into advance."[1] The rhetorical performance reflected the president's psychological warfare against economic depression as he mobilized uplift to restore public confidence in the US economy and the financial and governmental institutions deemed essential to its recovery. About a month later, Roosevelt proposed one of several new additions to the existing lineup of federal agencies. In a dispatch to Congress, the president urged lawmakers to pass legislation to create the Tennessee Valley Authority (TVA). The congressional response was swift, thanks to a solid bloc of support for FDR's agenda and a sense of urgency due to the severe economic crisis. Passage of the Tennessee Valley Authority Act of 1933 laid a cornerstone of the New Deal—the bold, sweeping array of policies and programs emerging in the early months of the new administration.

The legislation apportioned an area within the US South comprising Tennessee and parts of Virginia, North Carolina, Kentucky, Georgia, Alabama, and Mississippi to become the administrative purview of the new agency. There is truth in the popular expression that scores of people in this section of the country had suffered from economic hardship and social ills for so long that the collective response to the hard times of the 1930s could be expressed in the simple question often attributed to them anecdotally: what depression? The TVA agenda included a host of action items to redress decades of uneven development by rehabilitating the region according to the standards of progress in the governing philosophy of New Deal liberalism. In keeping with Roosevelt's martial rhetoric, the plan was to advance the TVA march on multiple fronts. For years, severe flooding because of deforestation and erosion had wreaked havoc on the Tennessee Valley. The loss of property was considerable; the loss of life was tragic. Routine outbreaks of malaria due to mosquito-infested standing water compounded the postflood devastation. The litany of debilitating economic, environmental, and social symptoms were endemic to a chronic condition influencing the common perception of the region as an outlier within the nation.

The TVA was conceived as a rapid response to the national state of emergency. As such, it deployed federal resources to achieve several goals. The primary focus was on the Tennessee River and its tributaries, where the construction of a network of dams, reservoirs, and power stations ensued. The extensive infrastructural development was designed to tame and remake the wild river by implementing flood control measures to save lives and property and improve inland waterway navigation to boost industry and commerce. A major objective was to generate hydroelectric power as a cheap and abundant energy source, making the TVA integral to a national push to expand rural electrification. Part of the plan for the Tennessee Valley was to facilitate economic recovery through modernization and development in the short term and give rural people ongoing access to the bevy of conveniences (and indulgences) of the modern consumer economy their urban counterparts already enjoyed. The TVA defined additional pursuits under the category of regional development: (1) promote sustainable agricultural practices based on the latest research to reverse the course of soil erosion and land degradation caused by decades of monoculture crop production; (2) enact social and economic reforms to alleviate poverty and improve health, hygiene, and education. The ambitious and controversial plans grounded in the belief that the federal government should guide the nation through troubled waters while setting the course for a more stable and prosperous future rendered the Tennessee Valley Authority a microcosm of the New Deal state. The TVA expanded in the decades following the Great Depression and

World War II. At this point, it is the largest public power company in the United States, providing electricity to more than ten million people in a bastion of political and cultural conservatism.

SETTING THE STAKES

The overarching objective of *Monumental Designs* is to present a cultural history of the Tennessee Valley Authority that examines representations of the agency in selected works from the New Deal era to the present. The TVA was successful at the outset because of the vital role culture played in promoting the near-total transformation of the Tennessee Valley through infrastructural development as part of a larger ideological and economic investment in public works. The dams were at the core of this undertaking; the majority were built between the formation of the TVA in 1933 and the end of World War II. An aura of monumentality suffused these structures, conveying their impressive symbolic and technological capabilities. Throughout this period, the TVA was at pains to portray the process as a natural development in geologic time and modernity. The sense of continuity complemented an emphasis on symmetry: clean lines, sharp angles, and smooth facades achieved through modernist architectural design were presented as evidence of harmonious integration into the existing landscape. Temporal and spatial measures helped chart the teleological path to the formation of the TVA, becoming a rhetorical staple of official narratives disseminated in the public sphere. To garner support from local people, members of Congress, and the public at large, the TVA mobilized cultural production to blend elements of local history and lore and the American mythos with a patented imprint of futurity defined by a sense of higher purpose and abiding faith in science, technology, and ingenuity as hallmarks of progress.

As discussed in the first three chapters of *Monumental Designs*, the phase of state-sponsored cultural production in the 1930s and 1940s emerged from some in-house projects but more often from cooperation with other New Deal agencies supporting arts and culture. This practice also extended to strategic partnerships with public institutions such as the Museum of Modern Art in New York and with venerable publishing houses in the private sector. The result was a body of work drawn from various mediums: architectural design; photography; documentary films and photobooks; mural paintings; theater; arts and crafts; and graphic design. While the content was geared toward promoting the TVA agenda, the artists working individually or in collaboration engaged with movements and figures on the domestic and international fronts to create cultural forms with aesthetic sophistication and appeal. TVA cultural production waned in the postwar years, as agencies and programs developed under the banner of the New Deal faced either sharp funding cuts or elimination. Yet this short-lived convergence of art and propaganda exerted influence in terms of formal innovations that eventually became standard practices in the various disciplines involved.

The culture that the TVA fostered provided material for subsequent generations of writers, filmmakers, artists, and musicians, especially those invested in portraying the Tennessee Valley's transformation with greater nuance and complexity than their predecessors working under federal patronage could manage. As the last two chapters demonstrate, these works have registered strong support, fierce opposition, and ambivalence in response to the TVA over time. In some cases, they operate as counternarratives by interrogating the logic and rupturing the temporal rhythms of infrastructural development, chiefly in the mode of historical fiction set in the New Deal era or infused with historical consciousness attuned to that period. A common practice involves shifting the focus from pro-TVA rhetoric to the upheaval and dislocation experienced by local people and the damaging environmental impacts of dam construction on a large scale. The historical and cultural context of this phase encompasses the transition to coal-fired plants as consumer demand far exceeded the capacity of hydropower and jeopardized the promise of ample and affordable electricity. Curiously, depictions of this major development are virtually nonexistent in fiction or film. Instead, the dams remain focal points, serving as infrastructural means of providing structural support to narrative frameworks. Nevertheless, a critical approach attentive to the material and symbolic functions of infrastructural development in selected texts produced since the New Deal era makes it possible to trace an ongoing process of constructing and contesting the Tennessee Valley as a cultural region defined by the

TVA's image of modernity and futurity. So far this body of work has attracted some scholarly attention, leaving plenty of room for additional contributions.[2] Developments in the fields this study most directly engages—critical infrastructure studies, the energy humanities, and US southern studies—offer useful theoretical and critical approaches and concepts for exploring the archive of TVA culture and appreciating the relevance and intellectual value of the artifacts.

The cultural project of making the Tennessee Valley an inflection point of rural modernity ran contrary to received notions about the more expansive regional designations to which it belongs, namely, Appalachia and the US South. Instead of dwelling on stock images and narratives of abject poverty and despair, hidebound customs, and fierce resistance to the federal government, the TVA worked to recast the valley as a demonstration site for presenting public works and neoteric economic, social, and environmental policies and practices as mechanisms for regional rehabilitation to aid national recovery. As *Monumental Designs* makes clear, this formulation was no less ideologically circumscribed than regional imaginaries steeped in idyllic agrarianism or Lost Cause nostalgia or those shaped by using southern exceptionalism as ballast for American exceptionalism to cast the regressive region as the progressive nation's internal Other. Indeed, the cultural initiatives were part of a concerted effort to sway public opinion and hold up the TVA as a model worthy of emulation. For this reason, the area apportioned to the TVA is a constructive geographical and critical framework for examining national and transnational associations and influences at local and regional scales—a network animated and sustained by forms of cultural expression.

The establishment of the TVA came at a critical point in history. The conditions of the Great Depression prompted a reassessment of core institutions, policies, and values considered elemental to the US brand of entwined democracy and capitalism. The Tennessee Valley was integral to this effort because of a comprehensive plan developed with scientific and technological innovation and economic development as guiding principles. That remained the case over time, as the TVA exerted considerable influence in expanding and exporting the public works model of regional rehabilitation elsewhere in the nation and the developing world. Consultations between TVA officials and representatives from the governments of India, China, Brazil, and Iran among others have been instrumental in the proliferation of massive hydroelectric dams based on the theory that infrastructural development is a fast track to closing the gap of uneven development defining relations between the Global North and the Global South for decades.

On the energy front, the TVA's rapid shift to coal-fired electricity illustrates deepening fossil-fuel dependence in the decades after World War II. On a related note, the important role the agency played in the production of the atomic bomb under the auspices of the Manhattan Project, its uneven record in experimenting with nuclear power, and its recent forays into renewable energy sources and natural gas have also shaped modes of energy production and consumption—for better or worse. Amid the catastrophic effects and willful denials of climate change as an anthropogenic force of nature, the New Deal inspired the Green New Deal—a similarly ambitious but embattled millennial heir to its predecessor because of the power and influence of the fossil fuels industry and entrenchment across an intractable political divide. During the Biden administration, the TVA made a public commitment to transitioning from coal as part of a long-range plan to reduce carbon emissions substantially. Not surprisingly, the pledge drew fire from Big Coal and environmental organizations, with the former concerned about the bottom line and the latter leveling charges of foot-dragging on renewable energy alternatives. The plan to make natural gas production a significant part of the TVA energy formula has garnered industry support and sparked public protests in the areas most directly affected. As political debates about infrastructure hinge on the related issues of energy policy, modernization, and economic development, *Monumental Designs* operates on the principle that reflecting on the enduring culture the Tennessee Valley Authority produced amid a global economic crisis is an illuminating exercise at this critical juncture.

TERMS OF ENGAGEMENT

Focusing on the Tennessee Valley Authority through the lens of cultural history makes *Monumental Designs* responsive to ongoing critical discussions in US southern studies about the efficacy, scope, and scale of a regional framework. At the center of a longstanding and sometimes contentious debate is "*the* South"—the monolithic conception that defined a nascent discipline in the post–World War II academy and remained the organizing principle for decades. Native-born status, religiosity, community, sense of place, rural folkways, the burden of history, and whiteness as the default racial setting became markers deemed essential (in every sense of the word) for an authentic claim to the "Southern" mantle. Among cultural conservatives, the imperative to apply strict standards derived from concern about imperiled regional distinctiveness. Anxieties about cultural erasure intensified as calls for accelerated modernization and development grew stronger with the onset of the economic crisis and the formation of the TVA and other New Deal agencies and programs. Eventually, critics began to expose the limits of this ideological framing and propose more inclusive practices. A case in point is Michael Kreyling's *Inventing Southern Literature*. Kreyling employs Benedict Anderson's theory of "imagined community" to expose "the South" as constructed rather than naturally occurring, forming from exclusionary practices by intellectual elites—namely, the Southern Agrarians—to establish their idea of the region as the standard measure.[3]

By the turn of the new millennium, the critical project of interrogating foundational terms, assumptions, and geographical boundaries emerged. In 2001, the assessment that "a new southern studies is long past due" turned out to be a galvanizing moment, courtesy of Houston Baker Jr. and the rhetoric of impatience.[4] For the purpose at hand, the most relevant strain from this critical discourse is the question of scale. Much of the scholarly work aligned with the new southern studies has relied on the region/nation model.[5] But more expansive perspectives have placed the region in illuminating hemispheric, transatlantic, and global contexts.[6] All the scaling up and down has led to intensified scrutiny of "South" as a critical concept. Jon Smith posits that it "increasingly appears to be an unhelpful scalar unit: far better to work at a larger scale (the nation, conservatism, plantation America) or a smaller one (consumer culture in Mississippi, desegregation in Atlanta or Milwaukee.)"[7] Leigh Anne Duck observes that individuals and groups assigned a regional identity tend to defy the supposedly fixed characteristics. After questioning whether an understood regional identity is necessary for sound critical practice, Duck supplies a speculative and provocative response: "The idea of Southern studies without the 'The South' may sound absurd, but exiting the realm of our most basic assumptions can occasionally prove enlightening."[8] Martyn Bone cautions against dropping the US South as a scalar unit, citing Neil Smith's influential work on uneven development to argue that a wider or more granular perspective is not necessarily more revealing than a regional one. Instead, Bone proposes a case-by-case method: "Depending on the object of (literary) study, the appropriate scalar unit might be more or less local, regional, or (trans)national; it might require too a dialectical 'jumping' between scales."[9] The object of study in *Monumental Designs* dictates the relatively small-scale setting, meaning that the TVA service area proves more useful than the US South for delineating the primary regional concern. But moving between scales also accounts for the profound local impacts, complex dynamics between region and nation, and transnational exchanges and influences entailed in the TVA enterprise and the culture it produced.

When constructing a critical framework for examining TVA cultural history, scholarship in infrastructure studies is a valuable resource. *Monumental Designs* takes a cue from the question that Patricia Yaeger poses about human emplacement in the built environments of modern cities rendered in material and fictional forms: "What is it like to be stuck, night and day, dreaming of infrastructure?"[10] The urban-centric focus of the special issue occasioning Yaeger's prompt does not preclude raising the same question about the largely rural environs covered by the TVA.[11] In this context, it conjures competing images of people longing for more leisure time made possible by rural electrification or beset by unsettling dreams as imminent dam construction forced compliance with the terms of eminent domain and TVA relocation programs. As the last two chapters of this study demonstrate, the experiences of upheaval and displacement became material for dramatic and sympathetic portrayals in works of fiction and film not beholden to New Deal patronage. While the administrators, architects, engineers, and construction crew workers were not stuck per se, they were in pursuit of a collective dream as they strove to implement the grand designs of infrastructural development. Such a heightened sense of purpose may seem at odds with what Michael Rubenstein, Bruce Robbins, and

Sophia Beal describe as the "boringness of infrastructure."[12] Similarly, the abstract and utilitarian tenor of Brian Larkin's frequently cited definition suggests an inherent lack of allure: "Infrastructures are built networks that facilitate the flow of goods, people, or ideas and allow for their exchange over space."[13] As such, infrastructural elements constitute "architecture for circulation, literally providing the undergirding of modern societies, and they generate the ambient environment of everyday life."[14] A challenge for TVA advocates and the creative people hired to develop compelling public appeals was to find the right balance between embellishing infrastructure with aesthetic and rhetorical flair to enhance interest and convey public meaning and making the fit seem so natural that the built environment could virtually fade into the contours of quotidian existence.

The dual objectives entailed in the TVA's public-facing profile resonate with an ongoing discussion in infrastructure studies about (in)visibility. In "The Ethnography of Infrastructure," Susan Leigh Star concentrates on the relational and ecological aspects of infrastructure to demonstrate that it means different things to different people, depending on the location and sector of society they inhabit. For Star, a defining feature of modern infrastructure is that it can seem "by definition invisible" until it ceases to function properly, at which point it demands immediate and urgent attention.[15] Scholars have tended to highlight this assertion at the expense of noting an important stipulation in Star's discussion of infrastructural awareness: taking infrastructure for granted is not an option for people displaced from their land and homes, living close enough to facilities that their lives are disrupted and degraded, or lacking easy or equal access to the basic services supposedly available to all. Larkin points out that invisibility is only one dimension in "a range of visibilities that move from unseen to grand spectacles and everything in between," adding that the goal should not be to argue that infrastructure is either visible or not "but to examine how (in)visibility is mobilized and why."[16] Rubenstein, Robbins, and Beal propose "infrastructuralism" as a mode of analyzing texts that "try to make infrastructure, as well as its absence, visible."[17] But Jessica Hurley and Jeffrey Insko observe that work outside literary and cultural studies has shown that "the visibility/invisibility paradigm" is quite limited; therefore, they echo the call to develop more effective ways of seeing and understanding infrastructure.[18] *Monumental Designs* stakes out a position amid these alternatives by focusing on the hypervisibility of infrastructure in cultural representations of the TVA in the New Deal era and beyond. In considering the complex material, aesthetic, and ideological implications, this study develops a line of inquiry within the parameters that Hurley and Insko set when describing US cultural history as a "rich archive of materials for a critical project that seeks to trace the genealogies and theorize the imagined futures enabled (or foreclosed) by infrastructure."[19]

In key respects, *Monumental Designs* aligns with studies of cultural forms that convey the material and symbolic aspects of infrastructure as part of public works: defining the parameters of state authority and intervention; registering collective aspirations and anxieties of futurity and modernity; and delivering (or failing to deliver) services deemed essential for modern life and for a sense of belonging that extends from the local to the national. Rubenstein traces the origins to Adam Smith's *The Wealth of Nations*, explaining that "public works are loosely defined as a kind of social imperative, a set of necessary institutions for any 'great society.'"[20] In this capacity, public works operate within capitalism but beyond the profit motive as they provide institutional support to the profit-driven machinations of the economic system.[21] The indelible mark of Smith's conceptualization was apparent in the congressional authorization of the TVA. The measure bestowed the unique and unprecedented designation of "federal corporation," enabling the agency to operate as a nonprofit electricity provider in the same market as private utility companies. Although not under the administrative umbrella of the Public Works Administration (PWA), also established in 1933, the TVA joined that agency in epitomizing the professed commitment to innovation and expansion that made public works a signature of the New Deal national recovery effort.

The network of TVA dams and reservoirs eventually spanning the Tennessee Valley was influential in setting the high expectations for economic stimulus attached to such projects. Jeff Diamanti explains the logic underwriting such projects: "Whether new, refurbished, or expanded, infrastructure has always functioned as a kickstarter for macroeconomic recovery, leading (so this fantasy goes) to long-term growth."[22] However, the heavy investment in dam construction to spur economic expansion altered the geographical and ecological conditions of the valley to a degree that is hard to overstate. In *Silenced Rivers: The Ecology and Politics of Large Dams*, Patrick McCully describes the effects:

> Nothing alters a river as totally as a dam. A reservoir is the antithesis of a river—the essence of a river is that it flows, the essence of a reservoir that it is still. A wild river is dynamic, forever changing—eroding its bed, depositing silt, seeking a new course, bursting its banks, drying up. A dam is monumentally static; it tries to bring a river under control, to regulate its seasonal pattern of floods and low flows. A dam traps sediments and nutrients, alters the river's temperature and chemistry, and upsets the geological processes of erosion and deposition through which the river sculpts the surrounding land.[23]

The consequential scale of dams made them centerpieces in cultural representations of the TVA from the start. Whether dominating the frames produced in photographs and films, enhancing special effects as projections onto scrims in stage productions, or challenging muralists to convey massive stature on a smaller scale, dams stood as expressions of towering achievement. This aspect of TVA cultural production was in keeping with the idea of *"art as grandeur"* Sharon Ann Musher cites as one of several ways to understand art funded by the New Deal state.[24]

The main reason for this representation scheme was the awareness on the part of officials and advocates that it would be advantageous to imbue infrastructure with public meaning to maximize operational capacity. McCully observes that "big dams have been potent symbols of both patriotic pride and the conquest of nature by human ingenuity," signifying progress for most of the twentieth century.[25] Accordingly, the TVA dams built for flood control, hydropower generation, and economic development became emblems of national resolve that registered democratic responses to similar infrastructural development plans in Germany, Italy, and the Soviet Union. As impressive feats of architectural design and technological prowess, the dams represented control over volatile forces of nature and economics heretofore impervious to human intervention. Such strategies were part of a concerted aesthetic and ideological initiative to make infrastructure seen in mass culture as a multivalent source of power "Built for the People" to provide "Electricity for All," as two prominent slogans declared. Nevertheless, as the works from the post–New Deal, postwar phase emphasize, opponents of the TVA, especially those most adversely affected by infrastructural development, were hard-pressed to see the dams in this light. Instead, they loomed large as ominous and imposing structures, conveying in material and symbolic form the unwelcome hand of federal overreach and the destabilizing forces of dislocation, cultural erasure, and ecological harm. In sum, as documented in the ensuing chapters, the public meaning ascribed to the dams through symbolic measures has not been cohesive but rather contested in the annals of cultural history.

Just as the hope for economic recovery in the near term and sustained growth in the long term were projected onto the TVA dams, so was faith in their technological capability to generate an ample supply of electricity at a relatively low cost for years to come. That this service was sold along with a program to replenish the land and promote soil conservation enhanced the appeal, diverting attention away from the potential for environmental damage. The promise of abundant electricity was pervasive in pro-TVA cultural production, as demonstrated by the representative works examined in this study. This legacy confirms how readily Frederick Buell's observation that "energy history is significantly entwined with cultural history" applies.[26] Once again, guidance from Yaeger helps refine the critical perspective—in this instance, through her insistence that "thinking about literature [and, by implication, other mediums] through the lens of energy, especially the fuel basis of economies, means getting serious about modes of production as a force field for culture."[27] In the case of the TVA, the initial force field was grounded in hydroelectricity as cultural expression empowered the fantasy of virtually limitless supply at low cost. The subsequent replacement of hydropower with coal-fired power in the infrastructural network was an effort to keep pace with demand so that the fantasy could remain intact. However, the dismantling of the New Deal cultural apparatus made the task increasingly more difficult as the harmful effects of coal dependence became apparent.

Curiously, depictions of the TVA in literature and culture from the postwar period to the present have remained narratively invested in the hydropower era signified by dams.[28] Granted, depictions of the hydroelectric fantasy usually accentuate the idealism of TVA agents and advocates who could not envision the destructive reversal of fortune that audiences now know was coming soon. Nevertheless, the preoccupation with returning to the mode of energy production that fleetingly prevailed in the New Deal era means that traces of the TVA's decades-long status as a prime locus of what Yaeger describes as this country's "constant entanglement with dirty energy" do not tend to register explicitly in cultural properties.[29] The dearth of representation calls to mind Imre Szeman's claim that "instead of challenging the fiction of surplus—as we might have hoped or expected—literature participates in it just as surely as every other social narrative in the contemporary era."[30] Szeman encourages urgent speculation in fiction about what happens if an energy surplus gives way to a deficit. "Contemplating energy futures prompts us to reflect on what we desperately need in our literary present: narratives that shake us out of our faith in surplus (there will always be more; things will always be better)," Szeman writes.[31] While the point is well taken, it is important to emphasize that contemplating *past* energy futures can have a similarly jarring effect. To that end, a cultural history of the TVA affords an instructive view of the modern faith in surplus taking shape and needing scrutiny—then and still.

MYTHIC PROPORTIONS: RECONSTRUCTING A CULTURAL REGION

Noting the inherent paradox in the federal corporation status, Senator George Norris, the progressive Republican from Nebraska who had first proposed an idea along the lines of the TVA in 1926, asked FDR how he planned to explain the strange hybrid to the American people. "I'll tell them it's neither fish nor fowl," the president answered, "but whatever it is, it will taste awfully good to the people of the Tennessee Valley."[32] Despite the geographic specificity, Roosevelt was careful in public not to pitch the project as a boon solely for the region. During his campaign, Roosevelt laid the groundwork for the TVA by defining public utilities as a yardstick for measuring fair and affordable rates for electricity nationwide.[33] With this model, the president anticipated arguments made by a vocal anti-TVA contingent including members of Congress and representatives of private utility companies. The latter decried what they perceived as unfair competition. The opposition complained that the cost of rehabilitating and modernizing the region far outweighed the benefits to the nation. Wendell Wilkie, who would run against FDR as the Republican nominee in 1940, stated the case succinctly as a zero-sum proposition, speaking as a corporate lawyer hired by private companies: "The Tennessee River flows through seven states and drains the nation."[34] Roosevelt was accustomed to addressing this complaint, having done so since his message to Congress, in which he called for immediate action "in the service of the people" defined as a national entity.[35]

The first step in making the TVA a reality involved repurposing existing infrastructure to become the foundation for subsequent construction on a large scale. The starting point was Muscle Shoals, Alabama, where Wilson Dam and the industrial site for which it generated hydroelectric power were originally built during the mobilization for World War I. Since the end of the war, the facilities sat idle despite periodic interest from potential investors such as the automobile magnate Henry Ford, who outlined an impressive plan that never materialized. Ford's vision paled in comparison to the one Roosevelt laid out in grandiose terms. The president claimed that the refitted Muscle Shoals operation was "but a small part of the potential usefulness of the entire Tennessee River. Such use, if envisioned in its entirety, transcends mere power development."[36] The aspiration of reaching beyond material concerns to fulfill a greater mission was key to the public appeal that enabled the TVA to assume mythic proportions as it moved from the planning stages to implementation. As William U. Chandler explains in his assessment at the fifty-year mark, "the history of the TVA rivals the myth of Hercules" in that the demi-god's ability to carve mountains in half and to defeat the river god Achelous parallel the capacity to claim dominion over nature and channel its resources toward human progress.[37] That Chandler was compelled to write in the lofty register that the TVA preferred when addressing the public demonstrates the mythic potency.

As Erwin C. Hargrove explains in *Prisoners of Myth: The Leadership of the TVA, 1933–1990*, the self-manufactured myth of the TVA was a major asset for many years but became an impediment as economic, environmental, and political conditions changed in subsequent decades. The time frame established in *Monumental Designs* accords with Hargrove's periodization comprising three distinct phases and the onset of a fourth. The first is the creation phase, running from FDR's call and the congressional response in 1933 to 1945 when changes precipitated by World War II set a new course for the postwar years. In the second period, 1945–1970, the TVA became a major power company increasingly reliant on coal to meet steadily rising consumer demand.[38] The third period, approximately 1970 to 1988, was distinguished by "the search for new missions to keep the TVA heroic" and by the fact that leaders were yoked to the idea of a mythic endeavor even though the political climate made federal action in the grand style of the New Deal untenable.[39] Hargrove draws from Philip Selznick's early work on the organizational culture to enumerate the ideological elements of the TVA myth: (1) insistence on the capacity for independent decision-making relatively free from the constraints of centralized bureaucracy in Washington; (2) belief that "the people," defined as local governments, groups, and individuals, must be participants in programs; (3) understanding that the agency was the coordinator of local, state, and federal policies and programs.[40] That TVA leaders seemed bound to these tenets and thus reluctant to adapt to changing conditions contrasts with the emphasis on innovation and transformation as signature features of the endeavor.

The cultivation of the TVA myth was in keeping with the vision of remaking the Tennessee Valley as a cultural region.[41] The strategy proceeded from the mindset articulated in Rupert B. Vance's *Human Geography in the South*, originally published in 1932: "The region which begins as a great complex of physical forces ends by being so reshaped by the human groups which occupy it that it emerges as a cultural product."[42] In the preface, Vance describes the intervening period between the first edition of his study in 1932 and the second in 1935 as encompassing "the creation of a great regional laboratory in the Tennessee Valley Authority."[43] Indeed, the TVA's experimental bent resonated with core tenets proposed by Vance and concepts developed in Howard W. Odum's *Southern Regions of the United States*.[44] These two academics were colleagues at the Institute for Research in Social Science at the University of North Carolina, Chapel Hill. Their work and that of others in the social sciences influenced the architects of the New Deal, who were persuaded by the argument that a new understanding of regionalism pointed to a way forward from the chronic sectionalism that had defined antagonistic relations between the South and the nation. Vance explains that regional planning involves steering "all regional changes and readjustments toward a desirable goal. This goal is determined after a consideration of both natural and cultural forces."[45] Wary of utopian thinking, Vance points out that "a survey of the region-as-is is followed by a blue print of the region as it can be reconstructed."[46] However, officials knew they would likely face local pushback if people perceived the TVA as delivering top-down mandates from Washington. That is one reason for the reiteration of the "grassroots" bona fides of the operation in TVA cultural production and public remarks by agency officials.

The TVA brand of regional planning is encapsulated in *TVA: Democracy on the March*, the 1944 memoir in which David E. Lilienthal took stock just over a decade removed from the launch. Lilienthal served with Arthur E. Morgan and Harcourt A. Morgan (no relation) on a board of directors appointed by President Roosevelt in 1933.[47] Lilienthal recognized the serious challenges posed by thinking along regional lines to organize national initiatives. Accordingly, his memoir acknowledges the concern that regionalism as an organizing principle might "'Balkanize' the country" while answering the charge that it is "a kind of provincialism that divides rather than unites the country, underlining sectional animosities and obstructing a really national outlook."[48] Lilienthal maintains that lawmakers tend not to think of states when crafting federal legislation. Instead, national policies emerge from wider conflicts, producing a spirit of compromise that "represents an attempted reconciliation between the interests of the various natural regions."[49] Although he adds that this is a post–Civil War phenomenon, the specter of sectionalism haunts the upbeat assessment. Ever the optimist, however, Lilienthal avers that a fresh perspective can get rid of the ghost, enabling a model that

> affirms and insists . . . that the solution of regional problems and the development of regional resources are *matters of concern to the whole country*. It proposes to harmonize regional advancement with the national welfare. That concern for and supremacy of the national

interest distinguishes "regionalism" from "sectionalism." Under the banner of sectionalism, states throughout our history have combined to support or to oppose federal action. Under the modern concept of regionalism, the federal government acts to meet regional needs to the end that the entire nation may profit.[50]

The promise of harmony between benefitting the region and the greater good of the country and the assurance that the national interest prevails were defining principles of New Deal regionalism—a "modern idea" Lilienthal says is "embodied in the TVA."[51] To make the case, Lilienthal found the trope of the yardstick to be an effective rhetorical instrument. By 1935 he had expanded the definition to apply to patterns of mass consumption, labor policies and practices, and rural electrification.[52] In turn, government-funded cultural works cast the TVA yardstick as a replicable model capable of strengthening national unity on regional grounds.

From the standpoint of the Roosevelt administration, the Tennessee Valley was ideal for putting the theory of modern regionalism into practice as a mechanism for delivering government services to people in need. One of the strategies in reconstructing the cultural region and overcoming the legacies of sectionalism was to incorporate elements of the valley's history and culture into an appeal to a national sense of purpose. FDR's message to Congress identified the valley as foundational to the unifying American mythos. The missive aligned the initiative with modernity while conveying a sense of continuity with the past through temporal manipulation. By this logic, the arrival of the TVA to move the valley forward on a path toward progress was also "a return to the spirit and vision of the pioneer"—the storied figure from the period of settler colonialism mythologized as a pathbreaking leader in the fulfillment of Manifest Destiny.[53] If successful, the bold endeavor would demonstrate how to "march on, step by step" to join "other great natural territorial units within our borders."[54] FDR's rhetoric enlisted the vaunted pioneer as a future-oriented icon in the emergent TVA myth.

The narrative convergence helped garner political support and favorable impressions in the public sphere. James Agee's coverage of the TVA during the first two years of operations is a prime example. Born in Knoxville and reared in the Cumberland Mountain area of Tennessee, Agee had local knowledge that suited him to the role of valley correspondent. *Fortune* magazine dispatched him to cover the TVA's arrival in 1933, leading to the publication of "Tennessee Valley Authority" in the October issue.[55] Echoes of FDR sound when Agee invokes "the mountaineer," an analogous figure to the pioneer. As the embodiment of the valley's lineage and cultural heritage, he is the protagonist of a mytho-historical saga that disregards Indigenous precedents to define the onset of settler colonialism as the point of origin: "TVA has a deep but realistic respect for what it calls the native culture of the valley and, far more directly than the citizens of Knoxville, the mountaineer is a part of TVA's plans."[56] Agee's piece illustrates the allure of the TVA myth to which the author sometimes appears in thrall despite instances of skepticism and the stipulation that a sound assessment cannot truly begin until Norris, the first new dam in the network, is operating at full capacity. Describing the "somewhat Utopian gleam in the eye" of an anthropomorphized TVA, Agee explains the desired balance between the Jeffersonian ideal of agrarian democracy and "the Power Age."[57] In further echoes of FDR, Agee describes the process in heightened language: "In this enormous machine the balance wheel is human. And here TVA becomes almost mystical in its earnestness and speaks of preserving and developing the native culture."[58] Agee's coverage set the stage for the wider reception that David E. Whisnant describes: "For most of its first two decades, liberals and progressives were almost unanimous in celebrating TVA as the most idealistic and comprehensive planning effort ever attempted in the United States."[59] Sections of Agee's "Tennessee Valley Authority" formed a virtual template for practitioners of the New Deal arts commissioned to promote the TVA.

Although formidable, the mythic power did not shield the TVA from criticism, particularly from detractors with roots in the region. A vociferous critic early on was poet Donald Davidson, one of the Twelve Southerners responsible for *I'll Take My Stand*—the noted pro-agrarian, anti-industrialization manifesto published in 1930—and later a diehard among the Southern Agrarians. In *The Attack on Leviathan*, published in 1938, Davidson issued a scathing indictment of central planning signified by the titular metaphor. The sense of urgency was due to the rapid implementation of modern regionalism under the New Deal—nowhere faster than in Davidson's native Tennessee Valley.[60] In 1948, a few years after the TVA's creation phase, Davidson extended the critique in the second volume of *The Tennessee*, his narrative history of the Tennessee Valley. The timeline in the subtitle, "Civil War to TVA," encompasses a pattern of historical resonances between what the author defines as comparable federal incursions. In some respects, Davidson's account is a rejoinder to Lilienthal's *TVA: Democracy on the March*, published four years earlier—not least because Davidson paints the young director as a defender of the bureaucratic faith. As in Agee's *Fortune* articles, Davidson employs elevated language, albeit in a mock epic tone that portrays the mindset as hubristic rather than heroic. Davidson recounts that the three directors appointed by FDR had unprecedented power to install "his Majesty Kilowatt II," the imperious embodiment of TVA infrastructure and hydropower, as the ruler of the "new river" and valley.[61] Where the teleological path forged in TVA cultural production conveys an air of inevitability, Davidson emphasizes irreversibility due to the political consequences of admitting anything short of success. "*They could not afford to make a mistake*," Davidson writes, further reinforcing the idea of hubris by accusing TVA officials of "playing God to the Tennessee Valley."[62] Surpassing the tonal heights of the TVA mythmaking he mimics, while echoing Agee's nuptial analogy, Davidson longs for the voice of "an exultant poet" like Percy Bysshe Shelley to mark the occasion, for "the wedding of the Tennessee and Kilowatt was expected to produce about the same utopian results as Shelley's symbolic union of Prometheus and the nymph Asia."[63] Although the TVA did not employ "an exultant poet," it effectively deployed creative talent to voice the expectation of "utopian results" and tout the many tangible improvements to the region that the TVA delivered. In so doing, cultural production helped amass a reservoir of public favor that would last for decades.

The volume held steady, for the most part, until the 1960s, the latter part of the second phase of the TVA defined by Hargrove. The ill-fated Tellico Dam and Land Between the Lakes recreational development projects (discussed in chapters 4 and 5) were key factors. The environmental consequences of coal dependence were a more critical concern. Harry M. Caudill's "The Rape of the Appalachians," published in the April 1962 issue of *Atlantic Monthly*, exemplifies the pointed criticism. Hailing from the Cumberland Plateau, Caudill was a Kentucky legislator whose staunch support of the TVA eventually turned into stern opposition. In the article, Caudill condemns the agency for abandoning its original grassroots mission and instead doing the bidding of a handful of rapacious industrialists. "The TVA, mighty benefactor of the Tennessee Valley, is subsidizing the destruction of the southern mountains," he writes.[64] Caudill adds another dimension to the dire consequences: "The wrecking of the southern coalfield is a national problem, and unless a national solution is found for it soon, the harm will be irreparable."[65] Another unfavorable turn in public opinion occurred in the 1970s as the TVA used its unique public-private designation to resist clean-air regulations issued by the newly formed Environmental Protection Agency (EPA). In *The Americanization of Dixie: The Southernization of America*, John Egerton charts the timeline of what he sees as a degraded reputation from the 1930s to the 1970s: "the government's most enlightened and progressive public works agency" eventually started "drawing fire for its contributions to strip mining, water pollution, destruction of free-flowing streams, regional development schemes, and manipulation of the real estate market."[66]

The accusation that the TVA had made the region a problem for the nation by the early 1960s was an ironic turn of events. In 1938, five years after the TVA was established, the *Report on Economic Conditions of the South*, which FDR directed the National Emergency Council to compile, found that "the South presents right now the Nation's No. 1 economic problem—the Nation's problem, not merely the South's."[67] A spate of severe flooding in Eastern Kentucky in recent years and protests against proposed natural gas pipelines are among the sobering reminders that a regional solution to the national problem has yet to come. For this reason, it makes sense that journalist and activist James Branscome has channeled Caudill to demand reparations from the TVA. The implication is that the plan to break free from coal dependence in due course is insufficient compensation for the damage done. The historical irony Caudill described is compounded in Branscome's condemnation of the strip-mining that has flattened mountaintops into tabletops: "No entity is more responsible for those tabletops than the Tennessee Valley Authority, an agency created in the first 100 days of FDR's New Deal to end flooding in the Tennessee Valley."[68] The time frame Branscome defines coincides with the period of cultural history covered in this study. The chapters are organized according to medium, focusing on photography and photobooks, documentary films, New Deal theater, a fiction film, and novels. *Monumental Designs* seeks to illuminate the related forms of infrastructural development and cultural production that have made the TVA a source of multivalent power and influence. In what follows, the foray into cultural history aims to foster critical thinking about the considerable benefits and unfortunate detriments of the TVA's transformation of the valley. The operating principle is that delving into culture along these lines can yield insights into how public works came to be regarded as modern engines of progress and sources of abundant energy defined in terms of perpetual growth and development and by what authority.

Chapter 1

A DAM SITE MORE MODERN
Developing TVA Monumentality in Visual Culture

WHEN PRESIDENT-ELECT FRANKLIN DELANO ROOSEVELT ARRIVED IN SHEFFIELD, ALABAMA, on January 21, 1933, to visit the Muscle Shoals industrial site designated as the first phase of the Tennessee Valley Authority, a bipartisan congressional delegation accompanied him. Among the group of lawmakers was Senator George Norris of Nebraska, a Republican who had envisioned the TVA in 1926. Also on hand were representatives at the forefront of the push to expand rural electrification through regional development projects across the country. In extemporaneous remarks before the tour started, Roosevelt made the symbolic staging explicit: "Every single part of the United States is represented here today."[1] The president closed his short address with a statement of purpose: "We are here because the Muscle Shoals Development and the Tennessee River Development as a whole are national in their aspect and are going to be treated from a national point of view."[2] Roosevelt's emphasis on the national scope of regional development was part of a strategy to rally public support by expanding the frame of influence and beneficial outcomes.

The TVA began not with bulldozers breaking ground but with the groundbreaking acquisition of an existing facility. An industrial site constructed at Muscle Shoals in 1918 during mass mobilization for World War I consisted of two nitrate plants dedicated to manufacturing explosives and a hydroelectric dam completed in 1924. After the war, potential investors showed periodic interest in repurposing the site for commercial manufacturing during peacetime. The industrialist Henry Ford was the most high-profile figure. Ford visited the area twice in 1921, bringing his friend Thomas Edison along on the second trip for inventive good measure. The Ford deal eventually fell through, as did others, paving the way for the TVA to acquire the dam and industrial facilities in 1933. The transaction established Wilson Dam as the first in a network that would eventually span the Tennessee River and its tributaries.

Claiming that the nation would benefit from the TVA and similarly designed regional projects, FDR insisted that the endeavor was ambitious and prudent. The incoming president declared, "I am very confident that the distinguished gentlemen who are with me from the Congress of the United States will be able to work with me and get something practical done."[3] The stress on practicality showed Roosevelt's hand in trying to counter the criticism that unfeeling technocrats driven by blueprints and statistics helmed New Deal projects. One complaint was that they were prone to generating ideas in theory without regard for the human toll of putting them into practice. Awareness of this pitfall guided the design of TVA infrastructure and informed the agency's promotional campaigns. As the most essential and impressive infrastructure, the TVA dams needed to work effectively and simultaneously on material and symbolic fronts. In addition to regulating the flow and volume of water for flood control and generating hydroelectric power, the dams would have to stand for something meaningful in the public imagination.

The art of constructing dams in line with composing national narratives did not begin with the New Deal nor did it end there. The TVA enterprise followed in the footsteps of the Boulder Canyon Project authorized by President Calvin Coolidge in 1928. That came to pass after several years because of the tireless efforts of Secretary of Commerce Herbert Hoover, who had been instrumental in brokering a deal among the states affected. The gigantic dam that was the cornerstone of the project took shape during Hoover's one term as president and eventually bore his name. Roosevelt presided over the Hoover Dam dedication ceremony in 1935, two years after the TVA congressional authorization. As Rob Nixon observes, Hoover became "the gold standard in the rush to emulation" for years to come.[4] Nixon points to numerous megadams subsequently built around the world, especially in the Global South, where defining dams and other public works projects as engines of rehabilitation and modernization became the modus operandi of global development initiatives. Nixon contends that Hoover Dam became a worthy model because it was perceived as an ideal convergence of form and function, "marrying a miraculous feat of American hydraulic engineering to a sublime spectacle of grandeur."[5] In this light, Hoover Dam and the structures it inspired developed into "places where the transcendentalisms of religion, nation, science, and art would converge."[6] It was convenient for proponents of these large-scale projects that such displays were useful for steering public attention away from the scores of people displaced and ecologies irrevocably altered by infrastructural development.

While Nixon traces a pattern that begins with the Hoover Dam, the Boulder Canyon Project and the TVA were part of a global trend in infrastructure that emerged in the aftermath of World War I, accelerated in the 1930s, and expanded globally after World War II. Kiran Klaus Patel, in *The New Deal: A Global History*, points out the transnational connections between the TVA dams and those built in France's Rhône River Valley, the Dnieper River Valley in modern-day Ukraine, and in service of "the hydraulic structure of Spain under dictator Franco" in Spain.[7] The most ambitious of the projects Patel discusses is Dneprostroi Dam, which was part of Joseph Stalin's first five-year plan and involved American and German engineers. "Americans had no problem finding Soviet dams fascinating," Patel observes, asserting a direct influence.[8] A common thread running through all these projects, in addition to other types of public works undertaken by Mussolini in Italy and Hitler in Germany, was the notion that public works would generate rapid economic growth and modernization for underdeveloped regions while projecting national prowess in a global theater of geopolitical posturing. In this context, Nixon explains, dam construction projects staged "a kind of national performance art."[9]

At the performative level, TVA infrastructure took on added meaning within the context of an international crisis and a program designed to bring about national recovery. Patel offers a sound assessment of how this process unfolded:

> For the New Dealers, the TVA was to be a marker of national strength, coherence, and the controllability of nature at the hands of seemingly apolitical, technical experts. It was to demonstrate what vigorous federal intervention could achieve. They saw the Tennessee River as a gigantic metaphor for the need for unbridled capitalism to be contained, channeled, and put to use for the public good. The

TVA therefore soon became a particularly potent—if not the most important—symbol of the New Deal.[10]

The TVA relied extensively on visual culture to reach the full symbolic potential for maximum effect. Photographs and public murals were prominent mediums in this mode of cultural production. Through the strategic composition and presentation of images, visual artists employed by the federal government rendered dams and other infrastructure monumental expressions of the desire for a fast track to experiencing the wonders of modernity and overcoming the debilitating conditions of uneven development. As such, the dams represented the technological capacity to shape the forces of environmental and economic volatility into steady and productive currents of energy and commerce. TVA cultural production sought to deter opponents who wanted to assign different meanings to the same elements of infrastructure by applying a set of destructive rather than constructive associations: erasure of local history, culture, and geography; displacement of local people with ties to the land; and federal overreach enabled by social engineering. Such charges demonstrate how, as Nixon observes, the meaning of public works is open to interpretation, given that dams function as screens for projecting "apocalyptic counter-images" that challenge those stamped with state authority as definitive.[11] In this regard, dams and the supporting hydraulic systems constructed in material and aesthetic forms and then reconstructed through visual culture became contested sites of representation. At such points of convergence, TVA cultural production defined symbolic value through a type of monumentality that could appeal to the desire for national recovery, progress, and belonging active in the public sphere.

ENVISIONING TVA MONUMENTALITY

A year after Roosevelt visited Muscle Shoals, one of the triumvirate of administrators he appointed to run the TVA toured the site to monitor the progress of the redesign. As part of his tour, David E. Lilienthal, who was serving as a director with Harcourt A. Morgan and Arthur E. Morgan, made a stop at Wilson Dam, where he posed for a photograph

Fig. 1. David Lilienthal, director of the Tennessee Valley Authority, at the Wilson Dam in Colbert County, Alabama, 1934. Courtesy of the Alabama Department of Archives and History.

(fig. 1). In it, he is wearing a dark suit, dress shoes, and a fedora and standing atop a concrete platform on the riverbank. Facing away from the camera, he gazes upward at the rush of water cascading down the dam's spillways. Viewed in context, the image documents a pivotal moment when the TVA became embroiled in a cultural debate about modern architecture as officials tried to decide on the signature style for subsequent dams in the network. A brief historical account posted on the TVA's website alludes in retrospect to the problem with Wilson's design for those who wanted the new dams to reflect modern aesthetic sensibilities: "[It] is the only neoclassical-style dam in the TVA system, integrating themes of ancient Roman and Greek architecture into the modern structure."[12] Wilson's features made the dam a vexing starting point, opening the photograph of Lilienthal to interpretation as a document that symbolically stages the aesthetic dilemma at hand.

An argument for making Wilson the template was that the design comported with the prevailing trend in monuments and public buildings. From the 1920s to the end of World War II, new construction in Washington, DC, reflected the rise of stripped classicism, a term coined to describe the modern revival and revision of an architectural style rooted in antiquity. Referencing Greco-Roman art and architecture was an aesthetic shortcut for adding historical gravitas to the relatively young American republic. Frank Capra's film *Mr. Smith Goes to Washington* (1939) dramatizes the intended effect, particularly in the montage sequence in which the protagonist, Jefferson Smith (played by Jimmy Stewart), visits several monuments and buildings upon his arrival in the nation's capital as an idealistic political novice.[13] As Smith moves from site to site, he marvels at the scale and symbolism of structures that recall the cradle of democracy in the ancient world and express American values in terms of monumentality. The photograph of Lilienthal against the backdrop of the Wilson Dam façade anticipates the cinematic composition, conveying a contemporary figure appearing to stand in awe of infrastructure built in the style of Roman aqueducts. The visual-historical allusion connects the TVA project in the present to Roman technological innovation and achievement dressed in the familiar trappings of ancient Greece. This aesthetic echo makes a statement about the American claim to the ancient Greco-Roman mantle as the brightest beacon of light in western civilization.

The contemporary display of Greco-Roman lineage was not confined to the United States. In Italy, Mussolini commissioned monumental architecture in the vein of stripped classicism to create resonance between the Roman Empire and the new order he was trying to bring about under authoritarian rule. Hitler orchestrated a similar movement in German architecture to confer legitimacy on the Third Reich. In *Modern Classicism*, Robert A. M. Stern explains how this strategy worked: "In the official architectural hierarchy, the most important public buildings were to be designed in an austere Classical style that stood for the *Macht* ('power') of the state."[14] Under the fascist banner, stripped classicism represented a new path forward in the cloak of the mythic past evoked to stir passions and a sense of belonging rooted in ethnic nationalism. The notion that the structures designed in the revived classical style could exist in harmony with those from antiquity added potency to the ideological persuasion.

The traditional approach was at base a refutation of modernism, which had emerged in the aftermath of World War I in opposition to the turn toward monumentalism. In Germany, for example, the vibrancy of modernism was apparent in the Bauhaus School fronted by Walter Gropius. Gropius also participated in the German Werkbund, an association of craftsmen reactivated by Ludwig Mies van der Rohe after the war. The Werkbund exerted a profound influence by staging exhibitions to highlight the latest achievements in modernist design. Stern explains that an aversion to modernist temporality motivated the proponents of stripped classicism in the 1930s. Citing Sigfried Giedion's concept of an "eternal present," Stern points out that detractors criticized modernism for producing a sense of temporal alienation in contrast to the proposed alternative: "Classicism propels us into a conversation between an idealized Ancient world and an evolving present."[15] From the standpoint of nation-states eager for infrastructure to become a conduit of economic development and a mode of nationalist expression, staging a dialogue between the past and present as grounds for imagining a promising future made sense.

The emphasis on classical elements in new construction on the international front and under New Deal auspices, particularly in Washington, DC, made the TVA's eventual choice of modernism for post-Wilson dam projects surprising. At first, the traditional approach held sway, as senior design team members pushed for the new dams to be cut from the Wilson mold. That changed because of the dramatic entrance of an upstart architect named Ronald Wank. An immigrant from Budapest, Wank was working in the trenches of the TVA design unit when his plan for the second dam in the system became the final blueprint, much to the shock and chagrin of his more experienced superiors. Built between 1933 and 1936, it bore the name Norris Dam in honor of the Nebraska senator and TVA stalwart. Christine Macy and Sarah Bonnemaison describe Norris Dam as "a modernist jewel set in the rolling uplands of Tennessee."[16] Such accolades certainly did not come from Wank's superiors in the unit. They felt that adopting the young architect's design was risky for an enterprise steeped in controversy. After all, it stands to reason that such a future-oriented approach would have seemed likely to play right into the hands of opponents who charged TVA officials with imposing a uniform transformation on the region without regard to local history and culture.

In the internal dispute between competing aesthetic ideologies, modernism prevailed despite concerns about the impact of large-scale structures designed in that vein on an existing landscape known for its natural beauty. William U. Chandler observes that the TVA responded by incorporating the new infrastructure into the old frame. Referencing a grandiosity bias toward so-called natural wonders pervasive in American conservationism, Chandler describes the process: "The nation's fifth largest river became the object of monumentalism of a different sort. The Tennessee and its tributaries were filled with concrete monoliths."[17] In dam construction, monoliths are the concrete panels connected to form walls, but they operate figuratively as façades open to definition and interpretation in the public imagination. In this regard, Norris Dam, Chickamauga Dam, and the others shaped by the modernist sensibilities that Wank brought to bear and artists rendered in visual culture were part of a significant trend in modern architecture. In this regard, the debate over the infrastructure of the TVA reveals monumentality and modernism as relational, even dialectical, rather than strictly oppositional. Stern acknowledges the animus toward monumental architecture that gave rise to modernism after World War I: "But in time, the desire of Modernist architects and propagandists to impose their way of building . . . universally, supplanting all that had preceded, naturally, led to a call for a Modernist monumentality."[18] At the intersection of modernist design and monumental aspiration, TVA monumentality emerged as an aesthetic ideology that shaped infrastructural development and, in turn, the production of state-sponsored visual culture commissioned to convey its meaning and purpose.

EXHIBITING TVA MONUMENTALITY

By the end of the 1930s, the TVA had made substantial progress toward completing its network of dams. The large-scale modernism of Norris, Hiwassee, Wheeler, and others concretized TVA monumentality as a significant development in modern architecture. In the eyes of many observers, these feats of architectural design and engineering were also forms of artistic expression. That was the case for curators at the Museum of Modern Art in New York City who staged an exhibition, "TVA Architecture and Design," in the spring of 1941. The exhibition was a testament to the TVA's success in collaborating with public institutions to project its image in the domestic and international spheres. After closing at MoMA, the exhibition went on the road, allowing people across the country to encounter the TVA in a format mediated and curated to present the agency as an exemplar of great achievements in public works. A book was published to document the exhibition in print form.[19] By this measure, the touring exhibition was a metaphor for the portability and suitability of the TVA model for other parts of the country designated for New Deal regional planning.

A preview of the partnership to come was the 1939 radio address delivered by President Roosevelt to celebrate the opening of the museum's new permanent home on West 53rd Street. FDR tailored his remarks to a national audience while alluding to international matters as he described the symbolic meaning of the occasion and the new facility. "We are dedicating this building to the cause of peace," he said. "The arts that ennoble and refine life flourish only in the atmosphere of peace."[20] In addition to acknowledging the international moment of heightened conflict, the president's message was an implicit comment on the notion of "art for art's sake." The debate surrounding that aesthetic stance had resurfaced in the US as writers and intellectuals weighed in on relations between art and politics amid a global economic crisis hitting hard at home and the threat of fascism mounting in Europe. Without mentioning New Deal state sponsorship per se, Roosevelt defined support for the arts as a way of advancing the democratic cause. As "a citadel of civilization," MoMA would strengthen its status among American institutions, becoming more intricately "woven into the very warp and woof of our democracy."[21] While the new building was the focal point of his address, Roosevelt pointed to outreach programs that would extend the museum's influence beyond the confines of Manhattan. He shared his conviction that exhibitions housed in the new venue would help broaden the scope of the fine arts as a discipline. Specifically, the president cited architecture, industrial design, and housing ("the great social art") as falling under a more expansive framework including other media: painting, photography, print-making, illustration, advertising, poster art, theater, and motion pictures.[22] Roosevelt concluded with trademark optimism, stating that "a nationwide public will receive a demonstration of the force and scope of all these branches of the visual arts."[23] The visionary and disciplinary elements of MoMA's mission that Roosevelt highlighted in 1939 aligned with the fundamental aims of the TVA such that collaboration was regarded as mutually beneficial.

The TVA exhibition opened on April 29, 1941. A museum press release announced the bevy of items on display. In addition, there was a daily screening of *TVA*, a twenty-minute documentary film produced in 1940 by the United States Information Service (USIS). The film detailed "the entire development of the project throughout the Tennessee Valley, with particularly beautiful sequences on the huge dams."[24] Among the dignitaries on hand for a members' preview and reception on the evening before the public opening was Mayor Fiorello La Guardia, who introduced David Lilienthal, the official representative of the TVA administration. Anticipating the memoir he published three years later, *TVA: Democracy on the March*, Lilienthal described the project as future-oriented despite its location in a region perceived as hidebound: "We realized that we were building not for our time alone, but structures that would stand for centuries, a thousand years or more perhaps."[25] Lilienthal explained that everyone involved in the construction of the dams was aware that nothing less than "the finest achievement of modern engineering skill" would be necessary to make them operational. Formal concerns were also paramount, Lilienthal added, waxing poetic:

> But what of their, [sic] esthetic quality, their form? These monuments would reflect for centuries the standard of American culture and the purpose of American life of our time. Should we follow the quite general practice of building the structures, and then add some decorations to make them "pretty"? Should we raise up monoliths to set their giant shoulders against the floods of a thousand years, and then embellish their strength with the doo-dads and columns of civilization now gone for a thousand years?[26]

In seven years, Lilienthal had turned away from the façade of Wilson Dam where he posed for the photograph showing reverence for stripped classicism. As an official representative of the TVA, he took a position in a longstanding debate about the course of modern architecture.

The criticism of outmoded "doo-dads" in Lilienthal's rhetorical question amounted to a public embrace of functionalism as a governing principle of dam construction. After all, it was Wank's stress on functionality over decorative flair that made his work stand out to Lilienthal.[27] The young architect was designing houses for the planned community of Norris when Lilienthal decided to give him a shot at a project on a vastly larger scale. Fundamentally, Wank took inspiration from the Bauhaus architect Alfred Loos, whose manifesto of functionalism, "Ornament and Crime," became a foundational text in the rise of modernism in architecture in the early twentieth century. The influence of Loos's polemical attack against embellishment in objects or structures made for use was on display in a scalar range from the utilitarian homes for Norris workers that Wank cut his teeth on as an architect to the smooth, clean faces of Norris Dam and the others built in the same style. Lilienthal's remarks combined allusions to the signature aesthetic features of modernism with assurances of practicality to cast public works projects as ambitious and innovative yet economical and practical. The framing of the exhibition was an attempt to reconcile two approaches to the overall scheme of TVA architectural design and engineering. On one hand, TVA officials wanted to stress aspects of Loosian functionalism by emphasizing operational capacity in the decision to forgo "unnecessary" flourishes that would have added classical touches. On the other hand, they celebrated the structures as imaginative feats of modern architecture worthy of distinction as fine art that a MoMA exhibition conferred.

The blend of items on display reflected the careful balancing act that the collaboration between the TVA and MoMA performed. Photographs of various sizes placed throughout the museum space formed a visual replica of the TVA network comprising several dams: Chickamauga, Guntersville, Hiwassee, Norris, Kentucky, Fort Loudon, Cherokee, Watts Barr, Pickwick, and Wheeler.[28] While the images of dam façades stressed their formal properties, those of control buildings, power plants, visitor facilities, and housing stressed the technical components. Also on display were several scale models: a rendering of Pickwick Dam; the powerhouses at the Chickamauga and Guntersville dams; the lock operations building at Kentucky Dam; and construction cranes at Hiwassee Dam. The visual appeal, sequential organization, and narrative framework of the exhibition conveyed to the public the overall design and essential components of the TVA enterprise.

The photographs must have stood out to exhibition viewers as a significant element of the multimedia visual arts display. That was due to the skill and artistry of the official TVA photographer, Charles Krutch. Krutch had been working since 1934 in the Information Division, where he remained until his retirement twenty years later. An article on Krutch available on the TVA website describes his penchant for creative experimentation even as he carried out what would seem to be mundane assignments. Tasked with taking pictures of infrastructure and machinery, the article notes, Krutch eschewed a rudimentary approach and instead "played with shapes and shades as few other photographers at federal agencies had ever dared to do."[29] Consequently, many of his photographs "looked like modernist paintings, dynamic studies in black and white," earning critical praise for Krutch as "an artist with a camera."[30] Since federal agencies hired photographers such as Dorothea Lange and Ben Shahn, characterizing his artistic eye as exceptional is an overstatement. Nevertheless, the modernist sensibilities evident in his work confirm the talent he brought to bear in presenting TVA infrastructure in a favorable light. Along with his assistant, Emil Seinknecht, Krutch was responsible for artful compositions that delivered to viewers through visual mediation the intended message that they were beholding modern marvels in photographic form.

Before Krutch's work figured prominently in the partnership between the TVA and MoMA, it played a role in another event at the museum. In 1937, two years before FDR's radio address celebrating the new facility, the museum mounted "Photography: 1839–1937," an exhibition commemorating one hundred years of photography as a visual medium. It drew praise from critics and attention from the public, traveling around the country in a touring format just as the TVA exhibition would a few years later. The curator was Beaumont Newhall, who had started working at MoMA as a librarian in 1935. For Newhall, helming this program laid the groundwork for becoming an influential figure in photography criticism and historiography. Four of Krutch's photographs were on display and appeared in a book based on the exhibition, *Photography, 1839–1937*, edited with a critical introduction by Newhall.[31] The visual rhetoric of these works shows Krutch's adept use of photography to reinforce the TVA's claim that it was committed to thoughtful integration of the new infrastructure into the natural landscape. Two of Krutch's photographs included in the exhibition ("Great Smoky Mountains, 1936" and "Early Spring, 1936") captured the natural beauty of the regional landscape, while the remaining images ("Wheeler Dam Roadway, 1936" and "Hydraulic Generator Scroll Casing, 1936") accentuated elements of design in the built environment. These images displayed an aesthetic projection of order and harmony that omitted the material conditions of disruption, displacement, and submersion of towns, cemeteries, historical landmarks, and Indigenous sacred sites entailed in infrastructural development.

A key aesthetic and ideological component of Krutch's TVA photography is evident in "Hydraulic Generator Scroll Casing, 1936" (fig. 2). The focal point in the frame is a man in work clothes standing inside the casing with a large wrench resting on his shoulder. The man is at a bend in the installation, facing to the right and peering down the tunnel into a distance that presumably extends beyond the frame. Like most of Krutch's photographs granting the viewer access to the interiors of TVA infrastructure, this one emphasizes the geometrical shapes of the industrial form as it simultaneously calls attention to the human touch required for the facility to function properly. Krutch took this picture the same year that Margaret Bourke-White's photographs of Fort Peck Dam in Montana accompanied the first cover story published in *Life*, Henry Luce's third magazine venture.[32] Although she was approaching a transitional point in her career, the *Life* spread reflected an ongoing preoccupation with industrial subjects and settings that began in her early work for *Fortune* magazine before she became a famous photojournalist.[33] The photographs in this mode often feature humans and machines engaged in industrial operations, with a propensity toward abstraction such that fascination with the latter can come across as cold indifference to the former. The industrial forms Bourke-White captured can seem ominous and threatening to the human subjects within the frame. As "Hydraulic Generator" illustrates, menacing machines are largely absent from Krutch's photography. It is possible to interpret the photograph by imagining that the casing has swallowed the worker whole, trapping him in the belly of the beast—photographic evidence of the TVA as the titular monster Donald Davidson envisions in *The Great Leviathan*. However, such an interpretation would amount to reading *into* rather than reading the image. After all, Krutch's photograph preserves a moment of human

Fig. 2. Charles Krutch, "Hydraulic Generator Scroll Casing, 1936." This photograph was one of the four by Krutch featured in the 1937 exhibition "Photography, 1839–1937" at the Museum of Modern Art and the representative work included in the book based on the exhibition. Photo courtesy of the Tennessee Valley Authority.

stillness and solemnity within the infrastructural setting, evoking the trademark sense of balance and harmony found in TVA cultural production. For this reason, Krutch's work stands in contrast to Bourke-White's aesthetically compelling but unsettling images of the Machine Age and, for that matter, to the iconic rendering of mechanized consumption in Charlie Chaplin's *Modern Times*, which also appeared in 1936.

As expressions of TVA monumentality, Krutch's photographs and the other items displayed in the MoMA exhibition lend themselves to examination informed by "Functionalism Today," the celebrated lecture Theodor Adorno delivered to the German Werkbund conference in 1965. In it, Adorno reflected on the post–World War II acceleration of modernist architecture as a response to recent history—specifically, as a rejection of Third Reich monumentality expressed primarily through stripped classicism. Adorno took issue with what he viewed as the dogmatic adherence to functionalism that had resulted from Loos's influential manifesto five decades earlier. As a countermeasure, Adorno issues a corrective to Loos's thesis that untethers functionalism from function: "The purpose-free [*zweckfrei*] and purposeful [*zweckgebunden*] arts do not form the radical opposition which [Loos] imputed."[34] Adorno contends that the abandonment of ornamentation in the interest of "pure" function is fundamentally flawed because "the absolute rejection of style becomes style."[35] Taking that maxim as a given, Adorno posits a tweaked Loosian formulation in which purpose and space might be held in creative dialectical tension. The capacity for imagining a new relationship between form and function is the basis of Adorno's proposition. "Architectonic imagination is ... the ability to articulate space purposefully. It permits purposes to become space," Adorno explains, charting an escape route from the trap of a false binary between purpose-driven or purpose-free design defined as "pure."[36]

The press release issued by MoMA in conjunction with the public opening of "T.V.A. Architecture and Design" included the full text of Lilienthal's remarks at the evening reception. While Lilienthal emphasized what TVA infrastructure was supposed to do by design, the description by MoMA's Architecture Department highlighted the creative energy that went into how it looked. The text cited the panoply of materials displayed in the exhibition as grounds for affirming the expansive vision of fine arts FDR articulated in his 1939 radio address dedicating the new MoMA. The departmental statement established that the state could bring "fine architecture" into being while serving public interests. By this reasoning, TVA projects could "handsomely combine dignity, logic and beauty—from the minor buildings built around them to the colossal dams themselves."[37] This process set the stage for a rhetorical performance in which language added the flourishes to TVA infrastructure that were absent from the modernist aesthetic. Stuart Chase, the bestselling author of popular economics books and advisor to FDR who had coined the term "New Deal," was a key player. Reading Chase's remarks alongside Krutch's photograph of the Hiwassee Dam (fig. 3) offers an instructive path to understanding the formation of TVA monumentality with the imprimatur of MoMA. In the Hiwassee photograph, the façade of the dam dominates the frame, creating the impression of a reflective surface, as the concrete pathway at the bottom mirrors the rectangular shapes of the monoliths. The

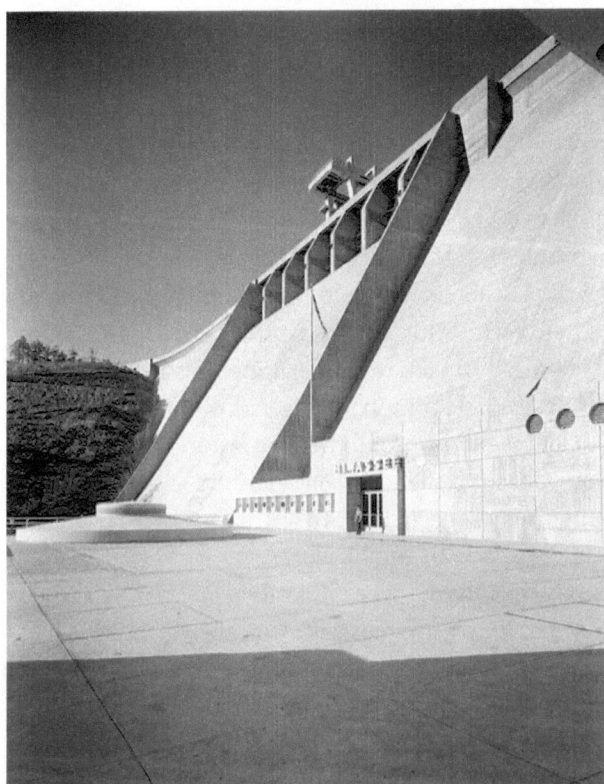

Fig. 3. Among the photographs of dams featured in the Museum of Modern Art's TVA exhibition was Krutch's shot of Hiwassee Dam in western North Carolina. Photo courtesy of the Tennessee Valley Authority.

symmetrical effect derives from the arrangement of the monoliths in a pattern of alternating vertical and horizontal etched lines. Adding to that effect are circular elements: a structure on the ground next to the dam resembles a science fiction B-movie flying saucer, and a series of circular impressions on the dam face look like portholes. Krutch's photograph foregrounds the unadorned design of Hiwassee Dam, yielding a veritable blank canvas ready in the frame to receive the symbolic meaning projected onto the surface by the official speakers.

When Chase followed Lilienthal in the lineup at the special reception, as the MoMA press materials document, he sounded some of the same notes but amplified them in terms of nationalism. He too stressed the capability of the TVA infrastructure to deliver on the bold promises expressed in the agency's mission. The key lay in a blend of tried-and-true methods and state-of-the-art technology that Chase touted in establishing continuity between the TVA as an American endeavor and those of past civilizations regarded as highly advanced and capable of great achievements. "To hold the river harmless for a thousand years requires dams like pyramids," Chase declared. "No architect, dreaming of Athens or Chartres[,] can alter the designs which this great press of waters demand."[38] The connection between the Nile Valley and the Tennessee Valley created an air of historicity that gave credibility to the embrace of clean lines, large scale, and monumental expression in the design scheme. Rising to the challenge of taming the river called for a "new architecture," Chase proclaimed.[39] In closing, he oriented viewers poised to take in modern marvels in the form of visual culture by appealing to an individual sense of national identity and belonging: "Look at it and be proud that you are an American."[40] A stirring excerpt from Chase's remarks greeted visitors at the exhibition entrance, welcoming them to participate in a deeply felt experience of affective citizenship generated by public works.

One visitor with a prominent media platform responded to the prompt in a manner that must have pleased TVA officials. Lewis Mumford, a critic interested in the philosophical implications of technology, published a review in the *New Yorker*. For his regular column, "The Skyline," Mumford focused on the TVA exhibition and a new book on architect Frank Lloyd Wright. Mumford extended Chase's historical analogy by putting the scale of the TVA infrastructure in context: "There is something in the mere cant of a dam, when seen from below, that makes one think of the Pyramids of Egypt. Both pyramid and dam represent an architecture of power."[41] Mumford noted the convergence of practical function and symbolic meaning, employing the dual connotations of "power" favored by the TVA. "The Architecture of Power," the title of this installment of Mumford's regular column, came from this passage. The review also addressed an aesthetic dilemma established in the first paragraph: the wide experiential gap between standing in front of a dam and standing in front of a photograph of a dam. The latter was the occasion of Mumford's review, but his description of the experience relied on a vivid recollection of the former. Disclosing that he had visited one of the TVA sites, Mumford described the dams as "even more breathtaking than the photographs indicate."[42]

Translating the sense of awe that Mumford experienced into the confines of a museum installation posed a significant challenge for the curators. Channeling nationalism as a complementary source of inspiration became a means of compensating for diminishing affective returns. In closing his speech at the preview reception, Lilienthal called attention to a common element of the TVA design scheme: "There is one phrase and only one you will find written over the doors of these structures; in large letters is this simple legend: BUILT FOR THE PEOPLE OF THE UNITED STATES."[43] The notion that "the people" could claim ownership of dams and other infrastructure echoed the call to view works of visual culture in light of an ambitious national project. This appeal was geared toward the conditions of a modern mass culture in which, as Walter Benjamin observes, "present-day perception" involves "a decay of the aura."[44] In Benjamin's view, the aura of an object derives from the "strange tissue of space and time" it inhabits, making the object unique in the eyes of the beholder.[45] The diminishment of this visual effect in mass culture is the consequence of two factors: "*the desire of the present-day masses to 'get closer' to things, and their equally passionate concern for overcoming each thing's uniqueness . . . by assimilating it as a reproduction.*"[46] "T.V.A. Architecture and Design" capitalized on this modern desire for visual reproductions by inviting the American public to "get closer" to TVA infrastructure via small-scale models they could tower over and photographs they could examine closely. The grandiloquent rhetoric defined the mediated encounter as an opportunity to take pride in ownership. In that regard, the sense of national identity and belonging proffered by TVA cultural production made the MoMA exhibition a component of the public works project it showcased.

EMBEDDING TVA MONUMENTALITY

The combination of word and image exhibited at MoMA was an essential element of the "photo-textual documentaries," or photobooks, that emerged in the 1930s.[47] By the early 1940s, photobooks were a well-established genre on the strength of publications such as Margaret Bourke-White and Erskine Caldwell's *You Have Seen Their Faces* and Walker Evans and James Agee's *Let Us Now Praise Famous Men*. In 1944, *The Valley and Its People: A Portrait of TVA* added to a substantial and expanding body of work, marking the first time that Krutch's photography was widely accessible to the American public. R. L. Duffus, a *New York Times* journalist and author, wrote the narrative. The text on the inside flap of the dust jacket describes the work as "a happy collaboration" between word and image, writer and photographer. This photobook illustrates the TVA's strategy of building on the success of the MoMA exhibition by forming a partnership with another cultural institution, the venerable Alfred A. Knopf publishing house.

The dust jacket copy sets the historical scope in familiar terms. It describes the narrative portion of the project as "an unfolding historical panorama of the Valley and its people" made more compelling by the "magnificent photographs" captured by Krutch's deft camera eye. The metaphor of the panorama offers significant insight into the aesthetic stratagems that Krutch and Duffus drew from the genre of photobooks and documentary realism more broadly. Tracing the development of the panorama as a form in visual arts and literature, Benjamin identifies the emergence of arcades as a benchmark. The creators of these immersive displays "sought tirelessly, through technical devices, to make panoramas the scenes of a perfect imitation of nature."[48] The practice of constructing "deceptively lifelike changes represented in nature" prompts Benjamin to link this form to contemporaneous panoramic literature and brand it as a forerunner to photography and cinema (silent and sound).[49] For city dwellers, panoramas in painting, arcades, and exhibitions provide opportunities to experience the vistas of rural landscapes in virtual form. Through mediation, this privileged position simulates command of distant settings, fueling the acquisitive desire that Benjamin identifies as a driving force of image consumption in mass culture. Affording mediated and simulated panoramic views of the Tennessee Valley's transformation became a recurring special effect in TVA cultural production. The staging of the MoMA exhibition, the murals on display in visitor centers and other facilities at dam sites, and the visual and narrative features of *The Valley and Its People* were examples of this aesthetic strategy at work in varying forms and to different degrees of scale, experience, and effect.

The ostensible starting point on the timeline of *The Valley and Its People* is 1933, the year of the TVA's congressional authorization, but the spatial-temporal field widens right away. Citing the high volume of water that a single acre of land in the Tennessee Valley receives per annum, the narrator abruptly shifts to a long view: "This water, moving as it must, seeking the ocean level, carries an energy almost beyond the imagination of man. It more than matches the great strength which thrust the hills up millions of years ago, for little by little it undoes what was then done."[50] The sense of time and space is expansive, stretching back into the past and juxtaposing ground-level and aerial points of view. In establishing the setting, Duffus prompts the reader to imagine looking down at the Tennessee Valley from the window of an airplane: "We could easily understand why this landscape, often so dreamy, so lazy-looking, is filled with power" (11). In effect, the narrative confers a feeling of omniscience to the reader in surveying the scene as it changes over time. "Power has been there from the beginning of man's time, and before," Duffus writes. "Power took the white pioneers downstream to make the first settlements, or to go through the Valley on their ways southward and westward" (13). From this vantage point, momentum reshapes the Tennessee Valley into a site of inexorable development and progress—notably one defined through the characteristic erasure of Indigenous history and idealization of settler colonialism in narratives that valorize pioneers as precursors to TVA visionaries.

To his credit, Duffus acknowledges an unchecked profit motive behind longstanding efforts to capitalize on the power contained in the valley. In a place once thought to have an inexhaustible supply of natural resources, "man has changed the scene, as invariably he does" (17). The combination of monoculture crop production and rapid deforestation means that formerly lush terrain has become denuded and eroded, leaving only "worn-out slopes, gullied, ruined" (17). These barren landscapes form an ecological archive, recording the anthropogenic damage that the myth of Manifest Destiny does not acknowledge. The objective, however, is not to dispel the myth, but to enrich the archive. The narrative records that "in the summer of 1933, a new human enterprise began to write its signature: the Tennessee Valley Authority. TVA!" (17). The perspective changes from distant to close in a "swoop" that brings the dams into view, revealing "the sharp perfection of their forms" and their "geometrical, effortless beauty" as features of the new signature on the Tennessee Valley (18). The symmetrical features of infrastructure contrast with the winding lacerations inflicted on the landscape by erosion. Like the MoMA exhibition, the photobook idealizes the dams as masterpieces of form and function that achieve perfect harmony by design. In this capacity, they "are as lovely as the hills, which they both interrupt and complete" (18). A visual effect of this description is to make the infrastructure seem a "natural" fit into the contours of geographic space and the continuity of geologic time.

The panoramic view of infrastructure in nature that the narrative simulates through visual imagery and perspective is apparent in the accompanying photographs by Krutch. Following the flyby passage, an aerial shot of Chickamauga Dam stretches across the fold to take up the bottom of two pages. From the perch given to the reader, the dam is the focal point, standing out but fitting in because of the design elements that Duffus highlights through figurative language. The placid scene conveys a relationship between the dam and the river that stresses balance and control. It is easy to forget that what lies behind the dam is a newly formed body of water—a reservoir made possible by anthropogenic intervention. The caption prompts the reader to feel aesthetic appreciation: "TVA structures, like this at Chickamauga on the main river, have an architectural beauty of their own" (20–21). Benjamin comments on the function of captions as photography transitioned from generating interest in the "*cult value*" of portraiture to attracting investment in the "*exhibition value*" that accrued from depopulated images of deserted streets, crime scenes, and architecture.[51] Since such images could "unsettle the viewer," Benjamin explains, "captions become obligatory" in orienting viewers to the scenes they encounter as observers.[52] In the photograph of Chickamauga, the caption notes the appeal of a design that balances formal and functional elements to harness natural forces and extract power for human benefit. The image of still waters tamed by hydraulic engineering contrasts with the earlier prose descriptions of currents running unchecked down eroded slopes and over barren terrain to inundate the area. The narrative punctuates the image with an explicit statement of the thematic intention: "Beauty, waste, and attempted redemption are simple ideas which this hawk's-eye view readily gives us" (20).

The photographs express the monumental consequence of TVA infrastructure in individual frames and their sequential progression. The initial images in the book display the majesty of nature in the region. A wide shot of a valley stretches across two pages, occupying three-fourths of the space. A mountain range comprises the backdrop, and the overcast sky and fog patches evoke a sense of misty memory that complements the (pre)historic timeline in the narrative. The next picture is brightly lit, revealing a winding river flanked by mountainous terrain. A towering tree in the left foreground of the frame, its limbs partially cropped, gives the impression of having a "hawk's-eye view" from atop a neighboring tree. Duffus fashions a complementary approach in the narrative through descriptive details that establish the visual perspective. The caption marks the location as the Great Smoky Mountains National Park. These images of natural wonder usher in the photographs that document the TVA's formation and development. The "unfolding historical panorama," to quote the dust jacket copy again, follows a teleological pattern that figures the recent anthropogenic intervention by the TVA as a logical progression converging with rather than interrupting the unfolding stretch of natural history.

Through the strategic interplay between image and text, *The Valley and Its People* posits an alternative to the invasive model of relations between nature and modern technology formulated in significant tracts of agrarian or environmentally conscious literature: Henry David Thoreau's *Walden* (1854), The Twelve Southerners' *I'll Take My Stand* (1930), Aldo Leopold's *A Sand County Almanac* (1949), and Leo Marx's *The Machine in the Garden* (1964), to name a few examples. Recording the observations of a visitor to the Norris Dam site after the completion of the project, Duffus describes "the peaceful charm of the scene," complete with "a quiet cabin up the draw on the right bank, the unmarred wood slopes, the green meadows, the cove and beach, and the dirt road that came out of them" (27). Now that the "fury of construction" is in the past, "everything is peaceful again, with the peace of quiet machinery, of controlled power, of the pure green water below the dam, always passing always there" (27). The implicit statement is that order and balance are possible because of the towering dam and supporting infrastructure, not despite them. Characteristically, Duffus succumbs to purple prose as he describes technology inhabiting the space without disruption: "The maze of wires in the yard beside the powerhouse hums gently, like an Aeolian harp in the wind" (27). Duffus crafts a technopastoral scene in which the dam enhances the natural attributes of the setting rather than effacing them with the brute, destructive force of mechanization, as detractors of the TVA claimed was the case.

While the portrait of the TVA that the photobook paints is understandably concerned with foregrounding infrastructure, the human element also comes into play. The text and photographs highlight the benefits of the TVA to the people of the Tennessee Valley, showing the transformation of the land and improved living conditions for the region's subsistence farmers. Furthering the interest in everyday people, several photographs feature rank-and-file employees operating machinery. In captions and the main text, they are cast as dedicated and productive supporters of the collective mission and vision. In trademark Krutchian fashion, these images show no sign of anxiety about relations between workers and machines. The implication is that the harmony between nature and technology in the Tennessee Valley landscape also applies to the working relations between the machinery of TVA infrastructure and its human operators.

Widening the contextual scope, the photographs of construction crew members bear a striking resemblance to images of robust industrial and agricultural laborers disseminated in Soviet propaganda to proclaim the virtues of the proletariat. Although the ideological imperatives are opposed, the composition strategies and visual rhetoric create dialectical tension between competing national forms of cultural production. In one of Krutch's photographs, a construction crew leaves a dam site at the end of a shift, forming a picture of solidarity. The man in the immediate foreground looks directly into the camera while his coworkers follow behind on a path. This image is one of only a few that include Black workers in the frame, indicating an attempt to counteract the argument that racial oppression compromised the moral high ground the United States claimed as a beacon of democracy. The photograph documents the hiring practices that challenged the dictates of segregation, albeit only to the limited extent that maintaining the support of southern segregationists in Congress would allow. The rugged work clothes and standard-issue lunchboxes add to an aesthetic expression of cooperation and camaraderie across the color line belied by the material conditions of Jim Crow in the society beyond the frame. Monoliths and scaffolding are visible in the background. The photograph is open to the interpretation that these men, like the laborers who constructed medieval cathedrals, can derive meaning and purpose from expanding the temporal frame to put a single shift into a broader perspective defined by the standard narrative of progress. Or so the caption says: "These men have done a day's work—work that will make possible for years to come a Valley civilization enriched by new skills and modern science" (22).

While the visual imagery in the text and views captured by the camera eye simulate distance and vastness, the photobook continues to grant readers access to the inner workings of TVA infrastructure. A case in point is a photograph taken in an engine room at Pickwick Dam in southern Tennessee. As in the shot of Hiwassee discussed above, large spherical structures appear in the frame, albeit this time front and center. The resemblance to B-movie flying saucers is the same but enhanced by the bright light reflecting off the metallic surfaces and the shadows visible in relief. The caption points to the single human figure in the frame—a worker standing atop the next-to-last generator. The visual effects evoke futurism, transforming the machinery of hydropower into a statement on the beauty and power of modern technology. The image runs counter to those usually associated with the region. In a paean to the Tennessee Valley penned by the likes of Donald Davidson, for example, a yeoman farmer drawing water from a well would likely be the extent of extolling hydraulic engineering.

From a low-angle shot of Hiwassee Dam at nighttime to a ground-level view of munitions fresh off the assembly line and standing in formation as though marching to battle, Krutch's photographs present light, dark, and shadow in proximity. The contrast accentuates symmetrical patterns of steel or concrete surfaces to accentuate mechanical precision as part of the beauty inherent to TVA infrastructure. In this regard, Krutch's aesthetic vision owes a debt to the New Photography movement of the 1920s. This turn in photography was part of the broader New Objectivity (*Neue Sachlichkeit*) in the German visual arts that formed in reaction to the excesses of Expressionism. A defining feature was the presentation of objects as they existed and functioned at a practical level. Whether on a large scale (modern architecture or industrial machinery) or in an intimate setting (glassware on a table), the focus was on harmony between design and purpose. Krutch tended toward abstraction in centering design elements when working in this style. Nevertheless, he could use visual expression to deliver the story the TVA wanted to tell. Consequently, these images were consistent with New Photography's aesthetic ideology given "the control and selection of images" by the architects and the editors who published them "to create a polemic: a highly edited view of the possibilities of architecture of their time, with aspects of the building concerned presented as evidence."[53]

The elevation of everyday objects through the aesthetic manipulation of images was of great interest to Benjamin. In Dadaism, he observes in "The Author as Producer," arranging random items in a photograph demonstrated that they could express as much as a painting simply because the "picture frame ruptures time."[54] However, as photography becomes "ever more *nuancé*, ever more modern . . . it can no longer record a tenement block or a refuse heap without transfiguring it."[55] As a result, "photography is unable to convey anything about a power station or a cable factory other than, 'What a beautiful world!'"[56] Photo-textual compositions documenting the TVA's role in war mobilization in *The Valley and Its People* seem arranged to elicit that very response from readers. Early in the book, for example, a photograph depicting a panoramic view of Watts Barr Dam on one page precedes images on two consecutive pages of TVA electric furnaces and the tower of a munitions plant, respectively (26, 28, 29). Following those images is a half-page photograph taken inside a factory, with the caption reading, "Out of water and power comes air power. Continuous aluminum sheet mill in Tennessee" (31). This arrangement of text and images traces the course of hydroelectric power through various stages, transfiguring the infrastructure of war mobilization to present its components as objects worthy of aesthetic praise. Roosevelt's martial rhetoric in the early 1930s casting the Great Depression as a foe whose defeat would bring about recovery assumes literal meaning in the context of the TVA's important role in munitions manufacturing. Duffus's soaring, jingoistic prose puts the images of mechanized mass production into the context of a national crusade. As in the MoMA exhibition, TVA infrastructure functions beyond the stated purpose of practicality to make a symbolic appeal to US nationalism.

EXPERIENCING TVA MONUMENTALITY

The visual and rhetorical appeal to the public crafted by the TVA officials and museum staff collaborating on the MoMA exhibition suggests that they understood the dynamic described in Brian Larkin's observation that "the deeply affectual relationship people have to infrastructures—the sense of awe and fascination they simulate—is an important part of their political effect."[57] Indeed, facilitating memorable encounters with public works appears to have been an organizing principle of the curation—an attempt to give the people a sense of what it might be like to visit the actual sites and experience remarkable feats of architecture and engineering. The visual language of TVA photography (figs. 3 and 4) prompted viewers to imagine themselves in the place of the human figure standing in proximity to the face of a dam. The option to make the mediated experience actual was available because the public-facing components and visual culture were part of the built environment at various sites, starting with Norris Dam. The facility the man is poised to enter in the photograph is the powerhouse (fig. 4). Assuming the logical sequence of events suggested by the image and the fact that the picture was taken between 1936 and 1945, the man would have opened the door and moved into a small entryway facing another set of doors leading to a reception room designed, as the name implies, to welcome the American public and visiting dignitaries or delegations from abroad to the facility. Making his entrance and turning left, in keeping with the natural flow of the room, he would likely have seen immediately to his left a large-scale painting of Norris Dam covering most of the wall, an impressive infrastructural canvas. Confirming Lilienthal's remarks at the MoMA exhibition opening, the standard TVA slogan would have stood out, emblazoned above the painting in metallic capital letters forged in a special "TVA font" complementing the Art deco design of the room and tailored to the construction of Norris: "1933—BUILT FOR THE PEOPLE OF THE UNITED STATES—1936." The prominent placement of the slogan reflected the purpose of the reception area: to issue the same invitation to public ownership extended in the MoMA installation. The mediation was more tactile and elevated in scale, considering the proximity and access to the dam and certain areas of its supporting facilities available to visitors.

Fig. 4. Norris Dam and powerhouse. The photograph is uncredited, but Arthur Rothstein took others in the grouping. Farm Security Administration, Office of War Information Photograph Collection, Prints and Photographs Division, Library of Congress. Public domain.

The mixture of form and function on display in the painting—the artist remains unknown as of this writing—creates a parallel between the visual rendering and the architectural philosophy that informed Wank's blueprint for Norris Dam itself.[58] The dimensions of the wall allow for a perspective that presents the built environment as part of the landscape seen from a distance. Instead of the visual implication that the dam fits the lay of the land as though by natural rather than human design, the infrastructure is thrown into sharp relief. The dark color scheme used for the reservoir and river makes the face of the dam and the angular symmetry of the powerhouse painted in a light beige stand out as focal points. Bright hues and light brush strokes bring the forest-covered mountains in the background into view. The vivid depiction of the modernist architectural design in the foreground set against the impressionistic vista in the background draws together elements of two distinctive artistic movements in a composition that adds a dramatic statement to the space. While the formal properties contribute to the aesthetic value of the painting, the functional component demonstrates its role in the public appeal the space was designed to proffer. The artist made infrastructure visible by rendering a section of the powerhouse exterior invisible. The visual effect afforded viewers a peek inside the facility at an area adjacent to the reception room but not open to the public—an engine room containing large turbines (the subject of one of Krutch's MoMA exhibition photographs) used in generating hydroelectric power. The painting was also a useful visual aid for tour guides tasked with translating the complex workings of the Norris facilities into lay terms. A caption in the lower right corner listing the dam dimensions further serves its instructional purpose. While the perspective on the powerhouse calls to mind the long-distance and aerial photographs featured in the MoMA exhibition and *The Valley and Its People*, it more closely resembles the view of the dam from the overlook at the top of a bluff on the eastern side of the Clinch River. Depending on the itinerary, the painting would be either an artistic representation of a vista that visitors had already taken in or a preview of what they would soon see at a much larger scale.

By 1956, twenty years after the dam's completion, another infrastructural canvas was displayed in the reception room. In a move that harked back to the New Deal era, when artists employed by the Federal Art Project (FAP) produced public murals in post offices, courthouses, and other public spaces, the TVA's staff artist, Robert Birdwell, who was hired in 1953, created a work spanning the entire wall opposite the painting of Norris Dam. Birdwell was affiliated with the Knoxville Seven, comprising faculty hired by Charles Kermit "Buck" Ewing, the first head of the University of Tennessee Art Department, and artists from nearby communities. In addition to Birdwell and Ewing, Carl Sublett, Walter Stevens, Joanne Higgins, Richard Clarke, and Philip Nichols were affiliated with the group. This cohort took inspiration from Abstract Expressionism, producing a local strain of this homegrown American movement that flourished in the 1940s and 1950s. While Birdwell's paintings associated with the Knoxville Seven connected to a contemporary art scene, his TVA work was not as cutting-edge. Still, the official account of Birdwell's tenure, which lasted twenty-nine years, portrays his art as fresh and innovative. An article about Birdwell posted on the TVA website features a subsection titled "A Modern Artist for a Modern Agency," which offers this observation: "His style was colorful, progressive and—above all—modern."[59] The concluding line reinforces the point: "It is only fitting that the modern, progressive painter's work should adorn the walls of one of the most progressive government agencies ever to be created."[60] The official assessment figures the artist's style as an expression of the agency's self-styled mission and legacy.

Most of Birdwell's work for the TVA is modern in that it evokes the brand of regionalism that Thomas Hart Benton developed in the 1930s. Birdwell achieved this effect by repurposing aesthetic elements of the avant-garde and modernist paintings he had done in the previous decade. The similarities are apparent in the Birdwell murals adorning the walls of Fort Patrick Henry Dam and Boone Dam facilities. That is not surprising since regionalism was the predominant artistic movement in Tennessee in the 1930s and 1940s and remained influential for years to come. However, the stylistic differences noticeable in the Norris mural are unexpected. It combines close-up scenes of farming, soil conservation, fishing, and a river barge in the foreground located to the left and right and across the lower portion of the wall near ground level, yielding an effect that resembles comic book panels. Large trees on the left side of the mural create a visual complement to the transmission tower on the right side. The background consists of a map of the entire Tennessee River watershed with the network of infrastructure represented, each facility marked by a rudimentary figuration and identified by name. Birdwell added to the mural over time, as the depictions of nuclear power plants at Browns Ferry and Watts Barr and other facilities constructed after the original period of composition confirm. The elongated bodies and faces of the human figures, the simplistic rendering of trees with bold lines and basic shapes, and the lack of illusionistic perspective in the scenes evoke folk art rather than regionalism. Foregrounding average citizens rather than dignitaries or celebrated historical or mythical figures registered an artistic echo of the statement on the opposite wall proclaiming that the dam was "built for the people."[61]

Considering the modernist sensibilities that prevailed in the design of TVA infrastructure, the mural's style and subject matter would appear to be at odds. Such tension is less pronounced when looking at the work with intersections between folk art and modern art in mind. In 1932, the Museum of Modern Art staged an exhibition, "American Folk Art: The Art of the Common Man in America, 1500–1900," curated by Holger Cahill, who later served as head of the Federal Art Project from 1935 to 1943. The museum's mission and the focus of the exhibition implied an affinity between folk art and modern art that countered the consensus view of irreconcilable differences. In "American Folk Art," an essay in the book published in conjunction with the exhibition, Cahill notes that in about 1920 an interest in old American furniture led many artists to scour antique shops and attics in search of cultural artifacts. In the process, artists "came across pictures which arrested their attention"; most of these works were "merely quaint, but some of them had esthetic value of a high order, and all of them had a quality which gave them a kinship with modern art."[62] Two subsequent MoMA exhibitions—"Masters of Popular Painting: Modern Primitives of Europe and America," in 1938, also curated by Cahill, and "Contemporary Unknown American Painters," spearheaded in 1939 by wealthy collector and museum advisory board member Sidney Janis—further cemented the fine art credentials of folk art in the cultural firmament. Birdwell's extension of this stylistic association at the midcentury mark was an aesthetic gesture that served a rhetorical aim, as Todd Smith explains about the broader category in which the artist's Norris composition fits: "The murals, created to enlighten the public, were purposefully traditional and modern at the same time and demonstrated the Authority's understanding that its avowedly modern design needed to be balanced with a more traditional aesthetic strategy."[63] In so doing, the Norris mural complemented other projects established in the area in the mid-1930s and still extant in the 1950s as expressions of the cultural continuity the TVA claimed to foster: adult education courses in artisan practices of weaving and woodworking; a shop dedicated to the crafting of furniture inspired by the style of local antiques; a ceramics shop that produced porcelain items from a refined form of local clay; and a collaboration with the Southern Highland Craft Guild led by Arthur Morgan, who helped establish outlets to sell the guild's wares in the area and New York City while he was a TVA director. In this context, the Norris mural, like the dam itself, expressed TVA monumentality shaped by an aesthetic ideology intent on resolving any perceived tension between the traditional and the modern.

The dams and other facilities dotting the painted landscape of the mural and the colors used to highlight the geographic area of the network show Birdwell engaged in creative cartography to craft a strategic welcome. This mural mapping diminished the importance of state lines in delineating the boundaries of the TVA region as the defining coordinates of a domain where local people were thriving in rural modernity. The foreground scenes in the Norris mural convey this theme, as reflected in the official account of Birdwell's work for the agency: "In Birdwell's TVA paintings, the Valley residents are progressive and modern, with an excellent quality of life."[64] As the focal point of the reception room, the mural worked with the other elements of the space to orient the public to the carefully curated Norris experience. Accordingly, it approached the mode of simulation illustrated in Jean Baudrillard's influential formulation: "The territory no longer precedes the map, nor does it survive it. It is the map that precedes the territory—the *precession of simulacra*—that engenders the territory . . ."[65] Carroll Van West notes that "comprehensive planning" made Norris the TVA's "signature project."[66] As such, the dam was at the center of a local hub comprising Norris Freeway; Norris Village, a planned community populated mainly by TVA workers; Norris Lake, a reservoir; and the overlooks, which were open to the public early on and allowed people to see the dam under construction and after completion.[67] On one level, this infrastructure network provided public services; on another level, it was a demonstration area designed to promote the TVA agenda. Many people accepted the open invitation, some planning family day trips and arriving in automobiles with picnic lunches to visit the various points of sightseeing interest. Others stayed longer, bunking in the rustic cabins and exploring nature trails in the nearby park developed as one of the earliest and most significant Civilian Conservation Corps (CCC) undertakings.

Donald Davidson describes a visit to Norris, circa the late 1940s, from the perspective of a hypothetical motorist arriving via the Norris Freeway. For Davidson, the curation was obvious in the idealized forms undergirding the overarching theme of balance between the rustic and the modern and the natural and constructed that the TVA presented to visitors as an experiential claim about what was possible and necessary: "an amiable wild park" demonstrating "how Tennessee ought to look"; "a neat filling station . . . designed to illustrate how very pleasant a filling station might be"; and Norris Village, "the model town, or ideal town, of the Tennessee Valley, as the authority conceived a rural town."[68] A prominent signifier of rurality on the scenic drive, as Davidson documents, is the gristmill visible to his hypothetical motorist on the east side of the freeway. The last significant landmark before the dam, the Rice Grist Mill was completed in 1798 by James Rice and his sons, who had moved to Tennessee from North Carolina in 1790. The two-story structure was fitted with a large wooden water wheel, which was repurposed over the years to generate power for a sawmill, a cotton gin, a trip hammer, and a dynamo that fueled electric lights in the mill and the Rice home at the end of the nineteenth century.[69] The functional history of the water wheel made for a crafty symbolic segue, allowing the modern dam to stand as a natural and logical extension—the next step in a pattern of technological innovation dating back over a century. Davidson describes the intended public meaning conveyed by the visual and temporal juxtaposition of the gristmill and the modern marvel: "TVA would, apparently, promote Norris Dam and likewise cherish with fond care the individualism, the homeliness, the folkways, the crafts of the old time in Tennessee. It could do both."[70]

Although Davidson uses different terminology, his critique of Norris portrays it effectively as a simulacrum. Indeed, the location of the gristmill gave the impression that the scenic route was forged near the spot where the structure had stood since its completion in the eighteenth century. In truth, it was the site where the structure had been relocated from Union County, Tennessee, nearly forty miles away. In 1935, Rufus "Uncle Rufe" Rice became the last in a patrilineal line to operate the mill after relinquishing his land to the TVA and relocating to Blount County to make way for the flooding that came with the completion of Norris Dam and Norris Lake. The CCC and the National Park Service oversaw the disassembly, reconstruction, and, yet again, repurposing of the mill—this time so that it could function as a historical landmark and tourist attraction.[71] Tellingly, the strategic and symbolic emplacement of the mill, apparently to convey a sense of continuity, balance, and harmony, gets unsettled by the reality of displacement that the visual enticements of the Norris experience prompted visitors to overlook. This curational strategy bothered Davidson because of his abiding concern about inauthenticity as a sign of historical and cultural amnesia or erasure even as he begrudgingly acknowledged that the TVA could have it both ways by exhibiting modernist and preservationist tendencies. The assertion of this dual capacity was an aesthetic and ideological imperative of TVA visual culture overall, as its practitioners sought to portray infrastructural development as part of an ordered, progressive transition from past to present to future with minimal disruption.

Chapter 2

DOCUMENTARY FORMS
Infrastructural Inevitability in *The River* and *The Valley of the Tennessee*

THE SCREENING OF A SHORT FILM ABOUT THE TVA IN CONJUNCTION WITH THE PHOTOGRAPHS and other works of visual culture on display at the Museum of Modern Art exhibition in 1941 can be understood as the ambitious documentary project fostered by the New Deal state in microcosm. Paula Rabinowitz traces the emergence of documentary films in the 1930s by referencing preceding developments in visual culture, mainly photography. Rabinowitz notes the features that defined the documentary films produced by federal agencies or with production companies supportive of the New Deal agenda: black-and-white imagery that prevailed due to aesthetic and technological factors; nondiegetic narration with gravitas derived from scripts with lyrical lines delivered in stentorian voice-over; and vivid, compelling sequences and shots "often wrenching part from whole" to create metonymic representations of abject living conditions and of labor on large-scale government projects designed for relief and recovery in the near term and prosperity in the future.[1] This approach to exposition "was at once didactic and narratological," an effective mechanism for "developing an inevitability to its argument" in the service of propaganda that "inscribed its audience within the public sphere" as stakeholders in and beneficiaries of US government initiatives depicted as essential.[2] Notable documentary films defined by the New Deal aesthetic blended elements of social realism and modernism, becoming counterparts to the photographs commissioned by the Farm Security Administration (FSA) archive and the photobook genre discussed in the previous chapter. This formal hybridity was in line with the imperative to capture—literally to document—the harsh conditions and seemingly intractable problems that the Depression exacerbated and to present New Deal solutions as foregone conclusions.

Based on immediate impact and enduring influence, the most significant of the New Deal documentaries was *The River* (1938), a pathbreaking short film written and directed by Pare Lorentz for the FSA. Clocking in at just under twenty-two minutes, *The River* chronicles a *longue durée* of exploitation in the Mississippi Valley for economic profit from agricultural and industrial pursuits. From this perspective, it tracks erosion and land degradation so severe that major floods are routine instead of rare occurrences. The narrative shifts course about two-thirds of the way through to follow the tributaries of the Mississippi River branching out eastward. This geographical scope encompasses a connection to the Tennessee River via the confluence between the Mississippi and Ohio Rivers. The conclusion, in terms of the runtime and argument, centers on the TVA as the solution to a set of related problems diagnosed as chronic: flooding, poverty, soil erosion, and land degradation. This approach was standard for the social problem documentaries produced to strengthen the case for New Deal programs.

The Valley of the Tennessee is a case in point—a 1944 film that runs along similar lines as *The River* even though the purpose and intended audiences for the two projects reflect a shift in historical context from the Great Depression to World War II.[3] Produced by the Bureau of Motion Pictures in the Office of War Information (OWI) and directed by Czech-American photographer and filmmaker Alexander Hammid, *The Valley of the Tennessee* was an installment of the *American Scene* series developed as part of a multimedia campaign coinciding with the D-Day invasion. The film was conceived to help engender warm and productive relations between the Allied forces and the local populations of Western Europe liberated from Axis occupation. In *The River* and *The Valley of the Tennessee,* as in the photographs staged at MoMA and featured in photobooks, the dams and other facilities register as documentary forms with practical and symbolic functions geared toward making infrastructure visible to create public meaning. In projecting the enterprise as a replicable and exportable model of future-oriented regional planning and public works to redress uneven development, these films further document the capacity of TVA cultural production to foster influential formal experimentation while adhering to the dictates of state sponsorship directing the narrative contours toward preconceived and overdetermined ends at a crucial historical juncture.

THE RIVER IN FORMATION

Pare Lorentz had already engaged extensively with New Deal cultural politics when he officially signed on as an advocate. In 1934, he published *The Roosevelt Year*, a book praising FDR and his administration. At the time, Lorentz was living in Washington, DC, and writing a newspaper column on espionage. During a meeting with Secretary of Agriculture Henry Wallace, Lorentz gave him a copy of *The Roosevelt Year* and "the seed of my idea about photographing the changes in America, such as Tennessee Valley Authority, that were presumably going to take place with the New Deal."[4] That seed sprouted in due course, but film rather than photography became Lorentz's medium of choice. In 1936, the director completed *The Plow That Broke the Plains*, a short documentary about the devastating effects of the Dust Bowl that nearly rises to the level of *The River* in terms of importance. It was produced by the Resettlement Administration (RA), a New Deal agency established to relocate displaced and dispossessed families to planned communities operated by the federal government. After the RA was declared unconstitutional in 1937, the viable agency operations were transferred to the newly established FSA. When Lorentz began working on *The River*, an FSA project, he joined a cadre of photographers and filmmakers whose compelling images of Americans beset by hard times would define the Great Depression in public memory. The topic of *The River*, like that of *The Plow That Broke the Plains*, was timely. As the film's production began, the devastating Great Flood of 1927 was a decade in the past but not forgotten. That was partly due to another major flood in 1936, which led observers to compare the two supposedly hundred-year floods. Then, as Lorentz and his crew were filming in 1937, severe flooding halted production. The dark cloud had at least one silver lining, as a few crew members captured dramatic footage that made the final cut and heightened the film's sense of urgency.

Lorentz's concentration on natural disasters resonated with that of contemporaneous works that explored the causes and assessed the devastating consequences. This cultural trend reached its apex with the fictional renderings of the Dust Bowl in John Steinbeck's *The Grapes of Wrath* in 1939 and John Ford's film adaptation in 1940. Michael Denning describes how these major events became rhetorical devices for illustrating alternative courses for dealing with the vagaries of capitalism to the American public. On the right, natural disasters provided a metaphorical means of defining the cyclical patterns of economic downturn and recovery as naturally occurring phenomena. The message to people enduring hardship, then, was that drastic alterations to the structure of the free-market economy were dangerous and that it would be more prudent to ride out storms with confidence that stabilization and recovery would surely come. On the left, where recovery plans ranged from the Keynesian to the Marxian, natural disasters were handy metaphors for a state of emergency arising from the economic crisis. Such figurations bolstered claims that state intervention to deliver immediate relief, spur recovery in the short term, and increase regulatory oversight to achieve greater stability in the long term were essential. The resulting "tensions between these rhetorics of 'the people'" meant natural disasters were "deeply embedded in popular discourses about the depression."[5] In this context, artists inclined to support the New Deal or those enlisted to promote it through cultural production, as was Lorentz, used the "trope of prefiguration" to convey a sense of longevity for a federal initiative presented as ambitious and transformative.[6] For the left, as Denning observes, "the New Deal programs were celebrated not as solutions in themselves but as prefigurations of a future democratic and collective social order."[7]

The River lends cinematic expression to the New Deal brand of futurity, affording a long view of history and ecology while charting a path toward progress leading to the TVA infrastructure under construction. Lorentz's mastery of duration involves a temporality that defies the bounds of the documentary short form to set deep time later recalibrated to what Hannah Appel calls "infrastructural time" as the measure of historical progression. As Appel explains, infrastructural time is a temporal construction that applies the broader concept of developmental time to infrastructure. Developmental time is associated with "linearity, progress, and teleology."[8] This perception of time facilitated "techno-developmental teleologies that animated ... orthodox modernization theories" and eventually influenced "people around the world to talk in terms of developmental time, progress and relapse, of being behind and needing to catch up."[9] In infrastructural time, developmental time functions as "a normative temporality ... a materialist insistence on a desired standard of living ... articulated through infrastructure."[10] It is important to stipulate that Appel defines this form of temporality and its discursive functions relative to the current global North/South divide, drawing on data and anecdotal evidence gathered while doing anthropological fieldwork in Equatorial Guinea. As the rhetoric promoting the TVA and similar public works projects in Europe and the Soviet Union attest, the elements of infrastructural time were extant in the 1930s and imposed on nonindustrialized nations in subsequent decades as building infrastructure to spark modernization and economic growth became the standard model.

Throughout *The River*, kinesthetic imagery in the narration and visual sequences express the momentum of repeating cycles that evoke infrastructural time, drawing together past and present in a scope that extends from prehistory to modernity. The Mississippi River and its tributaries conform to the forces of natural history and anthropogenic intervention converging on a course moving toward the only conclusion allowed within the framework: the formation of the TVA and the construction of large-scale public works projects. Lorentz develops this effect by adapting and reimagining filmmaking techniques associated with the avant-garde form of poetic cinema that emerged in the 1920s. Rabinowitz observes, "Cinema, photography, and poetry combine in a seamless teleological gesture wherein the end of the film offers the end of suffering and the emergence of a new world of mastery and modernity."[11] The result is a pro-TVA production that runs on infrastructural time so that the formal structure of the film and the infrastructure it highlights support the ideological imperatives and political agenda of the New Deal state.

TRANSNATIONAL CONNECTIONS: POETIC CINEMA, INFRASTRUCTURAL POETICS

Pare Lorentz's status as an important figure in film history rests on his skill at blending formal experimentation with topical relevance to push documentary filmmaking in new directions. The reception of *The River* indicates that this assessment formed early on. In 1938, the film earned the top honor in the documentary category at the Venice Film Festival. Among the competitors it edged out was *Olympia*, Leni Riefenstahl's infamous paean to the 1936 Olympic games in Berlin, which served as a showcase for Hitler's Third Reich. Riefenstahl's film did wind up taking home the festival's top honor, the Mussolini Cup, sharing the prize with Luciano Serra's *Pilot*, produced by Vittorio Mussolini, son of the Italian dictator. Nevertheless, Lorentz's win was significant considering the prevailing cultural politics.

The festival was in its seventh year in 1938, having been incorporated into the Arts Biennale in 1932 with the involvement of Mussolini's movie mogul brother and with support from the dictator himself. Marijke de Valck explains that the regime's imprint was relatively light during the inaugural run; however, by 1936 "the role of the Venice Film Festival as a consolidator of the ideological and cultural position of the Fascist party was unmistakable."[12] That Lorentz's film topped Riefenstahl's in this context is remarkable, and it has understandably invited comparative assessments of the two films and filmmakers.[13] *The River* and *Olympia* developed out of government-funded cultural production, albeit on different ends of the political spectrum. Both rely on epic grandeur to confer legitimacy on large-scale infrastructure projects as monuments to nation-building. In *Olympia*, Riefenstahl's camera eye gazes reverently at the infrastructure of the Third Reich, much of it constructed specifically for the Olympics. The aerial views of architecture precede ground-level shots of athletes striking statuesque poses or embroiled in the heat of competition. These images establish aesthetic connections between infrastructure and the human body, projecting both as exemplars of the muscular ideology of Aryan supremacy at the foundation of Nazism. Lorentz too directs the camera eye such that the perspective alternates between large- and small-scale perspectives. In *The River*, however, the bodies in motion and labor at dam construction sites or in engine rooms are presented as individual contributors to a collective enterprise painted with hues of democratic nationalism.

Such comparisons have led to the recognition of Lorentz and Riefenstahl as significant formal innovators. But it is crucial to add that emphasis on form should not come at the expense of considering ideological imperatives and propagandistic aims, especially considering attempts to cite aesthetic concerns as grounds for redeeming Riefenstahl.[14] While Riefenstahl makes for an instructive counterpart, Soviet avant-garde filmmaker Dziga Vertov has as much if not more to offer when examining Lorentz's filmmaking in a transnational context. In many respects, *The River* exhibits Vertovian influences traceable to *The Eleventh Year* (1928). Vertov produced that experimental documentary with the express aim of challenging conventions in the burgeoning field of nonfiction film. It centers on the building of the Dnieper Dam in Ukraine and includes footage from the Volkhov Dam construction site in northwestern Russia. Jeremy Hicks describes similarities between *The Eleventh Year* and other works in Vertov's oeuvre, noting that the filmmaker "continues to follow an agenda determined by journalism, even if his approach to the subject may be original."[15] The state-run production was billed as a newsreel even though Vertov blended elements of journalism with a new form of poetic cinema to create "something between newsreel and experiment."[16] Through this hybrid form, the film highlights public works projects constructed as part of Joseph Stalin's First Five-Year Plan to generate hydroelectric power for regional rehabilitation and development. At this pivotal moment, traditions rooted in the past contended with the forces of modernity at various scales. Lorentz addresses a similar predicament in the Tennessee Valley, displaying in his film the conventional formal properties and journalistic credentials of the newsreel while taking poetic license to portray rapid change in line with the TVA's ideological investment in the American myth of progress.

The Eleventh Year and *The River* both render scale through captivating cinematic imagery. Alternating long and close-up shots establish that the natural landscapes are transforming. *The Eleventh Year* opens with an aerial shot of mountainous terrain and then cuts to a ground-level view of water flowing over rocks in the Dnieper River. Similarly, *The River* begins with vistas of mountains engulfed in cloud formations, the peaks becoming more visible with each shot in the sequence. From the mountaintops and towering trees against the backdrop of majestic skies, the view in *The River* abruptly changes to tree leaves and water flowing filmed in close-up. This technique eventually became a convention of nature documentary filmmaking. In both films, the shifting perspectives on nature set the stage for comparable views of infrastructural development. Variations in scale convey the monumentality of projects in the making. In *The River*, this effect is enhanced by the commanding voice-over delivered by Thomas Hardie Chalmers, a Metropolitan Opera Company singer who first worked with Lorentz on *The Plow That Broke the Plains*. Lorentz's use of voice-over contrasts with Vertov's reliance on intertitles to serve as the sole device for narration.

Lorentz follows Vertov's lead in forging a vast temporal scope that contributes to the cinematic effect of imbuing nature and infrastructure with a sense of epic grandeur. In *The Eleventh Year*, the presence of the past affirms the legitimacy of Stalin's vision for the future. The camera moves in to reveal the skeletal remains of an ancient Scythian unearthed during the excavation phase of construction. Hicks observes that the juxtaposition of the remains and the project underway illustrates a clean break between the premodern and modern epochs consistent with the modernizing imperatives of the Soviet regime.[17] In *The River*, the images of mountainous terrain and flowing tributaries have voice-over accompaniment from a script written in verse by Lorentz. As narrator, Chalmers chronicles the "ancient valley" cultivated over time "by the / old river spilling her floods across the bottom / of the continent—."[18] The combination of imagery and narration is typical of Lorentz's approach to poetic cinema. Furthermore, it establishes a temporal pattern that extends from nature's shaping of the valley in deep time to the TVA's reshaping of it in infrastructural time. Lorentz's reliance on cyclical patterns to structure *The River* contrasts with Vertov's preference for collapsing time. Superimposition is one of the signature techniques used to achieve this effect. For example, in the "Conquering Dnieper" segment, Vertov superimposes a faint shot of the skeletal remains over a more vivid one of a construction crew worker handling a pile driver.

Although their styles are different, Vertov and Lorentz both draw from the aesthetic elements of poetic cinema to craft temporal frames in which historicity confers legitimacy on infrastructure built by the state. For both filmmakers, montage is the main instrument for crafting cinematic language geared toward poetic expression. Anna Lawton cites Vertov's employment of the technique in cinema as grounds for tracing connections to a contemporaneous movement in poetry: "The constant foregrounding in Vertov's films of the two basic structural elements of cinema—the shot and the montage—is analogous to the Futurists' foregrounding of the structural elements of verse—sound and rhythm."[19] Lawton's observation also applies to Lorentz, who organizes shots into montage sequences marked by repetition such that they convey the effect of rhythm and rhyme through film language. In this respect, Lorentz's technique mirrors that of Vertov, who "wove in each of his films a subtle net of semantic relationships by means of rhythmic patterning," which was "based on the same principles that sustain the creation of modern poetry."[20] But there is more to it than that. Lorentz traces and retraces the river's path through cycles of ecological and economic impacts. In so doing, the director makes the rhythmic scheme of verse and montage the framework for constructing a sweeping historical narrative and supporting the overarching claim through teleological progression. On this count, Peter Rollins credits Lorentz's deft editing, observing that "*The River* makes effective use of cutting to reinforce thematic messages."[21] As the film tracks insatiable materialism driving agricultural and industrial capitalism, the montage sequences expose a pattern of environmental degradation culminating in the current crisis. Rollins applies Sergei Eisenstein's concept of "intellectual montage" to illustrate how form works to rhetorical effect as the film moves from stating the problem to positing that the TVA is *the* solution.[22]

Like the works of visual culture discussed in the previous chapter, *The River* is structured according to the logic that the formal properties of infrastructure operate with but are also distinct from functional components. As Brian Larkin states, infrastructure is worthy of analysis as an aesthetic and semiotic mode of public address. As such, these projects "emerge out of and store within them forms of desire and fantasy that can take on fetish-like aspects."[23] Concentrating on form, "or the poetics of infrastructure, allows us to understand how the political can be constituted through different means."[24] The types of address in *The River*—verbal by the narrator, visual by the camera eye—suggest that the film enacts an infrastructural poetics that combines form and function in the interest of persuasion. From this standpoint, the structure of *The River* enhances the infrastructure of the TVA, projecting a collective fantasy that entices viewers to accept "representations as social facts."[25]

As a screenwriter, Lorentz pushed the concept of poetic cinema to the extreme. The script was published in the May 1937 issue of *McCall's* magazine as a feature story on the Mississippi Valley. A far cry from the original assignment, which had called for a conventional magazine article in the range of five thousand words, the script was composed in free verse. In 1938, Stackpole and Sons published an illustrated edition including stills from the film. At the time, recognition of Lorentz's gifts as a poet rivaled the kudos for his talents as a filmmaker. He earned a Pulitzer Prize in Poetry nomination in 1938 and drew praise from literary luminaries. James Joyce lauded Lorentz's writing style, declaring that it was the "most beautiful" he had encountered in a decade.[26] After reading the Stackpole edition, Carl Sandburg wrote a letter to the publisher praising Lorentz's achievement: "It is among the greatest of the psalms of America's greatest river."[27]

The lyrical narration delivered in voice-over by Chalmers unfolds over shots that range from panoramic views of the Mississippi Valley to images of cotton and timber production and steel manufacturing. Lorentz is careful to give the people working in these industries their due insofar as screen time goes. Critics have cited these and other qualities to characterize the film as Whitmanesque.[28] In the script, Lorentz, like Whitman, shapes an expansive point of view through which the persona employs acute powers of perception and a capacious historical consciousness. Often in Whitman's poetry, the persona sees through what can be termed a camera-I, with perspectives alternating between distant and close observation in assuming the proportions of the body politic and presuming to speak on its behalf. Similarly, the choice of "we" in *The River* establishes the narration as the voice of a national consciousness recollecting the exploitation of the Mississippi River for profit and eventually recommending the TVA as the remedy for decades of exploitation and ecological harm. Where the Whitman camera-I invites readers to identify with an individual persona, the repetition of "we" throughout the narration in *The River* incorporates viewers into the body politic by the mode of address.

The first instance of this technique occurs in the fourth stanza of the script, in which the speaker describes the construction of the levee system as an attempt to tame the mighty river. Reversing the natural course, the speaker chronicles the progress of construction upriver from New Orleans to Cairo: "We built a dyke a thousand miles long, / Men and mules, mules and mud; / Mules and mud and a thousand miles up the / Mississippi" (62). The alliteration, delivered by Chalmers with emphatic flair, is a formal device for establishing a pattern of repetition that mimics infrastructural time and frames the history of construction along the river. While the spatial path in the narration runs counter to the river flow, the temporality pinpoints key junctures on an extended timeline. A reference to levee projects started by the Spanish and French in the nineteenth century to protect New Orleans from flooding lays the groundwork for noting that over four decades, post–Louisiana Purchase, "we" extended the barrier for the full length of "the great alluvial Delta" (62). As members of the body politic, part of "we," viewers are implicated and incorporated into the temporal mapping of epochal phases measured in terms of natural history and the more recent history of anthropogenic intervention occurring in infrastructural time.

FLOWS OF CAPITAL, LABOR, AND PROFIT

The steady stream of water shaping the valley's contours foreshadows the flow of settlers arriving to seek their fortunes. At no point does the unfolding historical narrative acknowledge the existence of Indigenous people. At least it alludes to the enslaved people who built the infrastructure and performed the labor that enabled the ruling class to prosper. The narrator, in lines omitted from the published version of the script, recounts that "the planters brought their blacks and their plows and their cotton over to the river." The migratory pattern of settlers, capital, and labor is traced in the same dramatic tone as the earlier account of the Mississippi River and its tributaries forming. At this point in history, the river is a crucial hub in "the Empire of Cotton," the global network Sven Beckert defines. Beckert documents the work of cotton factors in New Orleans, Charleston, and Memphis, who "brought the global norms of capital accumulation and the manufacturers' demand for ever cheaper cotton at predictable qualities to the doorsteps of slave plantations."[29] Lorentz underscores this historical phase by creating resonance between word and image. "We rolled a million bales down the river for / Liverpool and Leeds . . . ," the narrator says, initiating a montage in which dockworkers load bales of cotton on the first leg of a transatlantic journey to the English textile manufacturing hubs cited. The narrator continues: "Rolled them off Alabama, // Rolled them off Mississippi, // Rolled them off Louisiana, // Rolled them down the river!" (63–64). The match cuts comprising the montage sequence, combined with the use of anaphora in the verse, convey the momentum of the cotton trade as it grew to dominate the global economy, dramatically altering the ecology of the Mississippi Valley in the process.

When the film turns to the mid-nineteenth century, the use of "we" to signify a singular national consciousness undergoes noticeable stress. Initially, the description of cotton production as a collective venture encompasses the experiences of the planters and manufacturers who reaped material rewards and the enslaved agricultural and exploited industrial laborers who were means to those profitable ends. However, the clear conflicts of interest glossed over here ultimately fueled sectional antagonism and civil war. This historical reality manifests as a contradiction in the narrator presuming to give voice to the body politic as a unified entity. The story of King Cotton's reign is interrupted by a visual interlude that adapts the newsreel aesthetic to a description of the Confederate surrender at Appomattox. The camera pans down a newspaper clipping transcribing Robert E. Lee's official remarks on the historic occasion. At the end of the shot, with the focus on Lee's signature, the narrator delivers a history of the Civil War, perhaps with unprecedented concision: "We fought a war. // We fought a war and kept the west bank / of the river free of slavery forever" (64). Despite the brevity, the account evokes the mythic conception of the Mississippi Valley as a cradle of freedom. It calls to mind Frederick Jackson Turner's description of the region as "the especial home of democracy," where "free land and the pioneer spirit," among other factors, created ideal conditions such that "democracy showed itself in the earliest utterances of the men of the Western Waters and it has persisted there."[30]

This account echoes Thomas Jefferson's vision of the Mississippi Valley becoming an "empire for liberty." Walter Johnson argues that this "dream" was the catalyst for the "history of slavery, capitalism, and imperialism in the nineteenth-century Mississippi Valley," which is the same history *The River* obscures or recasts.[31] Presumably designed to downplay sectionalism, the strategy of revising history to present opposition to slavery as part of a national commitment to the cause of freedom bolstered the Lost Cause instead, if the premiere of *The River* in New Orleans is any indication. Members of the audience reportedly rose to their feet out of respect when Lee's name appeared on the screen.[32] The irony of the gesture—standing to honor Lee while the narrator declared a triumph over the institution of slavery that the Confederate nationalist Lee and his soldiers fought desperately to preserve—points to a vexing question: who is the "we" that defines the point of view in *The River*'s narration?

At the time of the film's production, sectionalism was much on the minds of TVA advocates as they sought public support in the region and across the nation. After all, the New Deal was a federal intervention in the South on a scale not seen since Reconstruction. In his memoir, David E. Lilienthal explains the TVA strategy for dealing with sectionalism: "We avoid the word today, hoping perhaps that the evils of disunity and local selfishness will vanish if the syllables are forgotten. But it is not so easily exorcised."[33] An important component of the rhetorical strategy was to stress regionalism as the preferred design for administering New Deal programs—not least the TVA, which was held up as an exemplar. Lilienthal addresses the seemingly counterintuitive nature of this approach, insisting that the regional planning and delivery of federal programs "rests squarely upon the supremacy of the *national* interest."[34] The distinction between regionalism and sectionalism that Lilienthal tries to make plain in his book reflects the influence of modern regionalism, a concept formulated by Howard W. Odum and his colleagues at the Institute for Research in Social Science at the University of North Carolina in Chapel Hill. By this measure, sectionalism gives preference to regional or local authority, as in the belief that upholding states' rights should be the primary objective in governance; in contrast, regionalism places national interests first when making decisions at the local or regional level.[35]

Lorentz makes the case for regionalism as the organizing principle of the TVA by resorting to the trope of the South as the nation's problem. After the laconic account of the Civil War, the narrator stipulates that "we left the old South impoverished," adding that the region was "doubly stricken" due to the practice of monoculture for profit at the expense of sustainability (64). As the camera pans across a denuded and eroded landscape, Chalmers in the voice-over references the practice of "min[ing] the soil" without concern for the harmful effects (64). The mining metaphor foreshadows the destructive practices of coal extraction highlighted later in the film. The arc of the narrative continues a dark trajectory, with the speaker recounting that "we fought a war, but there was a double / tragedy—the tragedy of land twice / impoverished" (64). The accompanying shots of barren land reveal the extent of environmental damage caused by cotton monoculture, calling to mind a southern landscape ravaged by war and not yet recovered. If captured as a still, any of these shots might pass as one of the wartime photographs by Mathew Brady and his assistants as they created a visual archive of death and destruction with lasting legacies. Natalie J. Ring explains that the notion of the "problem South" was a common perception of the region from the late nineteenth to the middle of the twentieth century that delineated it as a "backward and a potentially catastrophic space" different from the rest of the country.[36] Leigh Anne Duck argues that the "backward South" stood in contrast to the "progressive nation," with the region perceived as a site of uneven development, alternate temporality, and hidebound customs such as racial segregation that were tolerated under classical liberalism.[37] In the section on the Civil War and its aftermath, the film rehearses the formulation of the region-as-problem and the need to solve it in the national interest. In this respect, *The River* is a companion to the 1938 special report commissioned by the Roosevelt administration that cited the South as the nation's primary economic problem.[38]

Lorentz's film illustrates how a cycle of interconnected economic exploitation and environmental degradation driven by the profit motive has worn out old modes of production and driven the formation of new ones. The profit motive is formulated as a product of human nature that registers with destructive impacts on the natural world. From the tale of King Cotton, the film turns northward to chronicle another monoculture crop, timber, which held the promise of "lumber enough to cover all Europe" (64). Close-up shots of an ax striking a tree initiate a sequence that moves from a long shot of the tree falling to match cuts of other trees falling in forests. The next sequence shows logs propelled by a stream of running water on a long conveyor delivering them to the riverfront for transport. Like the segment on cotton, the one on the timber industry shows how the downward flow of the river current has facilitated production and distribution, marking time and space in a narrative of rapid development. Industries converge in perpetuating the riparian flow of commodities into the marketplace: "There was lumber in the North / and coal in the hills. / Iron and coal down the Monongahela" (65). The story of iron and coal delivered to Pittsburgh and Wheeling is accompanied by exterior shots of factories in the distance, creating resonance between images of human-made structures blowing smoke and the footage of treetops immersed in fog earlier in the film. Likewise, the interior shots of a factory in which molten steel is poured into huge molds as sparks fly visually rhyme with earlier images of the river water moving in steady currents and then gaining velocity to form rapids that crash into rocks and spray water into the air.

The next segment chronicles a period of rapid expansion in which cotton and timber production moved west, enabling the prosperous cotton trade to continue and a boom in industrial and urban development to occur. "We built a hundred cities and a thousand towns," the narrator says, issuing a litany that moves from St. Paul and Minneapolis to Omaha and Kansas City to the mouth of the Mississippi at New Orleans as a montage of city skylines unfurls on the screen (66). Astrid Böger observes, "The cityscapes are treated in exactly the same way as the landscapes; both form a visual-musical continuum."[39] The narrator closes the stanza with a triumphalist declaration, "We built a new continent," evoking the myth of Manifest Destiny as rendered in *American Progress*, John Gast's iconic 1872 painting (66). But the effect is short-lived: the score turns ominous with a symphonic clarion call that diminishes to a single-horn dirge. The film lays bare the material history of accelerated development in an elegiac blend of word and image: the voice-over laments the loss of "black spruce and Norway pine, / Douglas fir and Red cedar; / Scarlet oak and Shagbark hickory" as the camera surveys the wasteland. The American myth of progress is subject to the countervailing force of recognition that development has come, "[b]ut at what a cost!" (66).

In this sequence, it seems as though Gast's Columbia, the angelic embodiment of Manifest Destiny, meets another angel from a painting—the figure in Paul Klee's *Angelus Novus*, as interpreted by Walter Benjamin. In his philosophical treatise "On the Concept of History," Benjamin imagines this figure as the Angel of History, suspended in a state of shock while looking back to the past and beholding it as a totalizing catastrophe rather than a linear path of progress. For Benjamin, the angel longs to mobilize the dead in a restorative enterprise, but strong winds blow from Paradise, propelling the angel with outstretched wings away from the scene while still looking back. "What we call progress is *this* storm," Benjamin concludes.[40] The metaphor relates to the subsequent sequence in *The River*, which illustrates how anthropogenic interventions in the Mississippi Valley have contributed to a perfect storm of natural disasters. A montage sequence begins with close-up shots, including water slowly dripping from melting icicles, establishing the spring thaw as the basis of eventual raging floodwaters that have been wreaking havoc with regularity: "1903 and 1907, / 1913 and 1922, / 1927, / 1936, / 1937!" (66–67). In retracing the river's path, the film reinforces through narrative and visual rhythm and rhyme the destructive pattern of a vicious cycle. The skilled editing lends formal expression to the historical repetition—a prime example of how *The River* documents the effects of an insatiable materialism that knows no bounds between agricultural and industrial forms of capitalism.

ON/OF COURSE: LORENTZ'S CLOSING ARGUMENT

The River takes a momentous turn when it recounts the devastation wrought by flooding between 1903 and 1937. In a lyrical tone that assumes biblical proportions, the film describes the damage done overall but does not single out the Great Mississippi Flood of 1927. In his historical account of that flood, the most destructive in the United States at the time, John M. Barry sets the stage with a dramatic prologue:

> The river seemed the most powerful thing in the world. Down from the Rocky Mountains of Colorado this water had come, down from Alberta and Saskatchewan in Canada, down from the Allegheny Mountains in New York and Pennsylvania, down from the Great Smokies in Tennessee, down from the forests of Montana and the iron ranges of Minnesota and the plains of Illinois. From the breadth of the continent down had come all the water that fell upon the earth and was not evaporated into the air or absorbed by the soil, down as if poured through a funnel, down into this immense, writhing snake of a river, this Mississippi.[41]

Barry's prose channels Lorentz's poetic style, resonating with the same momentum in moving from a wide scope to the narrower concentration illustrated by the simile of a funnel. Barry spends a considerable part of the narrative documenting the frenzied mobilizations and infrastructural reinforcements that the flood precipitated: the drive to fortify the levee system as the river stages continued to rise and, when that failed, the desperate coordination of the disaster response on an unprecedented scale. In *The River*, Lorentz dramatizes responses to impending floods through the martial metaphors prominent in New Deal rhetoric. In this vein, the floods serve as calls to arms: "We sent armies down the river to help the / engineers fight a battle on a two thousand / mile front" (69). A roll call citing the armed forces, the CCC, the WPA, the Red Cross, and the Health Service heralds the formation of an alliance. In each case, the mission would shift from flood prevention to search and rescue to recovery. The extent of the catastrophe leads the filmmakers to define the cause as noble and heroic rather than victorious, emphasizing the tireless commitment and bravery of the "soldiers" involved in the conflict between humans and nature.

The incorporation of 1927 into a series of flood years and the conflation of all those involved in the effort as part of a cohesive unit sustains the epic tone at the expense of documentary realism. In the Mississippi Delta, as Barry documents, the people on the front lines before the flood were African Americans coerced by local officials; after the flood, they faced internment in makeshift camps patrolled by armed guards set up on the levees out of concern that the agricultural labor force would flee en masse to escape the harrowing conditions.[42] Susan

Scott Parrish analyzes this response in terms of biopolitics, adapting the work of Giorgio Agamben from the context of Europe to the US South. Parrish stipulates, "A different biopolitical history pertained in the American plantation zone."[43] Unlike in Europe, where governments worked to alleviate conditions threatening the whole population, "plantation powers . . . designed one part of the population to protect the other."[44] These "Delta concentration camps" were set up because the planter class understood that its viability rested on the labor and positioning of Black bodies in response to the flooding and its aftermath.[45] As African Americans faced coercion and violence, "their role as a living buffer zone between whites and nature's dangerous vagaries was made literally manifest."[46] The leveling of the floods in a narrative of epic grandeur submerges the granular details of 1927 beneath a surface of idealized regionalism favored by New Deal advocates. Recalling the troubling history of coerced labor and forced encampment alongside *The River*'s narrative of heroic feats on behalf of flood victims calls to mind Agamben's observation in *Homo Sacer*, building on the work of Hannah Arendt and Michel Foucault, that the deployment of biopolitical power can produce moments of uncanny resemblance between liberal democracies and totalitarian regimes.[47]

The variable of biopower figures more substantially into the equation as *The River* draws closer to its endorsement of the TVA. The visual scheme at this juncture relies on the footage of the 1937 flood shot by members of Lorentz's crew. Lorentz deftly uses aerial shots of inundated communities, including shots of rooftops appearing to float on the surface of the vast floodwaters. The scene documents the devastation that had occurred with increasing frequency—a point underscored when the narrator, speaking from the perch of the Whitmanesque persona, repeats the timeline of recent history from 1903 to 1937. When the scene shifts to ground level, the destruction becomes visible at close range in footage of houses lifted from their original foundations and deposited upside down in random locations. Such images drive home the loss and displacement of life that resulted from each flood. Referencing the long history of profit-driven, anthropogenic manipulation of the river, the film zeroes in on the consequences for the land and the inhabitants of the Mississippi Valley. Long shots of oddly formed mounds and cliffs caused by soil erosion enhance the effect of surrealism, making it appear that a mad sculptor has carved the landscape in fulfillment of a distorted vision. The voice-over laments the fact that "four hundred million tons of top soil, / Four hundred million tons of our most valuable / natural resource have been washed into the / Gulf of Mexico every year" to set up the point that "poor land makes poor people. / Poor people make poor land" (71).

A montage sequence featuring a family picking cotton illustrates the hardship faced by the valley's inhabitants trying to eke out a living from the depleted croplands. The family members are portrayed as faceless figures "[d]own on their knees in the valley" foraging for literal slim pickings (71). Shot from various angles as they move slowly and mechanistically down the rows of puny cotton plants, they dramatize the experience of being trapped in a cycle of poverty and deprivation fueled by the harmful economic and environmental practices cited earlier in the film. The visual transition to the epilogue remains focused on rural families, exhibiting aesthetic features that became staples of documentary realism in the 1930s. Shots of tenant families crowded in ramshackle cabins confront the viewer with the disturbing proposition that the proud descendants of pioneers now comprise "a generation facing a life of dirt / and poverty; Disease and drudgery; // Growing up without proper food, / medical care or schooling, // 'Ill-clad, ill-housed, and ill-fed'— // And in the greatest river valley in the world" (72–73). The visual and verbal imagery, including a reference to FDR's Second Inaugural Address, marks a return of the problem South as a key trope employed to dramatic effect. The emphasis on abjection recalls FSA photographs capturing the hardship and despair of the Depression as the toll registered on human bodies and faces. For this reason, the visual sequences give the impression that subjects of Dorothea Lange's signature works have broken the spell of photographic stasis to spring into action. The solution presented in the epilogue hinges on connecting the lived experiences of the tenants with the broader historical currents *The River* has traced so far.

The rhetorical appeal to pathos evident in the sequence focused on poor tenant families is followed by an appeal to logos to set the stage for a soaring expression of TVA monumentality. Graphic maps appear on screen, one tracing the Mississippi River and its tributaries and another reiterating the issue of massive deforestation with illustrated trees dotting the map and then disappearing as the historical timeline of the narrative progresses. The narrative takes on qualities of a re-creation story as it arrives at the 1933 point. "First came the dams," the narrator proclaims (74). A shot of a dynamite explosion conveys the virtual Big Bang that brings the TVA into being, ushering in a sequence of shots from alternating perspectives: long shots of cranes moving debris, a construction worker filmed from a low angle as he operates a jackhammer, and an aerial view of dam construction. The narrator recites a poetic litany of the dams built in infrastructural time at the dawn of the TVA. The brief mention of Norris Dam as first in line occurs in the voice-over paired with a long shot of a construction worker. The positioning of the camera so that the worker is in the close foreground and the dam is in the distant background presents the individual worker on a scale closer to that of the massive structure his labor is partially responsible for constructing. The shift in relative scale alters the standard visual terms of images conveying the small stature of the lone figure against the backdrop of mammoth infrastructure.

The attention paid to construction feats imbues the dams with symbolic value such that they become monuments to the virtues and benefits of New Deal planning. The shots of dams completed or in progress provide visual reinforcement to the assertion that the TVA is bringing order to the region and releasing untapped potential. As in the historical overview, the concluding section uses the river's flow as an organizing principle for the argument. Once completed, the network of dams "will transform the old Tennessee / into a link of fresh water pools locked and / dammed, regulated and controlled, down six / hundred fifty miles to Paducah" (75). The linkage extends to the riverbank and the wider valley to make the point that "you cannot plan for water unless you / plan for land" (75), The film traces yet another force of change sweeping into the valley: a throng of young men of the CCC "working with the forest service and / agricultural experts ... to put the / worn fields and hillsides back together" by planting trees and clearing paths (75). According to the plan, putting the scientific theories of soil conservation into practice lays the groundwork for "a model agricultural community" (75). It is a microcosm of the ideological and biopolitical imperative of the New Deal to strike a balance between vaunted American individualism, especially the "rugged" kind, and the shades of collectivism necessitated by the severity of the crisis. Along these paradoxical lines, the newly formed town of Norris, Tennessee, becomes a model of self-reliance where people are once again following in the footsteps of their pioneer ancestors by "[l]iving in homes they / themselves built" (75). This claim belies what the visual images make clear: a community planned with such meticulous attention to detail that the residents and houses appear uniform. The uplift of the Norris sequence enabled by Chalmers's soaring tone, the shine of bright lighting, and the sheen of cleanliness apparent in homes and personal hygiene contrasts with the earlier abjection in depicting downtrodden tenant farmers.

The conclusion of *The River* establishes further ties to *The Eleventh Year*. Thanks to the Farm Security Administration, the narrator explains, farmers suffering from years of economic depression, "and in need of only a stake to be / self sufficient," have gained access to loans (76). Relying on the standard New Deal definition of relief as a hand up rather than a handout, this pitch prompts viewers to envision the TVA as delivering newfound power in every sense of the word: "But where there is water there is power. // Where there's water for flood control and / water for navigation, there's water for power— // Power for the farmers of the Valley" (76). The force of empowerment envisioned in *The River* has the capacity "to give a new Tennessee Valley to a / new generation," thus reinforcing the notion that the TVA enterprise amounts to a resettlement (76). For Vertov, as Hicks point out, formal properties are used to "enhance the sense of movement, of feverish but purposive activity, towards a socialist future" powered by the "magical ingredient" of electricity and military might.[48] In *The River*, the pioneering foray into modernity draws symbolic weight from the triumphalist claim of Manifest Destiny and another form of the hubris that drove previous anthropogenic designs to exploit the river for profit. The difference this time, the logic holds, is that sound planning and measured consumption of resources are operating "to make the river work!" (76).

The benefits of power generated by harnessing the river with the reins of hydraulic engineering are suggested visually through shots of towering TVA infrastructure imbued with public meaning. In one instance, the camera pans from a low angle up the incline of Norris Dam, ending in a long shot of the American flag blowing in the breeze atop the dam. After this overt display of nationalism, there is a cut to the engine room, where technicians operate control panels. From the controlled currents of the river, the film traces the path of hydroelectric power to the newly installed lines that are linking the valley to form an expanded grid. Such displays are in keeping with the tone of mythic grandeur that Lorentz maintains throughout *The River* and that aligns the film with a mode of TVA cultural production extolling infrastructural development as a generator of democratic freedom in the march toward progress taking place in the present and continuing into to the future. As Appel puts it, "Developmental time was always a myth."[49]

TVA OVER THERE

It did not take long for the impact of *The River* to become measurable in documentary filmmaking. As noted above, Lorentz's film has aesthetic, ideological, and infrastructural elements (along with international festival accolades) that invite transatlantic comparisons related to cultural geopolitics. In terms of audience, *The River* was mainly a domestic affair designed to encourage viewers to accept the problem-solution argument it presented to them through compelling cinematic devices. By the time *The Valley of the Tennessee*, a film heavily influenced by *The River*, appeared in 1944, the pressing issues of the Great Depression were trailing in the wake of World War II. Like Lorentz, the director of *The Valley of the Tennessee*, Alexander Hammid, was adept at drawing from elements of the 1930s documentary aesthetic to craft a visually compelling promotion of the Tennessee Valley Authority.[50] In this instance, the target audience was liberated inhabitants of a war-torn Western Europe mired in destruction and longing for the kind of reconstruction the film portrayed as a utopian enterprise in the Tennessee Valley.

Hammid's film blends overdetermined narration with innovative aesthetic features to lend cinematic expression to the geopolitical vision explicitly outlined in Lilienthal's *TVA: Democracy on the March*. The penultimate chapter title, "TVA and World Reconstruction," sets the stage for the former TVA director to broaden the scope by connecting regional and domestic matters in the United States to global concerns as the dawn of a postwar era that seemed imminent. Lilienthal describes a steady stream of visitors to the Tennessee Valley since the war began, noting that representatives from other countries were interested in touring the dams and powerhouses and that the TVA was now a "training ground for foreign technicians."[51] Officials from "post-war commissions of reconstruction" constituted in anticipation of an Allied victory had an especially keen interest in the TVA, Lilienthal explains, reflecting that of foreign journalists commenting on "what they believe are the lessons for their homeland in what is going on in this far-away and hitherto little known region."[52] Rather than a backwater suspended in arrested (uneven) development and bound by antiquated customs, the Tennessee Valley in this account is a region on course for a prosperous future shaped by modernity. Lilienthal asserts that the "TVA speaks in a tongue that is universal" so that no translation is necessary "when a Chinese or a Peruvian sees this series of working dams, or electricity flowing into a simple farmhouse, or acres that phosphate has brought back to life."[53] He takes great pains to persuade readers that visitors from abroad are more interested in how the agency works with local populations through "democratic methods of consent and participation by the people" than in the dams and powerhouses. This framing departs from the monumental meaning of these infrastructural elements in Lilienthal's memoir and TVA cultural production generally. *The Valley of the Tennessee* is a prime example, as it steers audiences toward the interpretation Lilienthal posits as a fait accompli: "The TVA has come to be thought of (here and abroad) as a symbol of man's capacity to create and to build not only for war and death but for peace and life."[54]

The Valley of the Tennessee's production history shows that the practice of federal agencies overseeing film projects and enlisting talented directors was still active in the mid-1940s. That was the case even though the bloc of conservatives in Congress had grown larger, more powerful, and at times more successful in trimming the sails of the New Deal. The remaining viability rested largely on changes reflecting the dramatic shift in priorities as the economic crisis of the Great Depression gave way to recovery fueled by mobilization for war and the massive reallocation of resources domestically and internationally to achieve an Allied victory. The Office of War Information was one of the agencies that underwent a major overhaul. Formed in 1942, the

OWI had been the Office of Facts and Figures (OFF), an agency led by Archibald MacLeish, the famed poet who joined the ranks of the Roosevelt Administration and served stints as the Librarian of Congress and in a research division of the CIA. The change in the agency's name signaled its redefined mission from gathering data and information for public use to shaping public opinion to promote unity on the home front and garner support for the United States abroad. Through its Bureau of Motion Pictures, as Ian Scott documents, the OWI was responsible for the "most ambitious collection of propaganda shorts that any government agency produced during the war."[55] The documentaries augmented the fiction films that were among Hollywood's contributions to the war effort, mirroring the thinking of the first OWI director, Elmer Davis: "The easiest way to inject a propaganda idea into most people's minds is to let it go in through the medium of an entertainment picture."[56] On this point, Davis was aligned with FDR, who "believed movies were among the most effective means of reaching the American public."[57]

Produced between 1943 and 1945, the *American Scene* series was "the centerpiece of the OWI's documentary project" and exemplified the office's mission put into practice.[58] It was first called "Projections of America," originating in the overseas branch helmed by playwright Robert Sherwood. *American Scene* fell under the more direct supervision of screenwriter Robert Riskin, head of the Bureau of Motion Pictures, and writer-director Philip Dunne, who oversaw the bureau's documentary film production unit. The guidance for filmmakers called for productions highlighting key themes such as the "American Character" rendered through a combination of "realism and idealism," the efficacy of US government policies and programs, and "the country's progress in science, industry, social reform, and modern agricultural techniques."[59] Another guideline stated the importance of downplaying social divisions, especially racial conflict, to depict Americans "as benevolent people with strong ties to the wider world, especially Europe."[60] The series comprised fourteen documentary shorts, according to the best estimate made by the National Archives from the remains of spotty wartime record-keeping. In addition to Hammid, Josef von Sternberg, Irving Lerner, and Arthur Arent, among other notables, were in the lineup of filmmakers; composers such as Aaron Copland and Virgil

Thomson were also involved. Marja Roholl documents that these films and other wartime Hollywood fare, along with magazines and books, made their way to Western Europe as part of the cultural arm of the military campaign that began on D-Day in 1944. This multimedia trove was "targeted at civilians rather than enemy soldiers"; it was deployed "not only to smooth the transition from occupation and war to liberation, but also to shape the post-war peace."[61] For screenings, the OWI relied on makeshift facilities, including damaged movie theaters and schoolhouses, meaning that the venues underscored the theme of reconstruction present in the documentary.

PIONEERS OF THE VALLEY

The opening sequence of *The Valley of the Tennessee* is reminiscent of *The River* in that it establishes nondiegetic narration to convey a sense of authority. In this instance, the commanding voice belongs to Fredric March, one of the prominent Hollywood figures who gravitated toward social and political activism in the 1930s. March was an outspoken antifascist and strong supporter of the Democratic Party and the New Deal. Like others in Hollywood with leftist political sympathies, he wound up on the radar of the House Un-American Activities Committee (HUAC). He eventually emerged unscathed to earn his second Academy Award in 1946 for *The Best Years of Our Lives*, a film directed by William Wyler portraying the difficulties of three veterans returning to civilian life after World War II. In *The Valley of the Tennessee*, the first lines March delivers set the tone vocally and thematically, serving as the voice-over in an aerial sequence featuring a Mainliner plane flying above city skylines, rural landscapes, and fields dotted with oil derricks. "More than three hundred years ago, the first pioneers crossed the ocean to a new world," the narrator intones. It is an interesting rhetorical gambit, given that the intended screening locations and audiences were exclusively "Old World." The ensuing lines herald "the promise of a land"—the phrase evokes the American myth of the Promised Land originating with the early pilgrims—where it was possible to stake an individual claim to freedom and prosperity. Realizing this potential, these steely pioneers "carved from the wilderness an empire of agriculture and industry."

As in *The River*, the mytho-historical narrative excludes Indigenous people, failing to account for their presence when the "first pioneers" arrived and for the genocide and forcible removal that were integral to settler colonialism.

Although the pioneers "set for themselves new and higher standards of living" and the realization of Manifest Destiny was largely accomplished, the narration points out that "in one of the great river valleys of America, something went wrong." Consequently, some three hundred years later, "the descendants of the pioneers were a neglected people living in a ruined land." An abrupt shift to the verbal imagery of the anthropogenic wasteland and visual images of abjection sound familiar notes from New Deal documentaries. While *The River* foregrounds families languishing in poverty, living in dilapidated shacks, and suffering from poor hygiene and malnutrition, *The Valley of the Tennessee* narrows in on children to establish a defining motif of futurity. March's lament of "a ruined land" makes the beleaguered Tennessee Valley a proxy for war-ravaged Europe. The voice-over accompanies a sequence in which children wearing tattered clothing file barefoot into a ramshackle schoolhouse. Alternating medium and close-up shots reveal smudges and forlorn expressions on their faces, serving as a visual focal point for narration steeped in pathos. March laments that "the hope and the promise were dead" for these children, adding in a line that echoes the script of *The River* that "the only future was poverty, ignorance, drudgery, the struggle to scratch a bare living from the reluctant soil." The bleak scenario is made plain with a cut to a montage sequence of despondent farmers toiling in the fields and staring into the distance. March explains that "the older men had forgotten that valley had once been bright with promise and hope." A brief explanation of soil erosion accompanies images of denuded land and March's stipulation that it "began innocently when early settlers cut down the forests." The erosion sequence is a prelude to the arrival of "destruction from the sky." Severe flooding unleashes "havoc caused by greed and neglect in men working alone against the forces of nature," illustrated by aerial footage of nearly submerged houses in a vast floodscape. In concise visual and narrative terms, Hammid's film employs the trope of the problem South to prepare for the arrival of the TVA as the model solution at the end. Although the argument remains fundamentally the same as the one made in *The River*, the circumstances of production and reception mean that it posits a wider range of applications in a postwar world of global initiatives involving public works.

While *The River* maintains a sense of detachment, *The Valley of the Tennessee* delivers a personal touch by grounding the salient issues in the quotidian experiences of two farmers trying to subsist in "a forgotten part of the United States" finally getting the attention it deserves. Horace Higgins is "one of many who had given up the fight," March explains, before putting words in the farmer's mouth: "It may have been good land once, but it's bad now."[62] Noticeably unkempt and missing teeth, Horace differs from his neighbor Henry Clark, who comes across as an updated version of the yeoman ideal, a fixture in the American mythos derived primarily from Jeffersonian agrarianism. With the focus on Henry, the film identifies soil erosion and severe flooding as immediate problems for him and his neighbors and a shared national concern: "a challenge for democracy and its ability to care for its own." At the heart of this challenge is "a problem of reconstruction: reconstruction of land, reconstruction of people." Repetition emphasizes the theme—much like the steady thematic beat of "down, down, down" in *The River* that connects the natural course of the Mississippi to development cycles—and registers with transatlantic import. The sequence ends by focusing on a mother bottle-feeding her infant—another instance of using children to represent the future—and then cutting to a scene in which two of the three TVA directors, Lilienthal and Harcourt Morgan, discuss plans with Senator George Norris. "Democracy met the test," the voice-over declares. "It found the men to supervise the job."

The visual contrast between Horace and Henry signals the farmers' different responses to the promise of better lives, labor, and land. Henry is cast as the TVA's version of a progressive farmer. As such, he is at the center of the frame as March explains that the mission is "to prove that human problems can be solved by reason, science, and education." Through this effort, "the Tennessee Valley was to be pioneered again, but this time to be developed, not plundered." By splicing shots of Henry into a sequence with footage of engineers, architects, and technicians hard at work, the film incorporates the longstanding frontier myth into the nascent TVA myth: "These were the new pioneers." Hammid's film underscores that Henry must accept the dramatic changes to the valley and farming practices of his own volition, not because of government mandates. A pivotal moment in this process comes when Henry visits a nearby dam site where he observes neighbors employed as construction workers engaged in various tasks. Significantly, this sequence features Black and white workers but not in the same shot or working in the same crews. This editing technically complied with the OWI guideline by avoiding racial conflict, but observant viewers would have been able to spot the policy requiring segregated work crews in practice. For Henry, the challenge is to make connections between the construction of the dam and the promised benefits to his farm and quality of life.

The introduction of John Warden, a TVA agricultural representative, provides the necessary explanation for the farmer and the viewer. Giving voice to Warden, March points out that the dams are "just a beginning" but ultimately "worthless" unless the local people are willing to cooperate with each other and the TVA. As Warden tries to convince Henry, Horace, and some of their neighbors to become "test demonstration farmers," he points out that doing so would make them individuals in a larger endeavor to serve the greater good. This theme, combined with visual and narrative components, evinces Hammid's mode of bringing elements of the 1930s documentary aesthetic into the postwar era. In particular, he employs the technique that Rabinowitz describes as focusing on the part to convey a sense of the whole in trying to depict the massive scale of public works projects, as noted at the start of this chapter. For Warden, the dams are "only part of the plan," the bulk of which is in the hands of the farmers. "The land is yours, the dams are yours, the whole TVA is yours," March says, ventriloquizing Warden's remarks to a group of farmers gathered at the local schoolhouse. Later, Henry is shown signing forms to join the demonstration program, meaning he will implement new experimental agricultural methods. March explains that the decision was difficult for Henry, "but he was a descendant of pioneers, of men who had taken a chance and who had known their salvation lay in cooperation." Through parallel editing, the film combines alternating shots of Henry driving his plow and a construction crew member operating a bulldozer at the dam construction site. The sequence visually elucidates the connection Henry has come to understand. March provides the narrative punctuation:

"The old spirit of the pioneers was reawakened—the dam builders, the farmers, the machines began to work as one." In contrast, Horace is portrayed as hidebound, refusing the new methods and farm implements offered to him. Consequently, he misses out on the replenished soil and abundant yields Henry reaps after only two seasons as a "new pioneer."

RUGGED (COOPERATIVE) INDIVIDUALISM

As *The Valley of the Tennessee* winds toward the inevitable conclusion, the film drives home the message of a common purpose at the grassroots level of the farmers and other people in the valley. Such cooperation was a bedrock of New Deal liberalism and of the cultural production commissioned to express its fundamental aims and principles. Robert S. McElvaine offers insight into this thematic concern in making the overarching claim that "two opposing sets of values" have prevailed in the United States almost from the outset: "acquisitive individualism" and "cooperative individualism" (201). While the former has reigned in periods of heightened conservatism such as the late nineteenth century, the latter has prevailed during ascendant liberalism, as in the Progressive Era. Moreover, identification with these values has tended to move toward the former during economic booms marked by relative prosperity and toward the latter during busts that bring financial hardship. McElvaine notes that the potent combination of heightened liberalism and economic crisis gave cooperative individualism a major boost during the Great Depression and a central role in the governing philosophy and policies of the New Deal.[63] The pervasiveness of this concept extended to popular culture, including movies produced in Hollywood, where support for the Roosevelt administration was consistently robust. McElvaine discusses Depression-era films that touted New Deal themes, culminating in *The Grapes of Wrath*. In that film, McElvaine observes, the director, John Ford, "addressed contemporary problems directly" and did "a remarkable job of presenting the moral economic values of the era."[64] As a result, embedded in this film and others "was a call for a kind of cooperative individualism that recognized individuals could achieve a degree of independence and self-respect only by cooperating."[65] In *The Valley of the Tennessee*, the narrator hits the same notes, explaining in one scene that Henry and others operating demonstration farms are "acting together cooperatively for a common purpose" by sharing a modern threshing machine designed by the TVA. "For the first time," he continues, "they were thinking in terms of each other, what they could accomplish together." The abundant crop yields at harvest time prompt a realization, which March attributes to Horace: "that the individual, through cooperation with his fellows, becomes a more important individual." In trumpeting a hybrid form of collectivism and individualism, *The Valley of the Tennessee* envisions a massive postwar reconstruction effort guided by the values of New Deal liberalism. In this respect, the film uses the trope of prefiguration, to return to Michael Denning's concept previously discussed, in envisioning the New Deal as still viable and assuming global proportions.

The closing sequence of *The Valley of the Tennessee* channels the theme of cooperative individualism into an impassioned expression of US democratic nationalism for consumption abroad. The film extends the visual rhetoric of the photographs on display in the MoMA exhibition and of *The River* by imbuing TVA infrastructure with an aura of monumentality. As March cites "the development of the people" as "the first concern of a democracy," the focus returns to the children of the valley. In contrast to the earlier scene featuring students mired in poverty and bereft of hope, the ending focuses on a racially integrated class of schoolchildren looking well-nourished and fully engaged in learning activities. This site of social infrastructure is a desegregated space, making it a product of cinematic fantasy rather than documentary realism. One group of students is gathered around a scale model of the Tennessee Valley to study how the network of TVA dams operates. The same youthful curiosity is evident earlier in one of the film's most visually compelling sequences: a long shot of a boy ascending a steep mountainside until he reaches the top and peers into the valley with wonder at a bustling dam construction site. The school activity segues into an information graphic designed to teach the school lesson to viewers.

The primer on the practical functions of flood control soon transitions to figurative expression, as March renders the dams "symbols of a nation's constructive energy" before reciting their names in a booming litany and proclaiming that they are "built for and owned by the people of the United States." As in the TVA exhibition at MoMA, citizenship confers ownership and benefits implied in the declaration that "the dams work for the people" to put "power in the hands of the people." The vow holds a double meaning: it refers to a pact with the people that the TVA will deliver "cheap and abundant power" to raise living standards and to the potential for the valley to prosper because of the transformation underway. As schoolchildren run toward the face of a dam towering into the sky above the frame, the narrator explains what they have learned: "that the TVA is . . . a yardstick, a measure of what men can build in peace, a measure of the stature of a new and better world." On a global scale, the signature yardstick metaphor resounds forcefully in the promise that adopting the TVA model will help bring about "a world with dignity, work, and hope for all." The framing of the promise in the context of a lesson learned by schoolchildren awed by the monumentality of infrastructure barely conceals the structure of *The Valley of the Tennessee* as carefully designed propaganda. As such, it channeled aesthetic and ideological currents from *The River* and joined its predecessor in shaping the contours of documentary filmmaking as an enduring cinematic form.

Chapter 3

POWER TO THE PEOPLE
The Spectacular Drama of Rural Electrification

THE ESTABLISHMENT OF NEW DEAL AGENCIES IN THE FIRST HALF OF THE 1930S RESULTED in a steady stream of acronyms from the public sector as the Roosevelt administration put the governing philosophy of bold government action into practice. Two years after the Tennessee Valley Authority joined those ranks, the Works Progress Administration (WPA) was established, functioning as an umbrella agency for various units and projects charged with providing relief and jobs to the scores of Americans who were out of work, down and out, and desperate for gainful employment. Through the WPA, the federal government offered opportunities for cultural work in the programs comprising Federal Project Number One: the Federal Writers' Project (FWP), the Federal Art Project (FAP), the Federal Music Project (FMP), and the Federal Theatre Project (FTP). For TVA officials wanting to make a case for the agency on the cultural front, in addition to the predictable legal and political grounds, these new federal entities afforded valuable resources for garnering public support.

The prospect of an interagency alliance materialized when the FTP, under the leadership of Hallie Flanagan during its run from 1935 to 1939, produced a play titled *Power* in 1937. The sponsorship of the Newspaper Guild of America, a union founded in 1933 to advocate for workers in the newspaper industry, extended the collaboration from the parameters of government to the Fourth Estate. The production dramatized the high stakes of the TVA's controversial project to make flood control, rural electrification, social reforms, and improved agricultural practices conduits of regional rehabilitation and economic development. As Kurt Eisen explains, Flanagan viewed the missions of the TVA and the FTP as complementary: the former spread light generated by electricity, and the latter sought to bring enlightenment through "cultural enfranchisement."[1] Another point of commonality was a commitment to regional planning as the most effective means of delivering essential public services. The FTP was organized into a network of regional production companies designed to draw from homegrown talent as much as possible and tailor material to local cultures and audiences. In this capacity, the FTP employed a strategy like that of the TVA by couching the promised benefits of the New Deal in terms of a grassroots appeal.

When *Power* started to take shape, a heated political debate about the TVA was in progress. Numerous legal challenges by privately owned utility companies and sharp ideological differences between advocates and opponents about the role of government in the industry stoked the flames of controversy. That made the subject matter appealing to the Living Newspaper Unit, a division of the FTP that drew creative inspiration and material from headlines of the day. For the artists producing living newspapers, in keeping with the broader mission of the FTP, the stated goal was for the dramatic arts to play a role in educating the public and encouraging meaningful civic engagement by heightening awareness and understanding of current events. The cultural politics of the moment helped the staging of *Power* align with Flanagan's fundamental production values, not least the "necessity for any living theatre to be of its own time and country."[2] As the premiere of *Power* drew closer, a key ruling on the unsettled question of the TVA's constitutionality was imminent. Consequently, Arthur Arent, a playwright serving as the managing editor of the Living Newspaper Unit since 1935, was on call to make a hasty revision that would supply an answer to the question about judicial action left hanging at the end of the production script.[3] To accentuate the aura of timeliness and sense of urgency, the director, Brett Warren, called for the actors to dispel the illusion of the fourth wall and engage with audiences directly. This approach was part of a broader effort to make the case that electric power should be an affordable and widely accessible resource—a public utility—rather than a commodity produced and sold for maximum corporate profit.

When *Power* opened at the Ritz Theatre in New York City on February 23, 1937, the audience was presented with a bona fide theatrical spectacle. The production consisted of thirty-three scenes and featured eighty-eight actors, many of whom were nonprofessionals recruited in a rush to fill empty roles in time for opening night.[4] In presenting a strong case for the TVA, the producers created a dramatic composite of seemingly disparate elements ranging from the theatrical traditions of vaudeville to dazzling visual effects with cinematic flair. The production design included a loudspeaker (a mechanical device for amplifying sound) and a character referred to in the script as the Loudspeaker (an actor speaking into the device and serving as narrator). There were also bright spotlights, a multimedia display of stereopticon text slides, and photographs and film footage projected onto a large scrim. The grand scale and innovative staging befitted a living newspaper positing that an embrace of modernity symbolized by the TVA was an exercise in American ingenuity and the pioneering spirit present in the local history and culture of the region. Jane de Hart Mathews aptly describes the essence of *Power*: "It was exuberant theater—melodramatic and exciting. It was also propaganda."[5]

Power is a cultural artifact of a historical moment when works commissioned by the state advanced the New Deal agenda. In the process, this mode of cultural production created intersections where distinctive aesthetic and ideological strains converged with significant implications for cultural history. This legacy is apparent in formal terms, as Laura Browder demonstrates in reading living newspapers as "documentary, modernist plays."[6] Browder points to the irony that these productions backed by the federal government were at times more radical than those produced by self-styled leftist companies such as the New Theatre League or avowedly experimental companies such as the Group Theatre. The notion that the living newspapers "used documentary and modernist pastiche not only to represent American history on the stage but to demand political activism from the mass audiences who saw the productions" illuminates hybridity in *Power* that positioned it relative to the prevailing winds of realism, radicalism, and popular culture in American theater of the 1930s.[7] The penchant for radical formal experimentation was consistent with modernism; the overtly social and political commentary drew on the radical impulses of agitprop. Combining mainstream theatrical traditions with elements of mass media aligned these productions with the cultural politics of the Popular Front as it facilitated a broad-based coalition by satisfying the tastes of the public. In this regard, *Power* illustrates Ilka Saal's argument that "the leftist stages of the New Deal solved the dilemma of form and public by persistently *vernacularizing* the political issues at hand—that is, by translating them into a language commensurate with the cultural experience of a broad public steeped in mass culture."[8]

A major objective in staging *Power* was to appeal to US nationalism while imagining a society and economy in which the excesses of capitalism would remain in check due to ethical considerations and regulatory controls. It was a hopeful, even utopian, vision of electricity as an abundant, cheap, and clean energy source operating at a capacity determined by controlled consumption. The mobilization for World War II and the postwar economic boom would soon precipitate a rapid shift to coal-fired plants that exposed the fundamental flaws in this hopeful projection. However, when it was originally produced, *Power* was an earnest paean to modernity that highlighted the prospect of a national grid rapidly expanding to facilitate rural electrification on the strength of hydropower. The representation of the grid in material terms cast it as infrastructure for redressing the effects of uneven development that had left rural locales such as the Tennessee Valley on the periphery and out of step with urban centers at the core of modernization in the United States. The harsh realities of disruption and displacement to local populations and the adverse impacts on local ecologies inherent to the construction of large-scale infrastructure projects were nowhere to be found on stage. In *Power*, electricity flowed as a multivalent force. On one level, it served the interconnected goals of regional rehabilitation and national recovery by empowering consumers to fuel economic growth. Symbolically, the expanding grid coursing with energy represented American ingenuity and democratic freedom in the interest of promoting national unity. On a continuum with pioneers flocking to the region in the previous century, the expansion of rural electrification staged in the living newspaper upgraded Manifest Destiny to advance the TVA's modern vision.

READING THE LIVING NEWSPAPER

The exaggerated theatricality of *Power* reflected the signature style of Joseph Losey, an influential director who made his mark on the Living Newspaper Unit before a departure clouded in controversy. Losey's conception of the living newspaper as a genre materialized, with help from the talented stage designer Nicholas Ray, in two controversial productions by the Federal Theatre Project in 1936: *Triple-A Plowed Under* and *Injunction Granted*. The former dramatized efforts to address the plight of farmers through provisions of the Agricultural Adjustment Act (AAA); the latter was a clarion call for worker solidarity to coalesce under the banner of the Congress of Industrial Organizations (CIO). Under Losey's direction, the living newspaper functioned as an instrument of critique with various applications and a mouthpiece for stirring calls to action. The scope of social and political commentary ranged from exposing coercive labor practices used to maintain a hold on power to faulting the federal response to the economic crisis for being woefully inadequate. As *Triple-A* and *Injunction Granted* attest, Losey was willing to take risks by drawing on radical aesthetics and politics to stake out ground decidedly to the left of the Roosevelt administration and champion policies and programs that would move the New Deal in that direction. In so doing, Losey was biting the hand that fed the FTP so aggressively that it could not go unanswered by Flanagan or unnoticed by politicians determined to shut down the agency.

Losey's attempt to advance a leftist political agenda highlighted an identity crisis at the FTP that had been evident since its inception. At the outset, Flanagan and Elmer Rice, the first director of the FTP's company in New York City, envisioned the living newspaper as an alternative to the print medium in form but not practice. The unit's organizational structure was modeled on that of a print publication. Each company would have an editor-in-chief with a staff of editors and reporters to develop "an authoritative dramatic treatment, at once historic and contemporary, of current problems."[9] Such measures were purportedly in place to bolster the claim for documentary status by ensuring accuracy and integrity. But they also appear to have been preemptive measures to give the FTP political cover. The inadequacy of this protection was evident early on as Rice resigned in the face of censorship by the State Department. Officials worried about potential diplomatic fallout from the Living Newspaper Unit's first undertaking, *Ethiopia*, a 1936 play about the brutal invasion of northern Africa by Mussolini's Italian forces.[10] The production never made it to the stage. It is no wonder that Flanagan was on high alert while monitoring the progress of Losey's productions later that same year. Tensions came to a head as Losey oversaw *Injunction Granted*, scripted by a team of writers under Arent's supervision. Mathews points out that the production "was supposedly an objective account of labor's treatment in the courts, but had been turned by Young Turks on the Project into a militantly pro–labor account of the working man's fight for liberation through unionization."[11] In extensive notes to Losey and Morris Watson, the director of the Living Newspaper Unit in New York, Flanagan called out what she perceived as a heavy hand undermining artistic integrity. She said the approach had made the play "special pleading, biased, an editorial, not a news issue," adding that it "lacks a proper climax, falling back on the old cliché of calling labor to unite in the approved agit-prop manner."[12] Given that "the project's treatment struck most who saw it as blatant and not very artful left-wing propaganda," Flanagan was likely more concerned about the potential political implications than any artistic compromises.[13] When Watson and Losey failed to heed her words, Flanagan threatened to stop the production. The result was that some scenes were revised to address Flanagan's concerns before the production closed in the fall of 1936. The creative differences that plagued *Injunction Granted* eventually prompted Losey's departure from the Federal Theatre Project and increased vigilance on the agitprop front.

Flanagan's intervention was part of a concerted effort to downplay aspects of the FTP that opponents could portray as "un-American." Alarm bells went off around membership in the Communist Party USA, as in the case of Losey, or fellow traveling, as the pro-union Watson was inclined toward.[14] In other instances, such as *Injunction Granted*, staging of an explicitly leftist political agenda was the sticking point. These factors conflicted with Flanagan's notion of the FTP as an objective arbiter engaged in public education and cultural enrichment rather than employed as an instrument of partisan politics. Flanagan's sternly worded letter to Watson after the *Injunction Granted* premiere encapsulates this viewpoint: "As I have repeatedly said I will not have the Federal Theatre used politically. I will not have it used to further the ends of the Democratic party, the Republican party, or the Communist party."[15] The origin of the living newspaper was a delicate matter that required some artful dodging by those defending the productions. In a 1938 essay, "The Techniques of the Living Newspaper," Arthur Arent claims that the theatrical lineage is "shrouded in mystery and confusion," speculating that the form could have emerged organically from the work of the Federal Theatre Project.[16] Arent's curious origin story is at best strategically attenuated and at worst disingenuous. In retrospect, it seems obvious that the fraught cultural politics of the moment influenced him to construct an alternate history of the medium.

Arnold Goldman convincingly argues that defining living newspapers as homegrown "should not obscure the extent to which the productions show lines of development from earlier left-wing American theatre, in particular the workers' theatre movement, and the radical theatres of Germany and Russia which fed that movement."[17] As Goldman and others have noted, for all the differences between Flanagan and Losey during the FTP venture, they had similar formative experiences that shaped their theatrical sensibilities. In the 1920s, both Flanagan and Losey visited the Soviet Union, where they were exposed to the theories of acting, directing, staging, and audience entailed in the system of theatrical realism developed by Constantin Stanislavski and advanced by innovators such as Vsevelo Meyerhold and Sergei Eisenstein, both of whom pushed the limits of formal experimentation. As for the German influence, Losey studied under Bertolt Brecht, whose brand of epic theater was a comparative model for thinking about what experimental theater might look like in an American context. Epic theater's opposition to theatrical realism involved formal properties of modernism deployed to call attention to the production apparatus and thus promote a form of alienation conducive to critical thinking. In the script used for the New York production of *Power*, the opening scene shines a light on the switchboard of the Ritz Theatre so the stage manager can explain how it controls the flow of electricity that makes the show's theatrical effects possible.[18] The idea was to disrupt the familiar assurance of empathetic absorption experienced behind an imagined fourth wall by engaging the audience as participants with a stake in the action. This moment of literal and figurative illumination was designed to draw attention to the infrastructure of the theatrical production and the city where the production was staged. The producers of living newspapers adapted these creatively useful but politically charged elements to develop a dramatic form tailor-made for mass consumption in the United States.

Considering the origins and aims, it stands to reason that living newspapers became flashpoints for intra-agency politics surrounding the identity and mission of the FTP and lightning rods for criticism from external quarters. In retrospect, the troubled run of Losey's productions in 1936 and the staging of *Power* amid the legal battle over the TVA the following year signaled the FTP's demise looming on the horizon. By 1938, that prospect appeared even more likely, as Flanagan was summoned to testify before the House Committee on Un-American Activities, more commonly known as the House Un-American Activities Committee (HUAC). The committee chair, Representative Martin Dies of Texas, was a showman in the political arena, performing his signature theatrics through red-baiting and political grandstanding. It was a preview of the coming attraction of Cold War McCarthyism. In the face of tough questioning, Flanagan tried to defuse charges lodged by detractors, arguing that the agency was not a perpetrator of the insidious activities cited by the committee but an ally in the fight against them. Regarding living newspapers, Flanagan insisted they were resources for educating the public and promoting civic engagement, not tools of leftist propaganda. When committee members inquired about her time in the Soviet Union, Flanagan tried to distinguish between aesthetics and politics, insisting that her interest in Russian theater was confined solely to the former. In contradictory fashion, Flanagan acknowledged the foreign influence on form but claimed that the FTP was producing a purely American brand of theater. If FTP productions were propaganda, Flanagan argued, they advocated for shared values such as fair housing and labor standards and affordable energy that were beneficial rather than detrimental to American democracy.[19] Predictably, this testimony was unconvincing to Dies and his colleagues opposed to the FTP; they summarily dismissed Flanagan's attempt to redefine the terms of the debate as a dramatic performance.

The complaints lodged against the FTP were Red Scare tactics neglecting the fact that the agency's leftist bent was decidedly mainstream relative to the prevailing cultural politics. The establishment of the FTP in 1935 coincided with the emergence of the Popular Front. This social formation comprised a broad-based alliance of communists, liberals, and fellow travelers mobilized against the rise of fascism. As Michael Denning documents, the Popular Front was responsible for a "laboring" of American culture evident in literature, film, music, theater, and other popular media.[20] The relationship between aesthetics and politics became a key issue, prompting a reassessment of the prescriptive standards issued in the throes of what Edmund Wilson dubbed "the literary class war" of the early 1930s.[21] The line in the sand public intellectuals such as Michael Gold had drawn to separate proletarian literature from the allegedly decadent tendencies of formalism faded as the Popular Front coalesced. In this context, living newspapers revealed intersections between realism and modernism and defied the logic used to underwrite highbrow, middlebrow, and lowbrow as legitimate and stable cultural designations.[22]

NETWORK OF *POWER*

The troubled FTP productions that preceded the New York opening of *Power* in 1937 did not bode well for the agency's future. But brisk advance ticket sales stirred hope among the producers that the Living Newspaper Unit could have a successful run with this venture. That turned out to be the case, as the production at the Ritz drew enthusiastic audiences and critical acclaim. Some sixty thousand theatergoers saw the show during the initial performances, with a favorable review in the *New York Times* by the influential theater critic Brooks Atkinson adding a boost. The critic cited the relish with which the "newshawks" of the Living Newspaper Unit performed, and he identified the endorsement of the TVA as the organizing principle. The review cited the pro-consumer stance taken "impartially against the electric light and power industry and for TVA."[23] Such blatant posturing for the government agency over private utilities informed the observation that "the most indignant and militant proletarian drama of the season has been staged with federal funds."[24] Although the proletarian credentials of *Power* are debatable, Atkinson's emphasis on federal funding highlighted the mutually beneficial partnership between the FTP and the TVA in dramatizing "the relation of consumers and the electrical industries."[25] This interagency alliance set out to create a network of pro-TVA theater productions—a cultural infrastructure to generate public support for energy infrastructure. Harry Hopkins, the director of the WPA, revealed the mission explicitly when he visited with the cast of *Power* backstage after attending a performance. Flanagan maintains that Hopkins delivered a frank but supportive message to the cast: ". . . you will take a lot of criticism on this play. People will say it's propaganda. Well, I say what of it?"[26] Since private interests had their propaganda machine, Hopkins figured that any means of educating consumers as a countermeasure would serve a greater good. "It's about time that the consumer had a mouthpiece," Hopkins declared. "I say more plays like *Power* and more power to you."[27] The enthusiasm Hopkins expressed testifies to the producers' confidence that *Power* could operate on emotional and rational levels to persuade audiences to support public ownership of utilities.

The initial run in New York was so successful that it spawned five productions by regional companies of the FTP within a year. Audiences in the Northeast, Midwest, and Pacific Northwest—from New York to San Francisco to Portland to Seattle—had opportunities to see a version of *Power*. The production in Seattle, which took place in July 1937, is notable when considering parallels between the dramatization of events on stage and the fraught politics of regional development. When *Power* opened, proposals to reshape the Columbia River Valley inspired by those implemented in the Tennessee Valley had sparked controversy. For several years, a private company, Puget Power, and a municipal operation, City Light, had been vying for market share supremacy. The battle involved legal and political maneuvers; an infrastructure arms race with duplicate installation of transformers, poles, and lines; and aggressive public relations campaigns mounted on both sides. The mayor, a staunch backer of City Light, instituted "Power Week" by official proclamation. The public show of support amplified the controversy as the political debate turned to *Power*. According to the production bulletin, public contentiousness influenced relations within the production company. The state director, Guy Williams, observed "interesting clashes of opinion" early in the rehearsal schedule, stipulating that a "conservative bloc" critical of the pro-TVA, pro–New Deal content were the instigators. Williams hastened to add that the criticism died down after the first week of rehearsals due to the effectiveness of *Power*'s dramatic appeal.[28]

The local politics made the staging of *Power* in the Pacific Northwest a crucial test for the argument by the Roosevelt administration that the TVA was not, as opponents insisted, a benefit to one region at a cost to taxpayers in others. For Williams, the Seattle run passed the test with flying colors. In the production bulletin, he documented that the initial response by audiences was like that of the conservative cast members. "For the first few scenes, each house appeared puzzled," Williams writes, singling out those theatergoers expecting to see an American version of German epic theater.[29] But the initial befuddlement gave way to enthusiasm as "about three scenes in, the audience would catch the rhythm and we never failed to close with at least four curtain calls." Williams's notes credit word of mouth and positive notices in local newspapers for giving the theatrical production momentum. The bulletin includes excerpts from a *Seattle Post-Intelligencer* review by J. Willis Sayre. Like Atkinson, Sayre called attention to the explicit pro-TVA agenda, gesturing toward its broader implications: "Above all it is propaganda for public ownership." The reviewer lauded the ambitious staging and adeptness at immersing audiences in the experience. Sayre described *Power* as "a historical pageant" enhanced by myriad special effects, adding that the "large and friendly" audience would release "a howl of delight" every time the profiteers were called out. An anonymous reviewer in the *Seattle Times* delivered a harsh response to the ideologically stacked deck. The reviewer observed that the "Old Debbil, the Power Trust is the villain and the TVA is the hero in as fine a piece of overdone propaganda as ever trod the boards," adding that "the play has the subtlety of a sledgehammer and the restraint of a groundswell." This political theater involved the content of the play and its staging in the context of the ongoing public debate. The *Seattle Times* reviewer mentioned that the mayor was on hand to give a speech before the curtain rose. Despite some negative reviews, *Power*'s successful West Coast tour led to a return engagement on the East Coast—a 1938 revival by the New York company at the 49th Street Theatre.

The production history of *Power* crystallizes the philosophy of regional planning that was a hallmark of the agencies involved and of the New Deal as a whole. At the heart of this strategy was the recognition that control too heavily concentrated at the federal level would create resistance at the state and local levels. The conception of the TVA as a federal enterprise administered through regional operations demonstrates the fine line officials had to walk in trying to put this New Deal philosophy into practice. The producers of *Power* were mindful that an appeal to regionalism could raise the specter of sectionalism. Tellingly, the dramatization of the Tennessee Valley in *Power* was never performed in the region. As Eisen explains, the FTP had trouble gaining a foothold in the valley and the South because of opposition to federal intervention in theory.[30] In practice, however, the response to the New Deal showed signs of cognitive dissonance. After all, there was staunch support for ambitious federal programs among southern Democrats in Congress—if they had a major say in how those programs were run.

One scene in *Power* showcases the legislative dynamics of rural electrification under the framework of the New Deal. In it, John E. Rankin, an influential Democratic representative from Mississippi, points to the growing congressional support for public ownership of utilities: "We have formed a bloc in the House of Representatives to save for the American people, now and for all time to come, the hydro-electric power of the nation."[31] Omitted from this dramatization is the fact that the progressivism displayed in energy policy did not extend to the arena of racial justice. Rankin and his fellow southern Democrats leveraged their support, making it essential to the advancement of the New Deal agenda and contingent upon preserving the status quo of Jim Crow segregation in the region. Ira Katznelson highlights a tendency in historical scholarship to neglect this crucial factor: "Despite its centrality, southern power has always hovered at the fringes of most New Deal portraits."[32] Positioning these legislators at the center of the Democratic coalition reveals that "the region empowered most New Deal initiatives in Congress, all the while holding fast to the ideology and institutions of official racism."[33] While these lawmakers acting on behalf of the southern ruling class held out one hand to accept funding from the federal coffers, they raised the other in defiance of perceived threats to the established social order of white supremacy. For the most part, the responsibility for distributing resources was in the hands of local elites who ensured the funds remained mostly on the white side of the color line. In effect, the system operated as undemocratic socialism. Notably, the propagandistic aims of *Power* and the elaborate staging designed to enhance its strength did not call attention to this integral component of New Deal politics and policymaking as the influential congressman from Mississippi enjoyed a moment in the spotlight.

SPECTACULAR *POWER*

When theatergoers arrived at the Ritz Theatre for the premiere of *Power*, they were met with a dazzling marquee doing more than its share to help the Great White Way live up to its name (fig. 5). Framed by bright lights, the marquee announced in brightly lit text:

> RITZ THEATRE
> W.P.A. FEDERAL THEATRE
> THE LIVING NEWSPAPER
> SPONSORED BY
> NEWSPAPER GUILD OF NEW YORK
> PRESENTS
> POWER

The play title appeared in large, bright letters descending diagonally toward the bottom right corner and superimposed over the center of a lightning bolt. The marquee illustrates David E. Nye's observation that electricity had transformed cities into textual landscapes by this time and "[s]pectacular lighting had become a sophisticated cultural apparatus."[34] Nye adds that corporate and government interests used this technology to "edit both natural and urban landscapes" to sell goods and promote civic pride as a public good.[35] The *Power* marquee was a preview of the show, preparing audiences for the coming flurry of special effects. An appeal based on the strength of pure spectacle was a common denominator of the productions in New York and other parts of the country. In a piece published in *The Oregonian* after the opening night of the Portland run, the reviewer marveled at how the play "made 'theater' out of whatever electricity is and sent sparks flying all over the stage."[36] The figurative description could have become literal depending

Fig. 5. *Power* premiered on February 23, 1937, at the Ritz Theatre in New York. Before people entered the theater, the luminescent marquee set the stage for a production with elaborate special effects. Photograph from the Federal Theatre Project Collection, Library of Congress. Public domain.

on the production and the capacity for elaborate and intricate lighting design. It is apparent from archival records and reviews that the two productions in New York were able to pull off the most dazzling feats of multimedia spectacle. Nevertheless, the other productions managed impressive enough effects to captivate audiences and satisfy most theater critics.

The lighting added a layer of meta-commentary that made audiences aware of electricity operating at every dramaturgical level to produce *Power*. Arent's script for the original production leaves nothing to the imagination once the cue for a spotlight on the lighting technicians comes in the first scene. "This is the switchboard of the Ritz Theatre," the Loudspeaker announces. "Through this board flows the electric power that amplifies my voice, the power that ventilates the theatre, and the power that lights this show" (10). The Loudspeaker commences the action proper by declaring, "Give us a demonstration of *Power*!" (10).

The blocking enacts the theatrical equivalent of montage, establishing a signature feature of the production design. The disembodied voice-over delivers the narration by the Loudspeaker, who presides in Whitman-esque fashion over a series of short scenes that demonstrate the crucial role of electricity in the quotidian contours of American life. The first scene is set in a factory where young women on the floor operate sewing machines at a highly productive rate. The lights fade out and rise elsewhere on characters named simply Mom and Pop at home listening to a radio program. A shift in focus to traffic lights mounted on stage underscores how electricity facilitates social order. Further illustrating the point, the Loudspeaker recounts the major blackout in Newark, New Jersey, in December 1936, describing it as the immediate onset of a "dark age" as the city descended into chaos (17). The life-saving potential of electricity gets further attention in a scene with a surgeon and his assistants engaged in a delicate operation under the glow of bright lights that optimize visibility. These contemporary illustrations of electricity affording modern conveniences and enabling vital functions signal the potential for greater capacity under an expanded grid able to reconcile the rural/urban divide delineated by uneven development. The next scene frames the progression in terms of technological innovation by presenting a brief historical reenactment of the triumphant moment when Thomas Edison completed work on the first electric light. "The happiness of man!" Edison declares. "I know of no greater service to render during the short time we live!" (17).

From great promise at the dawn of electricity to the examples of its fulfillment in the present day, *Power* tapped into the rich ideological reserves of what Nye terms the "electrical sublime," a concentrated expression of the American technological sublime. As Nye explains, the symbolic value of electricity in the American imagination was at a premium by the mid-twentieth century, having become "the panacea for every social ill and the key to a whole range of social and personal transformations that promised to lighten the toil of workers and housewives, to provide faster and cleaner forms of transport, and to revolutionize the farm."[37] The bright lights of skylines meant that the "electrified urban landscape emerged as another avatar of the sublime," and the effect was not lost on rural people, who developed desires that *Power* depicts as Promethean through innovations in stage and lighting design and references to a history of illuminating displays that mesmerized audiences.[38] The word "mesmerize" emerged from this history: the root derived from the German physician Franz Friedrich Anton Mesmer. Mesmer's experiments with animal magnetism in the eighteenth century were controversial in scientific circles but compelling for mass audiences drawn to the seemingly magical properties of electrical energy. For Nye, the invisibility of electricity added to the enigma and thus to the sublime encounter it could engender, creating a scenario by which "electric lighting became a visual representation of the new force."[39]

The special effects on display in *Power*—intricate lighting cues, projected stereopticon slides, and the use of scrims to create silhouettes of the actors transitioning from stationary to animated—illustrated with luminous flair how access to electricity could improve people's lives. These elements had roots in the performative aspects of electrical lighting that Nye traces to the 1890s, the decade in which the new vocation of the "illuminating engineer" emerged.[40] These technicians created dazzling displays for expositions, tethering theatricality to promotional campaigns and propaganda, as governments and corporations orchestrated ways to bask in the glow of modernity and inspire onlookers to imagine energy futures. "Dramatic lighting made possible the revisualization of landscapes," Nye writes, "filling them with new meanings and possibilities."[41] The script of *Power* calls for this technique at pivotal moments, such as the overture to the second act. A note directs the lighting technicians to project a slide with a map of the TVA region onto the stage curtain until it rises for the dramatization of a meeting in Dayton, Tennessee, in 1935 (70). In this scene, businessmen work through a cost-benefit analysis, concluding with minimal deliberation that forming a municipality to get energy from the government from the TVA is preferable to doing business with private utility companies. The lighting design creates a visual rendering of the new landscape of possibilities that the local leaders accept through reasoning depicted as commonsensical futurity (71–72). The scene exemplifies how the producers of *Power* used electrical lighting as a metaphor for the enlightenment made possible by the TVA. The projections of the region in slides and motion pictures designed to entice theatergoers with pro-TVA visual rhetoric were also projections onto the region that envisioned innumerable benefits in the wake of its transformation. Cast in this favorable light, the master plan appeared to be flawless. Achieving this special effect demanded strategically glaring omissions, meaning that audience members were left to their own devices to come up with any potential drawbacks.

THE BODY POLITIC ELECTRIC

Power relied on the familiar script of pointing out the region's problems to lay the groundwork for proposing the TVA as the only viable solution. Toward that end, the script of *Power* maps a geography of uneven development determined by access (or the lack thereof) to electric power and the modern conveniences it could deliver to the region's inhabitants. The prologue that opens Scene Fifteen describes the valley as cast in amber, relegated to the virtually premodern side of a geographical and temporal divide. The stage directions call for film footage projected onto a scrim as the Loudspeaker describes "a region blighted by misuse of land," with a culture deemed "primitive, a throwback to an earlier America" (61). As such, the Tennessee Valley is sorely lacking in the social and energy infrastructure deemed essential for modern living: "Here stand the results of poor land, limited diet, insufficient schooling, inadequate medical care, no plumbing, industry, agriculture or electrification!" (61). The temporal lag and the description of abject conditions are markers of the ills that rural electrification can help alleviate. In crafting this message for public consumption, the living newspaper anticipated documentary films such as *The River* and *The Valley of the Tennessee*. Though *Power* evokes stock regional tropes, it does so only fleetingly. The more pressing imperative is to chart an alternative course enabling the valley to join the rest of the nation in the march of progress. While this approach deviates from the trope of the "backward South," it hews closely to the narrative favored by the architects of public works projects in the 1930s (in the United States and elsewhere) who defined regions as sources of national identity. Natalie J. Ring points out that the perception of the South as a problem for the nation coexisted with the idea that it served as "the custodian of tradition," a "site of authenticity," and an object of "nostalgic yearning for the past."[42] In *Power*, the TVA is a steady hand guiding innovative ideas and transformative infrastructure into the valley while preserving its character. In so doing, it enhances rather than erases the vaunted "way of life" by liberating rural people from arduous labor and empowering them to preserve cherished traditions.

The framing of the Tennessee Valley in the production reveals parallels to other "souths" beyond the borders of the United States. Wolfgang Schivelbusch shows how the multifaceted approach undertaken by the TVA resembled that of the Agro Pontino project engineers in Mussolini's Italy. The Pontine Marshes, located southeast of Rome, was designated for reclamation and rehabilitation as part of the *bonifica integrale*, a package of measures geared toward land improvement while encompassing social, economic, and cultural programs. Residents of the region were described as inhabitants of a place that time had forgotten; they were simultaneously figured as guardians of a valuable cultural heritage and primitives who were sorely in need of the benefits only modernization could provide. The state aimed to cultivate "a new way of life" while preserving the best of the old.[43] This comparison places the depiction of the TVA in *Power* within the geopolitical theater where public works projects took center stage to tout regional rehabilitation as a sign of national resolve in the face of a crippling depression on a global scale.

To deliver this message effectively, the producers of *Power* relied heavily on the Loudspeaker to function as an instrument of amplification and a narrative device for ensuring cohesion. While living newspapers may have emulated print publications in many respects, they also took cues from newsreels, foremost among them the March of Time shorts that preceded feature films in theaters. The producers of living newspapers were not alone in borrowing elements from the newsreel aesthetic. As discussed in the previous chapter, filmmakers working on government-funded projects used the same tactic to lend an air of journalistic authority to propagandistic content. Arent explains that the original conception of living newspapers followed the newsreel model by envisioning a series of sketches dramatizing newspaper stories connected through timeliness rather than topicality. With an emphasis on content over style, living newspapers were distinguishable from newsreels because the latter was the "dramatization of an event," the former "the dramatization of a *problem*."⁴⁴ Although the ill-fated production of *Ethiopia* was an inauspicious start for the Living Newspaper Unit, it did allow the producers to settle on the role of the narrator in the context of the single-issue format. Accordingly, this figure would function "as a commentator—a kind of non-participating dateline which introduced various scenes" and maintained thematic focus and continuity.⁴⁵ The narrator's disembodied, amplified voice hails the listener to identify with the imagined community of the nation through a common historical perspective and a sense of belonging.⁴⁶

Power formulates a historical consciousness connecting the pressing issue of energy policy in the mid-1930s to the past by invoking defining national figures associated with the American mythos. At one point, the action shifts to a cabin in which a man identified only as Farmer is straining to read in a room dimly lit by a kerosene lamp and railing against the power companies that refuse to "string lights" to the countryside because they have calculated that rural electrification is not a sufficiently profitable enterprise (63; fig. 6). In response, the farmer's spouse, named Wife in the script, issues a call to action, urging him to channel the fighting spirit of "Andy Jackson": "Tell 'em you're an American citizen! Tell 'em you're sick and tired of lookin' at fans and heaters and vacuums and dish-washin' machines in catalogues, that you'd like to use 'em for a change!" (63). The invocation of Andrew Jackson in this expression of populist consumerism aligns *Power* with a feature of the technological sublime in the nineteenth-century United States. Nye explains that Jacksonians did not view industrialization in opposition to the natural world. On the contrary, the proverbial machine in the garden was a sign that "mechanical improvements would be harmonious with nature."⁴⁷ At the same time, resistance to centralized government as the primary driver led to a preference for localities to determine the pace of change. Arent's reference to Jackson as a historical figure associated with populism stands to reason: it reinforced the claim that TVA infrastructure accorded with the natural landscape of the valley and the people's will. It is important to point out that bringing Andrew Jackson into the picture raises the historical specter of Indian Removal that he championed and oversaw. Communities of Indigenous people in the Tennessee Valley faced land seizure and forced relocation under eminent domain, followed by the desecration and submersion of sacred

Fig. 6. Unidentified actors playing Farmer and Wife in one of the two New York productions of *Power*. Photograph from the Federal Theatre Project Collection, Library of Congress. Public domain.

ceremonial and burial sites and compounded generational trauma. As discussed in the following chapters, a common rhetorical strategy used by white landowners resisting orders to relinquish their land and relocate to new land provided by the federal government was to couch the process in terms appropriated from the history of Indian Removal.

Defining access to consumer goods in terms of populism resonated with the New Deal economic strategy of boosting getting and spending to bring about economic recovery. It was also consistent with Popular Front accommodations to economic tenets of classical liberalism to maintain a broad-based political alliance on the left. In this context, playing up consumerism in *Power* and other productions by the Living Newspaper Unit was a strategy for diverting attention away from the influences of radical European drama and the Workers' Theatre Movement. The call for union solidarity at the close of *Injunction Granted* was an exception rather than the rule for unit productions. Instead of staging a call to action aimed at workers, Saal explains, the idea was to envision a coalition "under the umbrella term 'consumer.' America's

'Little Man' is the average consumer struggling with utility bills and the housing situation, marveling about the price of milk and meat."[48] The strategy takes on allegorical dimensions in the script of *Power*, with the appearance in the third scene of a character identified as Consumer and described in the stage directions as "a meek-looking little man dressed in the period" (21). The dialogue between this character and the Loudspeaker serves as a primer on kilowatt hours as the standard unit for valuing electricity on the market and as an occasion for indignant speculation about price-gouging as an industry practice among private companies. The demand for access to the consumer marketplace by the "common man" parallels the inalienable right to the pursuit of happiness enshrined in the Declaration of Independence and lionized in expressions of American democratic nationalism. Saal explains that such grand gestures toward audiences were dramatic in every sense of the word: "Appealing to the democratic consciousness of its spectators, the Living Newspaper managed to elicit widespread support for Roosevelt's New Deal."[49]

The portrayal of the citizen-consumer as a populist mouthpiece underwrote *Power*'s endorsement of public utilities. The aspiring citizen-consumer of the Tennessee Valley became the descendant of the revered yeoman farmer, a stock figure in the American mythos since the nation's founding. By the time *Power* had its run, the South was a recurring site for expressing the yeoman ideal in the American imagination. In this instance, evoking the mythic past is a reorienting focus that views nostalgia for an agrarian idyll as grounds for a utopian imagining of energy futures. "We need light!" declares a small farmer cut from the yeoman cloth. It is another instance of a layman channeling the titular energy with a material and symbolic statement that frames consumer choice as a modern extension of the populist imperatives of Jacksonian democracy (84). This rhetorical move was responsive to charges lodged by TVA critics such as Donald Davidson, who invoked the Jeffersonian brand of the yeoman ideal to mourn the accelerated demise of local folkways through cultural erasure. In an account of the TVA's impact on the valley, Davidson laments the displacement of families "from homes where, in symbol or in fact, the Revolutionary sword or the pioneer rifle still hung above the mantel."[50] The inexorable winds of change are extinguishing fires once glowing warmly in hearths "as old as the Republic itself" and effacing "old graveyards."[51] For Davidson, historical landmarks regarded as sacrosanct and cultural artifacts used or displayed in rustic cabins attract the signature "backward glance" defined by the Southern Agrarians as a regional trademark. As such, they become objects of melancholic attachment deeply held and felt in the imagination because they are lost in real time. In contrast, the citizen-consumers of *Power* are willing to look away from the relics of antiquity to cast a forward glance toward a future in which modern conveniences reduce labor and increase leisure. As the state of emergency brought on by the Great Depression opened the valley to an ambitious and wide-ranging reconstruction, these competing ways of life exemplified common responses to rural modernity in general and to technological innovation as an engine of recovery in particular. On one hand, valorization of a mythic premodern era enabled Davidson and his ilk to take his stand against what the TVA represented in the public debate over the New Deal. On the other hand, the notion of a balance between tradition and technology suggested degrees of acceptance ranging from enthusiastic to opportunistic to begrudging.[52]

The alternative means of responding to the TVA were connected to ideological strains that surfaced on both sides of the Atlantic as the global economic crisis inspired dreams of escaping the volatile conditions of modernity by going "back to the land." Schivelbusch views the various expressions of this idyllic, idealized appeal in the context of a resurgent regionalism evident in aesthetic theories and practices that held sway in art, architecture, and other disciplines in addition to the work of prominent figures in economics, political philosophy, and sociology. In an overview of intellectual history, Schivelbusch points to the traditional and future-oriented possibilities shaped by the crisis. In Germany, the pre–World War I *Heimatstil* (native style) gave way to "a reactionary chauvinistic agenda for ethnic purity in architecture" that rose in opposition (literally as pitched roofs) to the flat lines of modernism.[53] Another example is the influential Swiss-French architect and urban planner Le Corbusier, whose ideological path led him to adopt the native style in the 1930s and to become a Vichy sympathizer in the 1940s. As an urban planner in the 1920s who greatly admired the embrace of electrification on display in major US cities, Le Corbusier had conjured the *ville radieuse* ("radiant city") as a visionary model;

in the 1930s, he added to that the ideal of the *ferme radieuse* ("radiant farm"). In 1946, he was part of a French delegation that visited the Tennessee Valley, allowing him to meet David Lilienthal and witness firsthand what had become a model for postwar reconstruction.[54]

The imagery of rural radiance evokes the bucolic countryside aglow with electric lights but free from crowding and other downsides of urban life. From this standpoint, achieving such harmony meant dialing back industrialization to the point that it could become compatible with customs, traditions, and forms of labor derived from antiquity. As Schivelbusch makes clear, the defining features of Le Corbusier's "radiant farm" were not unlike those that the influential economist and eventual Roosevelt administration appointee Stuart Chase envisioned for the United States after looking southward in *Mexico: A Study of Two Americas*: "The way out of the Depression, in the view of men like Chase, was to create a new synthesis of modern technology and 'humane,' preindustrial culture—by, for example, putting electricity to work for artisans and small, de-centralized, quasi-artisan industry."[55] The productive harmony between technology and culture and past and present that Chase describes found dramatic representation in *Power* through rural folks drawn to the light generated by electricity as a source of improvement and empowerment in everyday life and work. But the living newspaper took pains to insist that this desire was not a threat to the tried-and-true ways of old. On the contrary, *Power* declared that these customs were renewable and adaptable in the luminous era of rural electrification.

ON THE GRID

In the script of *Power*, the call to supply rural citizen-consumers of the Tennessee Valley with electricity is matched by the demand for affordable energy from those in urban areas who are already on the grid. The exchange between the farmer and his wife occurs in Act One, Scene Fifteen, comprising sub-scenes that alternate between rural and urban settings and feature parallel characters. The counterparts to the farmer and his wife are a couple labeled in the script as Husband and Wife. Set in an apartment in Chattanooga, Tennessee, this sub-scene presents the couple as disgruntled consumers who see their monthly utility bill as incontrovertible evidence of price-gouging by the power company. When the husband opens the bill, he initially directs the sticker shock at his wife: "Say, what do you do with the juice around here, eat it?" (64). From his standpoint, it "seems all out of proportion" since the bill is roughly equivalent to one-fifth of the rent (64). The husband and wife then trade charges of careless consumption, citing excessive use of the radio, the vacuum cleaner, and the lights as evidence. "Don't say anything, *do* something about it!" the husband declares in response to his wife's plea for energy conservation (64). The city dwellers eventually turn their attention from the household to the hold on the house that the power company enjoys because of its monopoly status. When the wife urges action, the husband balks that "I'm just one little consumer," adding that the State Electric Commission would likely not hear his complaint (65). She counters with a rousing appeal that parallels the pitch made by the small farmer's wife: "Make 'em. Tell 'em that your taxes are paying for their salaries. Tell 'em that that's what they're there for, to regulate things. Tell 'em you're sick and tired of making dividends for somebody else and it's about time the little fellow got a look-in some place" (65). The similarities between the scenes make it apparent that the play posits a close relationship between electrification and unification, as people on both sides of the putative rural/urban divide can find common ground in populist ire directed at corporate malfeasance and profiteering.

On the grounds of service denial in the country and price manipulation in the city, the play imagines the potential for consumer solidarity with equal attention to content and form. Through staging that resembles cinematic montage, *Power* collapses time and space in weaving together a pattern of visual rhetoric positing access and affordability as complementary issues relating to uneven development. In this figuration, the expanded grid that the TVA is constructing is a component of infrastructure that courses with material and symbolic possibilities for achieving consumer parity and promoting national unity. Additional sub-scenes flesh out the sequence comprising Scene Fifteen. In one, the manager of a rural electric company meets with the farmer now animated by the fighting spirit of Andrew Jackson his wife summoned in a call to action. "My God, I've got to have lights, I tell you!" he proclaims to the manager (65). Illustrating a common industry practice, the manager tries to assure the farmer that the company can meet his demand for power, provided the farmer is willing to pay for the installation of poles and wires at a cost of roughly four hundred dollars. The brief exchange ends with the farmer realizing he is at the company's mercy since it operates as a monopoly.

The following sub-scene finds the character City Man in the office of a public official identified as Commissioner pleading the case that "my electric bills are too high!" (66). The consumer's complaint is met with a defense of the industry status quo by a public official portrayed as beholden to private interests. The commissioner states that "the law permits any private enterprise to make a fair return on its investment" (66). These brief sub-scenes expose the corporate rhetoric of open access as disingenuous and highlight corruption in service areas as a feature rather than a bug of privately owned utilities functioning as regional or state monopolies. The end of the city sub-scene dramatizes an energy imaginary in which reforms can unleash consumer populism, activating a grid capable of delivering electrical, political, and purchasing power to citizen-consumers. "If laws like that are made for utilities," says City Man, "why aren't laws made to help people like me?" (67). With the stage fully lit, the farmer's wife, the city man's wife, and the farmer appear, each chiming in with "And me!" to form a quartet representing the vox populi (67).

The show of solidarity across the rural/urban divide ushers in the finale of the first act: a dramatic reading of the congressional measure authorizing the formation of the TVA. "May 18th, 1933," the Loudspeaker says, presumably with the intonation of newsreel narration. "The United States Government answers" (68). An actor portraying the Clerk of the Senate recites excerpts from the TVA charter laying out the agency's commitment to enacting social, environmental, and economic reforms. The emphasis is on new infrastructure for "*the generation and distribution of cheap electric power and the establishment of a cost yardstick*" (68). The prized yardstick metaphor favored by Lilienthal hits the mark by simultaneously speaking to consumer demands for access and affordability and calls for regulatory measures to bring laissez-faire capitalism under control. The script defines the moment when the clerk refers to regional rehabilitation as a musical cue: the start of "The TVA

Song," which delivers good tidings through loud cheers in unabashedly pro-TVA sloganeering.

In keeping with the established format of multimedia agitprop, the stage directions identify the phrase "*cost yardstick*" as the cue for a "motion picture of TVA activities and water flowing over Norris dam" projected onto a scrim to create a visually engaging backdrop for the parade (68). The cause of the TVA gets a ringing endorsement from a music man of the people—in this instance, a soloist whose credentials as a Tennessee Valley native lend him authority and authenticity. "My name is William Edwards," he sings in the first verse. "I live down Cove Creek Way; / I'm working on the project / They call the TVA" (69). The number, credited in the script to a songwriter named Jean Thomas, is a rousing march in the style of a John Phillip Sousa anthem.[56] The patriotic thrust of "The TVA Song" is to celebrate the state apparatus at work and to generate infectious enthusiasm with a clipped musical pacing that replicates the forward momentum of the valley's transformation. In a politically inflected turn, the soloist gets support from the chorus of parading actors, staging the capacity for individual expression to gain strength from large-scale collective action. The song continues with an account of a magical transformation now underway: "All up and down the valley / They heard the glad alarm; / The government means business— / It's working like a charm" (69). With the assurance that "things are surely movin'," the steady beat of the closing verses evokes the inexorable march toward progress that aligns the TVA myth with the broader contours of the American mythos (69). The scene dramatizes a process of emplacement and empowerment in which the electrical grid is a conduit of resources that will improve people's lives by connecting the valley to the nation and the wider world—at least the parts included in the sweep of modernity. Though effective as a means of stirring the audience to take up the cause at hand, the relentless positivity exhibited in the parade scene leaves no space for acknowledging the material reality of displacement and bureaucratic disregard experienced by people who did not march to the beat of the pro-TVA drum propelling William Edwards and his fellow enthusiasts.

FLASH FORWARD: *POWER* REVIVAL

The WPA and its subsidiaries comprising Federal Project One did not have the staying power to last beyond the 1930s. Hallie Flanagan's fight to keep the Federal Theatre Project operating ultimately proved unsuccessful, and it was officially shut down in 1939. That happened partly because mobilization for World War II dramatically changed the priorities of the federal government and the formulas for funding its agencies. Although the HUAC hearings did not inflict as much damage as intended by the orchestrators, the political theater in Washington was a harbinger of demise. For the Living Newspaper Unit, the timeliness of the productions it mounted was initially a great strength, promoting a sense of urgency in keeping with the hard times. But that eventually changed, and the living newspapers, like other forms of Depression-era cultural production (such as proletarian literature and agitprop drama), were classified at best as relics and at worst as "political art" unworthy of inclusion in the canon of American literature developed in post–World War II literary criticism and curricula. Despite critical reassessment of this exclusionary practice and the recovery of many discarded works in the 1990s, living newspapers remained in the annals of cultural history rather than getting reprinted or revived.

Power turned out to be an exception to the rule of obscurity. The Metropolitan Playhouse, an Obie Award–winning theater in New York City's East Village, staged the first revival of the play during a monthlong run beginning in mid-March of 2009. Founded in 1992, the Metropolitan eventually geared its mission toward productions exploring US culture and history, with special emphasis on recovering forgotten works. In keeping with the practice of setting a thematic focus for each season, the revival of *Power* took place under the banner of "Work." Compared to the elaborate original production, the revival was dramatically scaled down: in a relatively small space, it featured nine actors playing multiple parts under the direction of Mark Harborth. An announcement posted on the Metropolitan's website proclaimed that *Power* "hums out of the Great Depression with panache and surprising resonance today," adding that "this piece of the past has a great deal to tell us about our present."[57] The promotional pitch cited several current issues to bolster the claim of resonance: market regulations; water quality and access; the question of whether healthcare is a "public right" or "private privilege"; and the proposition that "our systems that supply electricity are founded on technologies that do more harm to the world than the good they provide."[58] The gist of the appeal was to reframe timeliness by drawing parallels between the pressing matters the living newspapers were conceived to address in 1937 and those much on the minds of theatergoers in 2009.

Reviews demonstrate that critics picked up on the historical resonance and point toward a consensus that it was the revival's *raison d'être*. Describing the Metropolitan as a "theatrical archaeologist extraordinaire," Karl Levett said that for people interested in learning more about the WPA and FTP "or just how little times have changed, *Power* brings history to living, breathing life."[59] Martin Denton praised the production as "a smart, funny, and fast-paced modern vaudeville that's as earnest, sincere, and utterly relevant as it must have been 70 years ago."[60] He cited the question of "whether electricity is a commodity or an entitlement," likening it to the healthcare debate in the twenty-first century before concluding that *Power* "feels of its own time and of ours simultaneously."[61] Other critics drew lines from the Great Depression to the severe economic crisis that erupted in 2007 and would come to be known as the Great Recession. An uncredited review posted on *Off Off Line*, a website devoted to Off- and Off-Off-Broadway theater, made the connection: "Moments of *Power* are eerily reminiscent not just of our economic crisis but of our heated conversations about how to deal with it. The parallels are powerful."[62] Alex Soloski, a *Village Voice* critic, offered a similar assessment: "With the country once again verging on a depression, the government contemplating semi-socialist interventions, and journalists and actors more underemployed than ever, it would seem a fine time to resurrect Living Newspaper plays."[63] Soloski ended the review with a cheeky nod to the play's enduring propagandistic charms: "By *Power*'s close, I wasn't entirely sure what the TVA was, but I knew I supported it enthusiastically."[64]

Not surprisingly, theater critics in New York defined *Power*'s timeliness relative to the ongoing economic crisis. After all, the Metropolitan Playhouse was just a few miles uptown from Wall Street and downtown from the headquarters of Lehman Brothers, the institution whose collapse on September 15, 2008, became emblematic of the deregulated, casino-style finance capitalism that brought about a debacle of major proportions. But this attention paid at the core neglects a far more apt point of reference on the periphery. In the early morning hours of December 22, 2008, a few months before the revival of *Power* opened, a rupture in a coal ash pond at the Tennessee Valley Authority's Kingston Fossil Fuel Plant in Roane County, Tennessee, sent more than 5.4 million cubic yards—1.1 billion gallons—of toxic coal fly ash slurry into the nearby Emory River and overflowing along its shores.[65] In short order, the spill engulfed a highway, a railroad line, and nearly four hundred acres of land. Gregory Button paints an uncanny picture of the catastrophe: "When the explosive force subsided, the fly ash deposits in the river were as deep as thirty feet and as high as sixty feet on land. Smaller *ash burgs* ten to twenty feet high were scattered throughout the moonlit landscape making it appear more like a distant planet than the idyllic landscape that existed only moments before. The surrounding countryside seemed transformed in geologic time rather than in a few horrific minutes."[66] As of this writing, the disaster at the TVA's Kingston site remains the largest industrial spill in US history—nearly ten times larger than the BP oil spill caused by an explosion on the Deepwater Horizon rig in the Gulf of Mexico in 2010. The full extent of the environmental damage is not—and may never be—known. The human toll can be calculated by accounting for lives lost, devastated, or uprooted due to the spill. For many workers involved in the cleanup, the fallout has become manifest in chronic or terminal illnesses likely caused by inadequate protection against exposure to hazardous materials.[67]

In the immediate aftermath of the spill, TVA officials began pouring energy and resources into disaster management, a response designed to mitigate the damage through environmental cleanup and an orchestrated public relations campaign. After cordoning off the affected area, the TVA built an elaborate car wash for transport vehicles so they would not be covered in coal ash when in view of cameras aimed by media outlets gathered at the scene to cover the cleanup. Respirators, protective suits, and dust masks were not allowed on site, leaving cleanup crew members vulnerable to contamination. In official public statements, TVA spokespeople avoided the terms "disaster" or "catastrophe," opting instead for "incident." In an internal set of "risk assessment talking points," the public relations division recommended the phrase "sudden accidental release," a euphemism that came to light after the memorandum was mistakenly emailed to a news organization in what also qualifies as a sudden accidental release.⁶⁸ The tendency toward euphemistic expression was on further display as spokespeople insisted that the substance unleashed by the spill was "inert" and nontoxic despite scientific studies that had long since determined the considerable toxicity of coal ash.⁶⁹

The Kingston disaster makes for a different resonance from what critics taking stock of the Metropolitan's revival of *Power* observed during its run. The treatment of hydroelectricity is a case in point. In the scene featuring Congressman Rankin, the script calls for the actor to deliver a remark taken verbatim from a 1937 *New York Times* article: "We have formed a bloc in the House of Representatives to save for the people, now and for all time to come, the hydro-electric power of the nation" (60). Rankin's promise of an inexhaustible supply in perpetuity encapsulates the prevailing view in the play and among the politicians and government officials who supported the TVA and considered it a model. The final scene—essentially a closing argument—punctuates the claim of abundance, articulating expansive aims by raising the question of the TVA's constitutionality pending in the US Supreme Court. The Loudspeaker proclaims that the decision will determine the "social and economic welfare" of people in the Tennessee Valley and other areas where similar projects might develop. The argument is that a favorable SCOTUS decision would allow for local control in harnessing "water power" to yield an unending supply of "cheap energy" (91). The investment in hydroelectricity as the energy of the future in *Power* comes at the expense of coal, which is not mentioned in the script. It registers now, if not then, as a glaring omission, considering how soon and heavily the TVA would come to rely on coal-fired plants to meet the growing demand that started in the mobilization for World War II and continued apace with harmful consequences.

The accelerated shift in energy resources is evident in Lilienthal's *TVA: Democracy on the March*, in which he argues that the coal industry's initial opposition to the TVA was a misguided stance influenced by "the ideal of restricted development" and based on the faulty assumption that the cultivation of hydroelectric power as an engine of rural electrification would necessarily result in lost market share.⁷⁰

Instead, the supposedly sound development practices implemented had the opposite effect: increased consumption of hydroelectric power boosted the use of other resources, mainly coal. "Never has as much coal been used for the generation of electricity, as since the river has been developed," Lilienthal writes, sounding a triumphant note that rings tragic in the aftermath of the Kingston spill.[71] In an author's note for the 1953 edition of his memoir, Lilienthal explains that "some of the valley programs have changed in scope, emphasis, and content," an understatement prefacing the bracing disclosure that the TVA is in the process of constructing "a huge system of coal-burning electric plants, and is becoming one of the largest users of coal in the country."[72] Built in 1955, the Kingston facility was considered the jewel in the crown of that "huge system" and operated as the largest coal-fired power plant in the world for more than ten years.[73] But the prized jewel had lost its luster as *Power*'s revival took to the stage, yielding a sharp contrast between the unequivocal failure of infrastructure at the Kingston site and the utopian vision of hydro-powered abundance on the New York stage. Along these lines, *Power*'s energy imaginary registered as a dated miscalculation rather than a visionary projection of an energy future that would come to pass by the time the living newspaper got a new and unexpected lease on life.

Chapter 4

BACK TO THE FUTURE
Crosscurrents of Development in Elia Kazan's *Wild River*

THE INITIAL PHASE OF TVA CULTURAL PRODUCTION DISCUSSED IN THE PREVIOUS THREE chapters involved New Deal agencies working within the parameters of the federal government or in collaboration with regional theaters, museums, and publishing houses. This body of work was part of a strategy to promote the TVA amid heated debates about its constitutionality and long-term viability. Photographs, documentary films, and other forms of cultural expression shaped favorable perceptions in the public sphere between the Great Depression and the end of World War II—a period during which the TVA achieved major accomplishments. The comprehensive vision it implemented unquestionably improved the quality of life for many people in the Tennessee Valley even as it upended the lives of those in areas designated for infrastructural development. In the postwar era, the TVA was faced with adapting to an economic boom in which an expanding consumer economy exhibited none of the restraint that the noted economist Stuart Chase assumed in models that had influenced the chief architects of the New Deal and the policies they implemented. On the contrary, the expectation that measured power consumption would become the norm was exposed as deeply flawed. As demand increased rapidly, the TVA made wholesale changes on the supply side to keep pace. In the 1950s and 1960s, a pact with dirty energy supplanted the model of virtually limitless hydroelectric power conceived in the 1930s. The move to coal-fired plants as the primary mechanisms for generating electricity contributed to destructive extraction practices and paved the way for colossal carbon footprints stepping into the future. In addition to reliance on coal, the TVA also had a hand in the nation's controversial development of nuclear energy as a source of military might and power for American consumers.¹

The transition to a new era for the TVA was well underway as the agency entered its fourth decade of operations. On May 18, 1963, President John F. Kennedy visited Muscle Shoals to headline an anniversary celebration. "Thirty years ago today a dream came true," Kennedy told the crowd gathered at the site where FDR launched the TVA endeavor in 1933 with great fanfare.² Praising the vision and tenacity of Roosevelt and his allies in Congress, Kennedy declared that the historic gains were only the beginning. The president recited a litany of positive outcomes in arguing that the naysayers of yesteryear had been wrong. The prediction that the TVA would undermine state and local governments did not come to pass, Kennedy insisted. Moreover, he claimed that concerns about imperiled free enterprise were unfounded. The president hailed the TVA's accomplishments on multiple fronts, contending that the seeds of modernization planted in the area had produced beneficial yields for the region and the nation. The record of success, he added, was good reason for standing firm against opponents still holding fast to the line established in the 1930s: that the agency was a product of egregious federal overreach responsible for introducing what Kennedy's predecessor, Dwight D. Eisenhower, called "creeping socialism" into a regional bastion of American self-reliance.³ To the detractors, some of whom were now comparing TVA infrastructure to the Berlin Wall, Kennedy responded by invoking the pioneering spirit, the same tactic that FDR used to optimal effect: "In short, the work of the TVA will never be over. There will always be new frontiers for it to conquer. For in the minds of men the world over, the initials TVA stand for progress—and the people of this area are not afraid of progress."⁴ On this special occasion, the champion of a burgeoning New Frontier was channeling the symbolic energy of the New Deal to reaffirm the TVA myth.

The connection between the New Deal and the New Frontier that Kennedy drew in Muscle Shoals had a cultural precedent in *Wild River*, a 1960 film directed by Elia Kazan.⁵ First envisioned in the 1950s, the film dramatizes the early days of the TVA in the 1930s. The source material, production history, and content reflect a shift in cultural production from promotion and advocacy to works in which the agency is subject matter for fictional, documentary, or historical representation without the direct influence of state sponsorship, inter-agency collaboration, or partnerships with public institutions. As an adaptation, the screenplay of *Wild River*, credited to Paul Osborn, blends elements of two novels: William Bradford Huie's *Mud on the Stars* (1942) and Borden Deal's *Dunbar's Cove* (1957).[6] The central conflict involves Chuck Glover (played by Montgomery Clift), a TVA official dispatched to a small community designated for flooding to form a reservoir as part of a dam construction project. Glover's main objective is to confront Ella Garth (played by Jo Van Fleet), an octogenarian widow who is the lone holdout against relocation under the terms of eminent domain. According to the mandate, Ella must relinquish her land—a small island in the middle of the Tennessee River—to the federal government. If Ella refuses to comply with the order, Chuck must ensure that she is evicted in time for the scheduled inundation. Laura Beth Daws and Susan L. Brinson describe Ella as "a fictitious 'Granny' sitting on her front porch with a shotgun, daring law enforcement to physically remove her from her home."[7] As such, she exemplifies a stock figure in post–New Deal fictional narratives that portray evictions orchestrated or perpetrated, depending on the perspective, by the TVA. The two novels on which *Wild River* is based were early entries in this category.[8]

While the source material was important, the initial spark of inspiration came from Kazan's experience as a young filmmaker on a project conceived in part to advance the TVA agenda. In 1937, Kazan was cutting his teeth with Frontier Films, a studio aligned with Popular Front cultural politics and supportive of New Deal policies. He was an assistant director of *People of the Cumberland*, a short film blending elements of documentary and dramatization to deliver a pro-union message in a narrative that, like Pare Lorentz's *The River*, eventually winds its way toward a conclusion in which the TVA emerges as the only hope for saving the beleaguered region. When Kazan first had the idea for what would eventually become *Wild River*, he wanted to cast the TVA in a favorable light. That inclination came from fond recollections of Frontier and the heady days of New Deal liberalism on the rise. As the film started to take shape, however, a substantial change in Kazan's relationship with the material was evident. In his autobiography, *Elia Kazan: A Life*, the director describes this development through identification with the principal characters, recalling conversations with Osborn after the screenwriter had agreed to take on the assignment of producing a script: "In talking to him, I discovered an astounding thing. I'd switched sides."[9] What was once intended as an "homage to the spirit of FDR" centered on "a resolute New Dealer" as the heroic figure in a quest to win over "'reactionary' country people" became something quite different now that Kazan found himself partial to "the obdurate old lady."[10] He describes having experienced a political awakening once he realized that his affinity with the "reformers" on the left in the 1930s was not based on conviction but rather on "believ[ing] that I *should* like them."[11]

The effects of the filmmaker's political conversion are apparent in cinematic and narrative elements that shape the historical representation of the TVA. A fundamental tension forms as the presence of infrastructure—an absent presence until the closing sequence—both shapes and unsettles the narrative structure. The impending flood necessitated by the construction of the dam and reservoir defines the stakes, plot, and conflicts within and among the characters. At the same time, it gives rise to shifting focal points and contradictory ideological perspectives that make it difficult to assign the roles of protagonist and antagonist with any degree of certainty. The result is a narrative clearly but compellingly at odds with itself. As such, it reflects the principal creator's initial investment in New Deal liberalism detectable as traces of nostalgia that are then countered by skepticism about the TVA's mission, policies, and practices. As Donald Chase aptly observes, *Wild River* "is an anomaly—a social-issue film from a major Hollywood studio that refuses to take sides."[12] In its evocation of state-sponsored TVA cultural production, the film stands as a cinematic return to the New Deal era that registers uncertainty about the renewed commitment to regional modernization and development at the cusp of the New Frontier.[13]

RESIDUE OF NOSTALGIA

Although Kazan had hardened toward the New Deal when *Wild River* went into production, the film retains aspects of the trip down memory lane he originally envisioned. In this regard, it anticipates what Fredric Jameson calls the "nostalgia film." According to Jameson, the first such film was George Lucas's *American Graffiti* (1973), in which the setting of the Eisenhower era reveals a fixation on the 1950s as a "privileged lost object of desire" figured as a prosperous and stable yet proto-countercultural moment of "pax Americana."[14] For Jameson, this rendering of the 1950s opens other eras to nostalgia-driven "aesthetic colonization" that lays claim to the present and near past or to a remote history beyond the reach of currently lived and remembered experience.[15] The nostalgia film does not attempt merely to represent historical material in realistic terms but rather to use "stylistic connotation" in conveying a sense of the past—what Jameson terms "pastness," as in "1930s-ness" or "1950s-ness."[16] While Jameson pinpoints the emergence of pastness in the early 1970s, this technique is discernable in the mise-en-scène of Kazan's 1960 film.[17]

The primary mechanism for evoking 1930s-ness in *Wild River* is drawing from elements of the New Deal documentary aesthetic. In so doing, Kazan was inspired by the firsthand experience he gained as part of the crew that produced *People of the Cumberland*, a collaboration between Frontier Films and the Highlander Folk School.[18] The school was founded in 1932 in Monteagle, Tennessee, by educator and socialist Myles Horton, poet Don West, and Jim Dombrowski, a Methodist minister. A protégé of theologian Reinhold Niebuhr, Horton was instrumental in modeling Highlander after the Danish folk schools he observed during a visit to Europe. The curriculum centered on adult cultural education and labor activism. Highlander's mission made it an ideal framing device for touting the potential benefits of progressive reforms for a region long debilitated by chronic social, economic, and environmental ills. As in other pro–New Deal documentaries, the force of the appeal in *People of the Cumberland* comes from a clear narrative structure. The focused and compelling script was written by Erskine Caldwell and narrated by Richard Blaine. Also essential to the film's success was a rousing musical score and characteristically impressive work by Ralph Steiner, the noted cinematographer and frequent documentary director who also shot Pare Lorentz's *The River*.

The film makes the case for regional rehabilitation by portraying "the forgotten Cumberland" as a wasteland of environmental degradation and economic exploitation perpetrated by the rapacious coal and timber industries. A montage comprising shots of the "ruined people" mired in abject poverty prefaces a turn toward resilience that recasts them as "the stock of the pioneers, the tough Scots and the English, descendants of a people who came here two hundred years ago with hope and a few grains of seeds." Taking a grassroots tack, the middle sequence showcases Highlander educators instructing people in everything from the traditional folk dances of their ancestors to the fundamentals of labor organization.[19] The argument is that this education and training promotes solidarity among the people in the region and with workers across the nation and around the world. A standout sequence mimics the style of a 1930s gangster film, depicting extralegal agents deployed to bust the unions engaged in a shootout with labor organizers determined to stand up to violent intimidation. The dramatic standoff prefaces the claim in the following sequence that steadfast commitment to the union cause will enable working people to prevail. In the final section, narrative and visual elements work in tandem to convey the impression of a seamless connection between the structures of labor organizations and the infrastructure of the TVA. Reminiscent of *The River*, a montage sequence composed of wide and medium shots of TVA dams accompanied by a musical crescendo in the score and soaring narration steeped in nationalism make the propagandistic strains of the film explicit by the time it concludes.

The influence of the documentary aesthetic is evident in *Wild River* from the outset, as cultural markers of the Depression era lend an air of historicity tinged with New Deal nostalgia. The film opens with footage shot during the major flooding that temporarily halted production of *The River* in 1937, as noted in chapter 2. The sequence conveys the magnitude of loss in the wake of the natural disaster as a survivor visibly in shock recounts how the water destroyed his home and claimed the lives of his entire family. It is a gripping moment in which pathos frames the implicit argument that flood control, and hence the TVA, is a necessity—literally, a matter of life and death. The subsequent transition from the black-and-white documentary footage to the film proper reveals a mise-en-scène replete with New Deal signifiers, albeit visually rendered with the bold palette of Technicolor rather than the black-and-white or sepia tones associated with the Depression documentary aesthetic. Art deco posters designed to promote the TVA and the National Recovery Act (NRA) are noticeable in the background as Chuck Glover walks to the local TVA headquarters upon arriving in town. The NRA poster forecasts a focus on labor issues, suggesting the influence of *People of the Cumberland*. Such details presented in vivid hues call attention to the mechanism of historical representation, of seeing the past through the lens of the present, since the Depression era in public memory lacks color.[20]

The production history of Kazan's film—from extensive drafting of the screenplay in the mid-1950s to its release in 1960—coincided with much of the decade commonly referred to as the classical phase of the civil rights movement. Brian Neve identifies "a degree of parallel between the New Deal mission in Tennessee in the thirties and Washington's later desire to dictate civil rights and other social policies of the Southern states."[21] A subplot involving segregationist resistance to recruiting Black agricultural laborers to work for the TVA aligns with the racial politics in and of the film and the struggle for civil rights unfolding at the time it was made. The depiction of infrastructure plays an essential role in creating this resonance. Anticipating Kennedy's rhetorical evocation of the idealized New Deal, the film presents the TVA enterprise as a metonym for the capacity of large-scale public works projects to deliver the liberating possibilities of modernity—but only to a point. Tellingly, the TVA's nondiscriminatory hiring policies and practices depicted in the film are more progressive than those of actual New Deal agencies. The blame for backtracking on desegregation and equal pay falls squarely on the locals, as though the Roosevelt administration's capitulation to southern members of Congress to ensure support for the New Deal were not a factor. In this and other aspects, it appears that *Wild River*, like the documentaries it references overtly and implicitly, is inclined favorably to the TVA. However, the lingering New Deal nostalgia is combined with counteracting shifts in focalization and contradictory ideological impulses that trouble the waters of *Wild River* and compromise its narrative and thematic cohesion.

BARGAINING WITH THE FAUSTIAN MODEL OF DEVELOPMENT

Despite the ambivalence in *Wild River*'s approach to recent history in general and the TVA in particular, the film paints a compelling portrait of the disruption and displacement that occurs when underdeveloped locales experience accelerated modernization. For this reason, Marshall Berman's trenchant reading of Goethe's *Faust* as a modern tragedy hinging on the "Faustian model of development" offers a constructive analytical framework for reading the film's engagement with material history and culture. Among the qualities that make *Faust* recognizable to contemporary readers, Berman avers, is that it "expresses and dramatizes the process by which, at the end of the eighteenth century and the start of the nineteenth, a distinctively modern world-system comes into being."[22] Berman holds that Goethe's version of the story departs from its antecedents because the animating feature is "the desire for *development*" forging "an affinity between the cultural ideal of *self*-development and the real social movement toward *economic* development."[23] Fundamentally, the Faustian enterprise is not capitalistic but utopian, prefiguring socialism because of the overriding concern of bringing about a prosperous future for society through central planning and organization. Toward this end, the Faustian model "gives top priority to gigantic energy and transportation projects on an international scale" and establishes "a new mode of authority" derived from the capacity of leaders "to satisfy modern people's persistent need for adventurous, open-ended, ever-renewed development."[24] By the twentieth century, this approach reached its apogee, marked by "the proliferation of 'public' authorities' and superagencies" invested in the expansion of public works as a means to redress the adverse consequences of uneven development.[25] It is apposite that among the real-world Faustian developers Berman cites is David Lilienthal, whose ideas find expression in *Wild River* through the TVA agent charged with convincing Ella Garth to leave her land.[26]

The Developer at Odds

When Chuck Glover arrives from Washington, DC, the TVA has secured all the land designated for flooding except Garth Island. Until now, Ella has stood her ground against multiple representatives tasked with convincing her that she has no choice but to leave. After a briefing on Ella's noncompliance, Chuck expresses a begrudging admiration for her resolve, telling a gathering of officials holding a strategy session at the local headquarters, "That is the American way of life. Rugged individualism is our heritage. Three thousand people sell, and Ella Garth won't sell. We applaud that spirit. We admire it. We believe in it. But we've got to get her the hell out of here." While he pays homage to Ella as a paragon of American individualism, he insists that she must back down for the greater good. The conflict between the lone holdout against eminent domain and the TVA representative reflects a longstanding dispute in the United States that intensified as the New Deal materialized. At this point, Chuck's assessment of the dilemma is optimistic. "I do think we often underestimate the intelligence of people," he tells the mayor and TVA officials. "We can talk to them, and they will listen." Such confidence comes from the belief that the benefits are self-evident and that a messenger need only deliver the TVA gospel with conviction and reason to convert skeptics or opponents.

As an agency disciple, Chuck takes on the role of the dreamer in Berman's Faustian development model. To play this part, Berman explains, is to occupy a "closed society" as "the bearer of a dynamic culture within a stagnant society" and, accordingly, to feel increasingly "torn between inner and outer life."[27] The split along this fault line in Chuck's character takes effect as he interacts with Ella Garth. In so doing, he finds himself increasingly sympathetic to her cause even as he is bound by official duty to make it a lost one. In this regard, Chuck is fashioned from Crawford Gates, the TVA agent in *Dunbar's Cove* whose steadfast determination to convince the recalcitrant Matthew Dunbar to leave his cherished ancestral plot of land is tempered by mixed emotions. This shared trajectory parallels Kazan's experience of initially identifying with Chuck and his commitment to the TVA and then later believing that Ella is justified in defying the eviction order. Although Chuck's characterization tracks with the phases—or metamorphoses—of Berman's Faustian model, reluctance rather than certitude shapes *Wild River* into a "*tragedy of development.*"[28] The psychosocial divide Berman identifies in the Faustian dreamer is a function of perceiving places deemed underdeveloped as lagging and remote by modern standards and thus urgently needing modernization. Robin L. Murray and Joseph K. Heumann observe the correlation between this logic and the mapping of the region in *Wild River*: "Chuck's introduction to Ella's premodern island demonstrates the extent of the contrast between North and South, between the technological progress promised by the TVA and the stagnant rural economy of stolid unchanging Southerners."[29] Indeed, Chuck's first visit to Garth Island—the name is taken directly from Huie's *Mud on the Stars*—exposes divergent courses and stark cultural differences that raise the specter of sectionalism as an obstacle to winning over local converts to the TVA cause.

When he arrives at the dock to make his way to the island, Chuck sees a sign on the opposite bank emblazoned with a territorial warning: "TVA Keep Off." It marks the boundary of Ella Garth's domain and the sovereignty she claims over it as proprietor and matriarch. The brief sequence in which Chuck commandeers a floating pier to make the short crossing evokes the mythic River Styx. In this scenario, the land of the living is the town, the realm of modernity bustling with activity due to the dam in progress and anticipation of the economic boon it promises to bring upon completion. By contrast, Garth Island is the land of the dead, established when Chuck makes landfall and sets out on a path toward the Garth home winding through a field of dried cornstalks left in the wake of harvest. The Styx analogy extends further given that the island graveyard where Ella's husband is buried later becomes a symbolically important site.

The juxtaposition of the town and Garth Island as discrete spaces presents them as oppositional models of development in microcosm: the former runs on infrastructural time regulated by the TVA; the latter disrupts that flow with stasis. In this respect, *Wild River* evokes the southern modernism of the New Deal era. As Leigh Anne Duck explains, formal experiments in this regional branch of the literary-cultural movement explored "the potentially unsettling experience of modernity's multiple temporal forms," including the "temporal disjunctures of uneven development," yielding "representations of the imagined temporal divide between the region and the larger nation."[30] The temporal mapping of uneven development according to the imagined split between region and nation corresponds to the countervailing ideological perspectives in Kazan's film. From a perspective supportive of Ella Garth, the season of death on Garth Island makes it symbolic of the passing "way of life" mourned in conservative intellectual circles, particularly among the Southern Agrarians. As such, the island stands in for the local places and people facing cultural eradication due to the rapid modernization imposed by the TVA. From a position favorable to Chuck Glover, he is the emissary from town who promises a new and better way of life to engender the regeneration of the wasteland and reconciliation across the temporal and developmental divide.

As Chuck approaches the Garth home, brimming with confidence that he will succeed where his predecessors have failed, Ella relies on her territorial advantage. Spotting him from her front porch, Ella quickly goes into the house—a strategic retreat signaling that she dictates the terms of their first encounter. Failing to coax her out, Chuck follows the instructions provided by Ella's widowed granddaughter, Carol Garth Baldwin (played by Lee Remick), to look for Ella's three sons. He is disappointed to learn they are united behind their mother's defiant stand. Unlike Ella, however, love of the land is not the primary motivation. Instead, the key factor, as Hamilton Garth (played by Jay C. Flippen) explains, is that getting jobs in town requires "too much work." In response to Chuck's question about who does all the work on the farm, Hamilton makes a head gesture toward three Black men visible in the background as they sit in a boat cleaning fish. The filming of this exchange establishes the Garths' dependence on Black labor as a recurring theme expressed through visual cues and plot developments. When Chuck presses the issue further by asking how the brothers have managed to avoid working for so long, he gets a laconic rejoinder from Hamilton: "Just never started."

An aversion to labor, along with the costume design, cues the audience that the Garth brothers fit the mold of the "poor white," a longstanding staple of American culture. In *Not Quite White: White Trash and the Boundaries of Whiteness*, Matt Wray traces the origins of the derogatory concept to the nation's founding. By the first half of the nineteenth century, Wray explains, American literature presented a "dual image": "poor frontier white as hero or poor white trash as villain."[31] Wray coins the term "stigmatype" to describe the latter figuration, adding that it "proved ideologically useful to both northerners and southerners" and so "appeared with greater frequency in the national popular culture."[32] Stigmatyping the Garth brothers delineates Chuck as the outsider relative to the insiders of Garth Island he believes he can win over by bringing enlightenment to the benighted island. Chuck's strategy in trying to achieve this end immediately reveals his deficiencies in the art of persuasion insofar as the Garths are concerned. After he suggests to Hamilton that Ella's stubbornness could be a sign of senility, Joe John Garth (played by Big Jeff Bess) responds by hoisting Chuck in the air and tossing him, suit-clad, into the river. This comic relief calls to mind the frontier sketches of southwestern humor, in which cartoonish depictions of poor whites as quick-tempered and prone to physical confrontations abound. In the Depression cultural milieu, the Garth brothers resemble the poor whites rendered by Erskine Caldwell in *Tobacco Road* (1932) and the photobook *You Have Seen Their Faces* (1937), for which the author supplied dialogue to accompany abject photos of poverty-stricken southerners taken by Margaret Bourke-White. Despite the similarities, the Garth brothers fall into a gray area, exhibiting traits of the stigmatype at the same time they defend their mother's honor in a manner that is impulsive but understandable. As the scene concludes, the gray area also encompasses Chuck's position vis-à-vis the roles of protagonist and antagonist, with the Faustian dreamer literally and figuratively exposed for being all wet.

Having failed in his first attempt to reach Ella, Chuck returns to his room at a local boarding house to change clothes. On the telephone with a TVA official, Chuck insists he is up to the task, and he gets the opportunity to prove it when Hamilton shows up to apologize and to invite him to meet with Ella. Before Chuck even arrives on the scene, Ella has full command of the stage, addressing a gathering of the Black tenant families who live and work on her island. It is a compelling introduction to Ella and the skilled performance that Jo Van Fleet delivers—even more impressive given that she was in her thirties and portraying a woman in her eighties—as a steely matriarch with steadfast devotion to the land she calls home. "Well, they say that President Roosevelt's got some kind of new government," Ella declares. "It's called a New Deal. Now, what do you think of that?" The composition of this shot positions Ella at the center of the frame, with a small group of tenants, including a small boy, close to her as they listen intently. Although she addresses them directly, she projects her voice so that everyone in earshot can hear what she has to say. The dramatic monologue amounts to a Sermon on the Isle. "Mr. Roosevelt is going to flood this land," Ella says, infusing her oration with biblical energy before declaring that "he's going to take the best piece of land in these here parts and put it right smack under the Tennessee River!" Ella rhetorically fashions herself the suffering Job to FDR's indifferent God. The quasi-religious fervor lays the rhetorical groundwork for aggrieved populism: Ella describes the president "up there in his big, white house" dictating that the only course of action is "putting my island underwater." The implication is that the use of eminent domain to make way for infrastructure projects gives new meaning to the trope of the "forgotten man" at the heart of New Deal political messaging. From Ella's point of view, the term applies to people like her—the displaced persons whose concerns about the loss of land and liberty are falling on bureaucratic deaf ears. The force of Ella's monologue runs counter to the New Deal nostalgia established through visual cues in the opening sequences.

Ella's strategy is to make the grounded argument, in every sense of the word, that the traditional way of life on Garth Island is preferable to living under the yoke of federal authority. Against the dream of prosperity and lives transformed for the better by modern conveniences that Chuck promises the TVA will deliver, Ella marshals the emotional strength of land attachment and the sense of reassurance that comes with the familiarity and stability of the closed society on the island. Continuing her address as Chuck arrives on the scene, Ella cites "our friend" who left under cover of darkness as evidence of the new upheaval. She blames the tenant's flight on fear rather than conceding that better prospects in town are a more reasonable explanation. To dispute the enticements of the TVA, Ella suggests that joining its fold undermines a strong work ethic and the preservation of individual liberty. "I understand they're going to put you on relief," Ella says scornfully to the tenants. "Well, you just go ahead and get yourselves relieved. Any time you want." Using reverse psychology, Ella makes the freedom to leave the grounds for staying put, warning that exercising the option to flee may appear liberating but that it will lead to entrapment in a cycle of dependence. A landlord touting sharecropping as the way to preserve individual liberty makes for a dubious proposition at best. Such a disingenuous stance exposes a level of manipulation commensurate with Ella's interest in retaining the cheap labor she relies on to sustain her farming operation. Although on a much smaller scale, Ella has the same concern as white planters in the Mississippi Delta who feared a mass exodus of Black labor during the Great Flood of 1927.[33]

Where the planters used power and influence to coerce labor, Ella relies on rhetorical cunning.

Continuing in the vein of the sermon, Ella stages a parable of sorts to illustrate the validity and moral authority of her stance. She turns to one of the tenants, Sam (played by Robert Earl Jones), and informs him that she has decided to buy his dog for one hundred dollars and that Sam has no choice but to sell. When he objects, insisting that even she cannot force him to part with beloved "old Blue," Ella seizes the moment to drive home her point: "Sam and me, we don't sell. Sam don't sell his dog, and I don't sell my land that I've poured my heart's blood into." Just as separating Sam from Blue would break a loving bond, so would forcing Ella to sell her land sever spiritual ties. This belief resonates with the philosophical musings of the Southern Agrarians, who imagined a mystical connection to the land as an organic birthright possessed by the rural people they valorized as model citizens of "the South" defined in monolithic terms. It also reveals ties between the characterization of Ella Garth and the source material from which *Wild River* derived. Like Matthew Dunbar, the protagonist of Borden Deal's *Dunbar's Cove*, Ella draws energy and resolve from a sense of place that she considers beyond the purview of the federal authorities to comprehend, let alone claim. In this regard, she also resembles Mattie Randolph, the real-life matriarch who stood her ground against the TVA during the construction of Norris Dam in 1936 and provided additional inspiration for *Wild River*.[34] By staking her claim to Garth Island on moral and quasi-spiritual grounds, Ella counters eminent domain with what might be called immanent domain, eliciting sympathy from viewers in the manner Kazan describes having felt after his politics changed.

In responding to Ella's demonstration, Chuck remains in the mode of the Faustian dreamer, pointing to progress and the communal ideal of the greater good as reasons to change her mind. Respectfully, he tries to explain to her that "sometimes it happens that we can't remain true to our beliefs without hurting maybe a great many people. And I'm afraid this is one of those times." Clift plays the scene with intensity, his facial expressions and eyes conveying passion and urgency. Ella asks Chuck if he knows anything about the land, suggesting he grab a handful of soil on his way back to the mainland to get a feel for it. "That's real bottom," she says, implicitly reinforcing the contrast between her deeply rooted connection to the place and his outsider status. Instead of letting the charge stand, Chuck revises the terms of Ella's land attachment such that it is no longer bound by physical proximity: "Mrs. Garth, you don't leave the land; you love your land." By this logic, Garth Island will remain with Ella even though Ella will not stay on Garth Island. It is a distilled presentation of the case that the TVA agent Crawford Gates makes in a series of repetitive encounters in *Dunbar's Cove*. Crawford argues with conviction, but to no avail, that Matthew Dunbar's stubborn resistance to the TVA is misguided individualism that is futile in terms of his effort and detrimental to the neighbors he claims to hold in high regard and to serve as a champion of local values.

While Chuck appeals to pathos in recasting the terms of Ella's ties to the land, he emphasizes the tangible benefits of the TVA as a mechanism for alleviating social ills and economic disparities. Using standard talking points, he argues that the dams will stop the rising death toll and destruction caused by severe flooding. He cites the data point that 98 percent of people in the area do not have electricity and thus stand to gain from an abundant and affordable energy source capable of freeing people from the shackles of tedious, backbreaking labor. "I expect that's what you call progress, isn't it?" Ella says derisively, before offering her assessment, again in terms of spirituality: "Taking away people's souls, putting electricity in place of them, ain't progress. Not the way I see it." For Chuck, electricity generates both light and enlightenment as benefits of the technological progress associated with modernity; by contrast, Ella uses homespun theology to cast rural electrification as a veritable deal with the devil—or, in terms of the Faustian model, with Mephistopheles—cast in a false light that exposes the soul to irreparable damage.

Undeterred, Chuck refines his approach, conjuring a proleptic vision that evokes the technological sublime for inspirational effect. He describes the intentional flooding as though it has already happened. Forecasting the formation of a reservoir in the future to shape circumstances in the present is a common refrain in works that use dam projects for plot construction. The frequent references to the imminent flood in *Wild River* are verbal parallels to the visual technique in Dziga Vertov's documentary film *The Eleventh Year* discussed in chapter 2: superimposing faint images of flowing water onto footage of sites and structures in the planned reservoir zone to yield the special effect of a simulated inundation. Chuck's defense of flood control within the overall TVA design brings the film's titular theme to bear: "Dam after dam after dam, we aim to tame this whole river," Chuck says. Here is an instance of how, as Murray and Heumann point out, "*Wild River* asserts that rerouting the river to battle flood problems counters individual rights and liberties fought for during the Civil Rights period in which the film was produced."[35] Ella's response mounts a folksy critique of the anthropogenic logic underwriting this assertion: "I like things running wild like nature meant." She tallies the existing dams as "already enough," decrying how they are "locking things up, taming them, making them go against their natural wants and needs." To underscore the point, Ella declares, "I'm against dams of any kind," essentially mounting a defense of the natural order of things. Nevertheless, in the context of debates over infrastructure, economic development, and rural electrification at the time, the meaning of "natural" remains contested rather than settled.

While forceful and passionate, Ella's plea on behalf of untamed nature is dubious, forming a key component of an exercise in mythmaking enabled by historical whitewashing and glaring omissions. The remainder of her argument unfolds in a scene in the island cemetery, where Ella leads Chuck to her husband's graveside to further impress upon him that she has no intention of leaving. There are matching tombstones for husband and wife on this hallowed ground—the highest point of the island, untouched by floodwaters since Ella can recall. In a solemn tone, Ella shares an origin story of mythic proportions, casting her husband, Woodbridge Garth, as the hero. Kazan composes the sequence to film Van Fleet from a low angle, lending authority to her oration. Ella says Woodbridge "was looking for an island, and he took this one." She alludes to the extensive clearing and cultivation necessary to make the land conducive to farming, implying that he worked singlehandedly to achieve dominion. The implication is that Woodridge was an exemplar of pioneer-settler self-reliance, possessing the necessary fortitude, strength, and determination to prosper from the land.

As is usually the case, the myth of the self-made man fulfilling a Manifest Destiny obscures the harsh realities of material history rooted in violence and exploitation. Noticeably absent from Ella's story is the fact that the removal of the Indigenous population would have been the reason land in this part of eastern Tennessee was available for men like Woodbridge Garth to claim in the first place. For this reason, Woodbridge and his ilk were not self-made men so much as they were men whose fortunes were made possible by settler colonialism and the federal government, an earlier incarnation of the institution Ella is now indicting as intrusive and oppressive. In making this assertion, Ella relies on a rhetorical appropriation, borrowing terms of forcible removal entailed in Indigenous history while failing to acknowledge the debt. In this regard, *Wild River* takes on an added dimension as a nostalgia film, resonating with Michael Truscello's reading of fictional narratives, including *Dunbar's Cove*, engaged in "white settler nostalgia" that "erases Indigeneity."[36] Accordingly, this pining "for a mythical landscape before the flooding, or for a mythical white agrarian culture, naturalizes 'settler jurisdiction' and other quotidian modes of occupation without explicitly engaging the dispossession of Indigenous people."[37]

Notably, the film's erasure of Indigeneity denies traces found in the source material. The origin story at the opening of *Dunbar's Cove* recounts David Dunbar's arrival in "the land of the Five Towns," an enclave where "white men entered only by becoming Chickamaugas, white Indians, irreconcilables themselves."[38] And so it was with David Dunbar, who was "enough Indian even though it was Chickasaw rather than Cherokee but with the wild, turbulent blood that gave him belonging."[39] By this reasoning, David's claim to the land that would bear his name gained validity from his mixed-race ancestry and hybrid cultural identity. The author thus makes him the remnant of a "national disgrace," the dispossession and removal of Indigenous people.[40] Although this depiction perpetuates the myth of the Vanishing Indian, it does exhibit at least some awareness of Indigenous history. However, this limited historical acknowledgment was lost in adaptation, as the script of *Wild River* makes Ella a mouthpiece for the white settler nostalgia that defines the point of view and delimits the scope of the tragedy of development.

Within the framework of the plot, the visit to the gravesite achieves the outcome Ella intended. Chuck leaves the island with diminished confidence in his powers of persuasion and a burgeoning admiration of Ella for standing firm. Considering this plot point, Chuck might be read as Kazan's proxy relative to Ella Garth even though the director went further than the fictional TVA agent in feeling sympathy for the steely matriarch. The scenes comprising the initial encounter between the two principal characters are a distilled form of material from *Mud on the Stars* and *Dunbar's Cove*. In these novels of ideas, the authors include long dramatic monologues or extended, often repeated, debates between characters about the TVA, the New Deal, and the finer points of central planning versus federal overreach among numerous other topics. The debate staged in the opening sequence of *Wild River* is indicative of the ideological ambivalence that pervades the film as the dream Chuck tries in vain to express as an agent of the TVA meets the dramatic force of Ella's claim (to the land and as argument) that she makes as the agency's fierce opponent.

Developing Romance, Romancing Development

The first forays onto Garth Island establish the terms of the conflict between Chuck and Ella, with the roles of protagonist and antagonist interchangeable based on where the given viewer's sympathy lies. At the same time, these opening scenes establish a budding romance with Ella's granddaughter Carol that determines Chuck's transition from Faustian dreamer to lover. Berman explains that this "second metamorphosis" of Faust occurs because of his involvement with Gretchen, the romantic heroine whom contemporary readers find "simply too good to be true—or to be interesting" because of "simple innocence and spotless purity" more suited to "the world of sentimental melodrama than to tragedy."[41] To counter such skepticism, Berman posits that reading the work as both a story and a tragedy of development reveals greater complexity and depth in Gretchen as a character and the narrative structure of the section in which she meets her demise. Berman identifies three protagonists at this stage: "Gretchen herself, Faust, and the 'little world'—the closed world of the devoutly religious small town from which Gretchen emerges."[42] The tripartite relationship in *Wild River* consists of Chuck, Carol, and Ella, with the latter embodying the "closed world" of Garth Island. In a variation on the classic love triangle, Carol plays the pivotal role because Chuck and Ella vie respectively for her romantic or filial devotion during their dispute over eminent domain. For Chuck, as for Faust in Berman's reading, becoming the lover who inspires a transformation in his beloved enables him to connect with the place he will ultimately destroy—an outcome he regards as salvation through the lens of creative destruction. Berman's assessment of Faust and Gretchen applies to Chuck and Carol in *Wild River*: "Their love affair will dramatize the tragic impact—at once explosive and implosive—of modern desires and sensibilities on a traditional world."[43]

Carol is present but remains at the margins while the tense negotiations between Chuck and Ella play out in the foreground. In the graveyard scene, cutaway shots reveal Carol lurking nearby, watching and listening as her grandmother recounts the origin story of Garth Island. Nevertheless, there is a brief exchange in which Carol describes to Chuck the tragic stakes for her grandmother: "If she has to leave this island, it will kill her." The reaction shot captures a sympathetic expression on Chuck's face, underscoring the complex dilemma he now faces. Although Carol is deeply devoted to Ella, she does not share her grandmother's life-or-death attachment to Garth Island. After all, as Carol discloses to Chuck in a subsequent scene, she technically left the island for a brief period when she and her husband decamped to a small house on the mainland just across the river. After her husband died, Carol stayed there and attended college for a year on Ella's dime before eventually returning to the matriarchal fold, presumably because going to college while caring for two small children as a single mother was not manageable. Still, Carol's explanation that going to college was an attempt "to better myself" suggests to Chuck the possibility that she, unlike her grandmother, is keeping an open mind about the TVA.

Because Chuck sees Carol as an opportunity to reach Ella and perhaps change her mind, distinguishing between the development of romantic feelings and the infrastructural development of the area engineered by the TVA can be challenging. Chuck's approach to courtship demonstrates the entanglement of his dedication to his professional mission with his burgeoning romantic desire. His initial overture involves an attempt to reframe eminent domain by shifting the topic from the fact that Ella must move by legal decree to the promise that her quality of life will improve markedly because of resettlement to one of the planned communities where modern conveniences are available. Later, he explains to Carol that he is also concerned about her present circumstances and prospects for the future. Ironically, while Chuck tries to convince Ella that taming the wild river is possible and essential, he aims to steer her granddaughter away from still waters. Before Chuck came along, Carol got engaged to a local businessman in town, Walter Clark (played by Frank Overton). Chuck surmises that her decision to accept the proposal came from the head rather than the heart, and he implores Carol not to marry a man she does not love. "You're a real romantic, aren't you?" she says, indicating that his transition from dreamer to lover is in progress. For Chuck, the language of love contains traces of his vocation: he implores her to end the engagement by explaining that the steady erosion of emotional life in a passionless marriage is worse than land degradation. Carol takes the plea to heart, joining Chuck on the floating pier to cross the river. Kazan stages the scene as a reversal of the earlier crossing and a revision of the Orpheus and Eurydice myth, with Chuck determined to deliver Carol from the land of the dead to join the living. Unlike his mythical counterpart, Chuck is successful in this endeavor, earning Carol's backing in his effort to convince her grandmother to leave Garth Island voluntarily. Predictably, Ella describes this move as "siding with the enemy."

The path from courtship to marriage exposes a truncated narrative arc, suggesting that a key scene or two to establish mutual attraction wound up on the cutting-room floor. Consequently, the relationship is open to the interpretation that Chuck's passion stems as much from wanting to enlist Carol in his cause as from genuine romantic desire. This possibility becomes evident when he visits the small house on the riverbank after Carol and her children have moved back there. While he is animated when speaking to Carol about the TVA vision, he is reticent when she expresses feelings for him. When Carol confesses that she has fallen in love with him, she calls out his initial unwillingness to reciprocate with an allusion to the impending flood: "What's the matter, Chuck? Afraid you're getting in too deep?" External consequences of development rather than internal feelings of affection are responsible for forcing Chuck's hand. Specifically, Hank Bailey (played by Albert Salmi), a local landowner angered by the upheaval the TVA is causing in the Jim Crow labor regime, shows up at Carol's house with a gang he has gathered. These men aim to take vigilante action to make Chuck retract his promise to implement fair hiring practices and pay equity for Black workers. The tone of the scene is uneven, depicting an overt show of white supremacist mob mentality mixed with incongruous attempts at dark humor that fall flat. Moved to defend Carol's home and her honor, Chuck proves ineffectual, suffering two hard blows from Bailey knocking him unconscious. As she did when declaring her love, Carol assumes the role of the traditional romantic hero, mounting a defense of her beloved in a fight with his adversary. The injection of physical comedy is as incompatible with the circumstances as the earlier instance of failed dark humor involving the prospect of mob violence. Although she momentarily holds her own, Carol winds up on the ground next to Chuck after Bailey clocks her. This violent turn is a prelude to the marriage proposal, which Chuck proffers while they are still on the ground in a mud puddle. Deflating the romance even further, he stipulates that they will probably regret getting married. Unlike Gretchen, Carol does not meet her demise in the throes of intense passion for the Faustian figure. Instead, the marriage in *Wild River*, performed in the next scene by a Justice of the Peace, signals that the future of Garth Island is firmly on the course dictated by the TVA, making Ella Garth the focal point of the tragedy of development's final act.

The Developer's Prerogative

The rapidity of Chuck and Carol's move from new acquaintances to newlyweds parallels the accelerated pace of modernization and development overseen by the TVA. The progression of their relationship, like the dam construction project, unfolds in infrastructural time. The one exception to this temporal rule remains Garth Island. Up to this point, Chuck's conflict with Ella has mirrored the divide between inner and outer life that Berman identifies in the Faustian dreamer. As the TVA's designated representative, he is duty-bound to see that Ella follows the law. Nevertheless, the more he engages with Ella, the more conflicted his personal feelings and professional obligations become. With the formation of the reservoir fast approaching, the pressure to settle the matter once and for all reaches its peak. Seeking a resolution, Chuck takes a forceful approach and, as justification, becomes even firmer in his commitment to the TVA vision. In the final act, Chuck enters the last phase of the Faustian model: that of the developer. In this capacity, he perceives natural resources as potential energy sources that go to waste if not exploited to fuel the engine of progress. From this perspective, the developer understands the natural world he inhabits in abstract terms—specifically, as a site for building infrastructure to facilitate energy production and economic development. As Berman explains, the developer is "convinced that it is the common people, the mass of workers and sufferers" who stand to gain from the epic transformation of nature.[44] Chuck operates in this mindset, believing that forcing Ella to leave her land is purely for her good and that of her neighbors.

The deadline for eviction brings the tragedy of development to a head. Berman's observation about Faust applies to Chuck in that "his tragedy will stem precisely from [the developer's] desire to eliminate tragedy from life."[45] By the time he plots Ella's move to one of the modern tract houses in the TVA planned community, insisting that there must be a porch for her cherished rocking chair, Chuck has convinced himself that he is unburdening her from the toils and hardship of daily existence on the island. Surely, he reasons, it will only be a matter of time before she sees the light and comes to appreciate the superior quality of life the TVA is making possible. Such calculation suggests that Chuck is trying to assuage his guilt over the reality that Ella's way of life, if not Ella herself, is being sacrificed to development figured unequivocally as a greater good. In this respect, Ella parallels the elderly couple in *Faust*, Philemon and Baucis, who live on the one remaining parcel of undeveloped land within the realm of Faust's grand design. For Berman, they are the first modern figures in literature to represent "people who are in the way—in the way of history, of progress, of development; people who are classified, and disposed of, as obsolete."[46] Indeed, Chuck's determination to upgrade Ella's life stems from his inability to acknowledge her obsolescence within the modern space he prepares for her as though he is carrying out a rescue mission instead of a mandatory relocation.

Chuck's self-fashioning as a deliverer obscures his motives as a developer. This facet of his character emerges as he shifts gears to play up the idea that he is acting mainly out of concern for Ella and play down his primary interest in fulfilling his mission on behalf of the TVA. It is also apparent when he hatches a plan to attract the Black tenants living on Garth Island to the mainland. The mayor rejects the idea out of hand, pointing out that such a move would violate the local customs of Jim Crow segregation and, in turn, lead white men already employed by the agency to quit en masse. But the mayor's dismissal of the idea only strengthens Chuck's resolve, at least momentarily: "Look, this is TVA. We're new. We don't have any customs yet. I'm going to hire those men, and every man, black or white, gets paid the same." This principled stand has historical resonance, evoking the rhetoric of change that made many Black people optimistic about the TVA—initially, at least. As Nancy L. Grant documents, "[t]he most marginal people in a marginal region," whether they were in rural areas laboring under the sharecropping system or urban areas such as Knoxville or Chattanooga, had a vested interest in an agency committed to regional transformation.[47] "No group had more to gain than blacks living in the valley," Grant points out.[48] Like their cinematic counterpart in *Wild River*, actual TVA officials initially pledged to make racial equity a standard operating principle. However, the entrenched status quo dashed the hopes raised by this professed commitment, as Grant explains: "Unfortunately, the promise of nondiscrimination in job opportunities, housing, and community development was translated into a reality that, at best, maintained existing patterns of discrimination and, at worst, brought about racial exclusion and heightened tensions."[49] In *Wild River*, the promise of equality is enough to spark an exodus from Garth Island. With their belongings in tow on wagons, a caravan of Black tenants enacts a scene of migration rendered with striking cinematography and a heightened sense of drama aided by the musical score. The lone tenant who remains on the island is Sam, the man who refused to part with his dog when Ella orchestrated an object lesson about not giving in to coercion by the powers that be. Although Sam is intrigued by the electric light switches when Chuck takes him on a tour of a TVA tract house, he ultimately decides to remain loyal to Ella—a relationship redolent of the paternalism commonly associated with romanticized depictions of antebellum southern plantations. The notion that Chuck's progressivism is far removed from Ella's paternalism is undercut by factors that call the TVA agent's nobility into question: his capitulation to business leaders who claim to be "responsible for the town" (particularly in meeting their demand that workers must be divided into "segregated gangs") and the fact that his plan to help people escape the island is part of his ploy to remove Ella from it. These aspects of Chuck's character further underscore the transition from New Deal idealism to disillusionment that Kazan had made when production began on *Wild River*.

In response to the exodus, Ella takes an ax to the ferry pole, severing the connection between the island and the mainland. But it is to no avail—a symbolic gesture at best. Several of the people who left Garth Island and their lives as sharecroppers soon return, only this time as employees of the TVA assigned to the crew carrying out the eviction order. Sensing that Chuck has lingering guilt despite his determination to move forward, the local US marshal puts the forcible removal in perspective: "It all goes under the general heading of *Progress*." The scene in which the crew arrives has visual echoes of Chuck's first crossing to the island, except now he is not steering the floating pier but riding on a tugboat flying an American flag at full mast. The presence in the frame of this steam engine vessel powered by coal fire can be read as an instance of fuel registering as a "cultural code or reality effect" within the film's "imaginary resolutions of real social contradictions," to apply Patricia Yaeger's gloss on Fredric Jameson in formulating an "energy unconscious."[50] The shot calls to mind the vast difference between the past energy future of abundant hydroelectric power supplied by the TVA envisioned by Chuck and the outcome by the time *Wild River* was released: the proliferation of coal-fired plants in the Tennessee Valley. When Chuck arrives, he finds Ella appropriately clad in black for the mournful occasion; she carries only two small bags, signaling her steely resignation with a silent bearing and cold glances at her foe. As she is taken away on a rowboat, a closeup reaction shot conveys Ella's sorrow at the sound of the first old-growth tree falling. "There she goes!" shouts a crew member, one of her former tenants, delivering a line that marks the tree's demise and foreshadows Ella's in the immediate future. Just as Carol predicted, being forced to leave the land is more than her grandmother can bear. Kazan vividly conveys Ella's alienation from the modern trappings surrounding her in the new house she cannot think of as home. An asphalt truck paving the street outside the house evinces the new infrastructure taking shape because of the dam project. At the same time, Ella's forlorn expressions signal that she is rapidly fading away. With her trademark feistiness yielding to lethargy and despair, Ella eschews her rocking chair, revealing that it is not the source of spiritual connection to the island that Chuck imagined when he insisted that her house have a front porch. No object can ease the deep sense of loss felt by Ella, a character who, like Philemon and Baucis in *Faust*, represents the scores of people displaced for the sake of development. Berman explains that such people are unable "to adapt and to move" in response to the spatial, temporal, and ontological dictates of modernization.[51] And so it is with Ella. When she asks Carol to take money from the household kitty to settle her only outstanding debt—sixteen cents for a bag of sugar—the impression that she is not long for this (modern) world is palpable.

Faust's method of removing Philemon and Baucis amounts to another kind of displacement: he shifts the burden of responsibility by dispatching Mephistopheles and his henchman to handle the matter. When Faust learns how the mission was accomplished—burning down the elderly couple's home and killing them in the process—he is stricken with horror and guilt. Confronted with the realization that he has deluded himself and others into thinking that he could "create a new world with clean hands," he is reluctant to accept it as fact.[52] The outcome is similar in *Wild River*. After clearing trees from the lot, the TVA work crew sets fire to Ella's house as Carol arrives to tell Chuck that her grandmother has just died. Unlike Faust, Chuck is on hand to witness the destruction carried out to the letter of the law. That Chuck is acting on authority—a cornerstone embedded in the very name of the agency he serves—is underscored in dramatic long shots of the crew departing the island. Flames and a cloud of black smoke from the burning house are visible in the background of the frame as the American flag attached to the tugboat billows in the wind in the foreground and signals the federal stamp of approval (fig. 7).

Fig. 7. Still captured from *Wild River*. Members of the work crew look on as Ella's house on Garth Island is engulfed in flames.

In Berman's analysis, the tragic demise of the elderly couple, like that of Gretchen earlier, takes a toll on Faust. Disavowing the means is insufficient to ease his guilt over what happens in the end. Returning to the idea of split consciousness, the destruction the Faustian figure unleashes has existential consequences: "It appears that the very process of development, even as it transforms a wasteland into a thriving physical and social space, recreates the wasteland inside the developer himself. That is how the tragedy of development works."[53] Signs of the inner life that Chuck Glover leads are more difficult to discern. Although he responds to the news of Ella's passing with sadness, he does not seem to feel culpable now that his mission and the final phase of the dam project are complete. Through aerial shots of the dam and reservoir, the infrastructure lending shape and meaning to the narrative structure finally moves from abstract (references in dialogue, shots of blueprints, and so on) to actual (concrete) form.

In closing, as in the beginning, Kazan relies on cinematography to evoke pastness or 1930s-ness, to return to Jameson's formulation. The final sequences of *The River* and *People of the Cumberland*, featuring dramatic shots of dams accompanied by swelling musical scores and stentorian narration, are useful for illustrating how Kazan draws from the New Deal documentary aesthetic but tones down the fanfare. In *Wild River*, the camera that affords panoramic views of the dam capable of inspiring awe derived from the technological sublime also captures countervailing images that diminish the uplift. First in a medium shot and then an aerial shot, the Garth family cemetery, the only part of Garth Island not submerged by the reservoir, appears in the frame. The image of the waterscape calls to mind a line from Isabel Duarte-Gray's poem "Tennessee Valley Authority," a haunting meditation on submerged communities: "This lake ain't lake the way a god / shapes lakes with claws of ice."[54] The peak of the hill where Ella and Woodbridge Garth are buried protrudes from the surface of the water so that their tombstones remain visible on the tiny remnant of the island. The conclusion features a medium shot of the small-engine plane transporting Chuck, Carol, and the children to their shared lives. After looking down at the gravesite, Carol turns forward, tapping Chuck on the shoulder and prompting him to behold the dam as they are poised to fly over it. The final shot offers a spatial rendering of the future-oriented vision of the TVA developed in the New Deal setting of the film and reauthorized at the cusp of the New Frontier encompassing its production. Instead of the certainty about the TVA endeavor in the documentaries that provided aesthetic inspiration, *Wild River* hits a final note of characteristic ambivalence. By not going away, unlike their counterparts in *Faust*, the remains of Ella and Woodbridge Garth stage a final act of resistance from the grave. The lingering presence of the dead haunts the air of inevitability surrounding the TVA, injecting a dose of tragedy that reduces the symbolic capacity of the dam to stand for an unqualified triumph of development.

A RELATED TRAGIC DEVELOPMENT

When *Wild River* was released in May 1960, the issue of dam construction in the Tennessee Valley was more than a source of creative inspiration and historical representation—it was a pressing issue of the day. Fifteen months earlier, Aubrey "Red" Wagner, the TVA's general manager—the title for the chief administrative officer—summoned agency officials to the Watts Barr hydroelectric plant for a planning session. Wagner's opening remarks "set the tone for the meeting" and revealed that he "wanted to build more dams, create more reservoirs" in charting the TVA's course for the future.[55] Because this path was a return to the strategy of the agency's formation, it stands to reason that the signature component was a dormant project that originated then. The idea for what eventually became the Tellico Project emerged in the mid-1930s around the same time Kazan was with Frontier Films. Tellico was unusual for the first phase of the TVA in that it was not designed for flood control and hydroelectric power but for economic development. The main goal in constructing the Tellico Dam was to create a reservoir for recreational use and freight transport—a means of mobilizing infrastructure development to build a local commercial, leisure, and tourism economy. Included in the blueprint was the planned community of Timberlake, named for Henry Timberlake, a cartographer who explored the area during the colonial period when it was dotted with Cherokee villages. The Tellico Project did not proceed as originally intended because it was scrapped in 1942 when budget priorities changed during wartime. After Wagner tapped the project for a potential reboot in 1959, it soon got a boost from the election of JFK in 1960. The feeling among the agency's leadership was that this "neo-New Dealer ... would look with favor on TVA" and that "historic forces seemed to favor Tellico as the showcase of TVA's 'new mission.'"[56] By May 1963, when the president lauded the TVA during the thirtieth anniversary celebration in Muscle Shoals, the governing board had already approved a plan to seek appropriations from Congress to start the Tellico Project in 1965.

The renewal of Tellico meant the return of land seizure under eminent domain and, in turn, opposition from local people who did not want to comply, especially to increase the fortunes of developers invested in the new economy. In short, it was a replay of the TVA's beginning—the historical conditions depicted in *Wild River*. Suffice it to say that all did not go according to plan on this front or others, as the Tellico Project became embroiled in a multifaceted controversy and a series of legal challenges with implications lasting beyond the official completion date of November 29, 1979, and lingering to this day.[57] As was the case during the TVA's emergence, the response to its expansion was contentious. A fault line separated opposing political factions and special interest groups, giving rise to disputes within communities and families. Among the ranks of the divided were Indigenous people, primarily the Cherokee—descendants of those omitted from Ella Garth's dramatic graveside oral history shrouded in settler colonial mythology. With few exceptions, such erasure was repeated in media coverage of Tellico over the years, as stories tended to focus on the plight of white farmers or the snail darter, a three-inch fish that became the focal point of efforts to halt dam construction on the grounds that it violated the Endangered Species Act. The serious attention paid to the snail darter relative to the lack thereof devoted to the fact that the formation of the Tellico Lake reservoir would submerge cherished and sacred Indigenous sites mobilized the self-described Cherokee and Appalachian poet Marilou Awiakta. In the genre-blending *Selu: Seeking the Corn-Mother's Wisdom*, Awiakta recalls the moment of her activist awakening tempered by self-doubt after a friend's urgent call to action in 1978 as the closing of the gates at the Tellico Dam to form the reservoir appeared imminent: "'All I can do is write,' I said. 'I'm not well known. I don't have any clout. Who will publish it? And even if somebody did, what good is it to sling a poem at a dam?'"[58]

Despite her feeling that a writer was powerless against developers fueled by the profit motive, Awiakta pitched stories to national publications, to no avail, and wrote letters to the editors of newspapers in Tennessee. Eventually, she found a receptive venue, *The Dixie Flyer*, an underground newspaper in Memphis. Awiakta's article, "Tellico: End of the Trail," was published in November 1979 and reprinted in *Selu*. In it, Awiakta stages a reclamation of the language of removal to limn the presence of the past in the tragedy of Tellico. Speaking with members of the Eastern Band of Cherokee Indians in preparation for writing the piece brought deep historical resonances to light for the writer/activist: "To them, as to me, the Trail of Tears was not only a vivid memory, it was an old pattern they saw repeating in the Tellico Dam controversy. Their eyes were deep with pain, anger and sorrow."[59] To convey the affecting sense of historical repetition, Awiakta begins the piece with a poem, "The Covenant," in which the speaker is Tsali, the revered Cherokee leader who rallied his people against forcible removal from their ancestral lands in western North Carolina in 1835 and later surrendered to face execution by a firing squad. The poem depicts Tsali's martyrdom by emphasizing his insistence that "a remnant shall remain" in defiance of removal, making that claim the foundation of a prophetic declaration: "And the Trail of Tears / shall be made dry / as by a mighty wind."[60]

Awiakta responds to the concluding simile in the first paragraph of the main text, treating Tsali's prophecy as a prompt to take stock at a pivotal juncture for the descendants of the remnant: "Will the Trail of Tears be made dry as by a mighty wind? Or will the gates of Tellico Dam slam shut and rising waters drown the historic and spiritual heartland of the Cherokee nation?"[61] To make the stakes clear, Awiakta explains that the imperiled heartland comprises Choto, "the capital of the nation" regarded as "a holy city"; Tuskegee, the birthplace of Sequoyah, inventor of the Cherokee syllabary; and Tenase, from which the state of Tennessee derives its name.[62] There was hope among opponents of Tellico that the sites might be spared after the passage of the Historical Preservation Act in 1966. Archaeological surveys funded by the National Park Service and the TVA uncovered evidence of twelve thousand years of

Indigenous history in the Tellico area.[63] Nevertheless, Awiakta points out that the hope proved fleeting upon the realization that historical significance, cultural heritage, and spiritual practice were relative terms in federal policymaking and the logic of economic development. In a haunting variation on the idea that "a remnant shall remain," Awiakta notes that "non-Indian graves" had been moved in anticipation of the reservoir deluge while Cherokee bones were either in storage at the University of Tennessee or soon to be submerged.[64]

Throughout the chapter of *Selu* dedicated to the Tellico Dam controversy, Awiakta shifts between poetry, journalism, and creative nonfiction to weave together various threads into this tragedy of development. A common refrain is a critique of storytelling modes that shape and perpetuate dominant narratives in public discourse and historical memory through instances of selective emphasis or exclusion that enable collective amnesia and enact marginalization. Awiakta references two examples of the national media shining a spotlight on Tellico, noting that in the final months of 1979, a story in the *New York Times* and a segment airing on the *CBS Evening News* focused on people defying mandatory evacuation orders. A standout among the holdouts was Nellie McCall, an eighty-four-year-old widowed white woman whose mixture of determination and sorrow in the face of impending loss added a human dimension to the abstract arguments about infrastructure and economics. A line can be drawn from the people who stood firm against the TVA in the 1930s to fictional analogs such as Ella Garth to Nellie McCall and others facing the seizure of land under eminent domain. For Awiakta, the focus on these experiences and the reductive framing of the Tellico issue as the snail darter versus the dam evince "a long period of indifference" to the Cherokee.[65] Such neglect failed to recognize their painful and compounding losses defined within the historical framework of Indian Removal and the appropriation of that history to craft narratives about the displacement of people with ties to the land rooted in white settler colonialism.

In concluding the chapter, Awiakta draws further historical parallels, this time between the series of court decisions in disputes over Indian Removal and the fifteen-year effort to protect ancestral homelands from the Tellico Project. With the reservoir already formed and developers busy reshaping the seized territory that had been ceded, the 6th US

Circuit Court of Appeals denied a Cherokee appeal to protect ancestral burial grounds based on the claim of unequal treatment in the exhumation and reinternment of remains. Returning to Tsali's simile in "The Covenant," Awiakta figuratively reclaims the land and seizes the means of infrastructural development by rebranding Tellico Lake a "Lake of Tears." With this name, the reservoir becomes a vessel for expressing an inclusive, transcendent lament by all who have mourned or will mourn the lost land. "Tears from everyone who loves the beautiful valley of the Little Tennessee and had tried in vain to save it," Awiakta writes. "And tears welling up from the bottom of the lake, from the eyes of the Cherokee ancestors. We are all part of the web. What affects one strand affects us all. In time, even the fish of Tellico Lake would have cause to weep."[66] Awiakta is remarkably generous in the end, making the web of tearful connection as wide as possible rather than trading one form of exclusion for another. She even extends an olive branch to the TVA by giving the agency credit for becoming more mindful of informing the public about the conditions of the rivers and lakes it controls, scrapping a planned nuclear project, and helping establish the Sequoyah Birthplace Museum overseen by the Eastern Band of Cherokee Indians. Awiakta's web of emotional attachments is useful for rethinking narratives of removal that are not so inclusive but rather complicit in cultural appropriation and historical erasure—Kazan's *Wild River*, for instance. Recalling the final sequence with that in mind makes it possible to read the shot in which Carol points forward before the plane crosses the dam as a harbinger of the Tellico Project, of more dams and more reservoirs, as Wagner put it to the TVA officials a year before the film's release. Such a perspective also affords a different view of the aerial shot framing the small crest where the markers on the graves of Ella and Woodbridge Garth are all that remain visible. There is more than meets the eye if we bear Awiakta's words in mind and look deeper, below the surface, trying to recover what lies beneath.

Chapter 5

FROM *FLOOD* TO *LONG MAN*
The Rise of the TVA Novel

IN A LETTER TO LOUIS RUBIN JR. DATED JULY 6, 1963, ROBERT PENN WARREN ANNOUNCED that he was nearly finished with a new novel. Warren disclosed that it had a wide expanse, reaching from the 1930s in the back story to the onset of the 1960s in the present. He added that the main setting was Tennessee, but Hollywood, Greenwich Village, and Spain would also figure prominently. The work in question was *Flood: A Romance of Our Time*, Warren's eighth novel, published in 1964 by Random House. Although Warren made the imminent construction of a hydroelectric dam and reservoir in the Tennessee Valley the driving force behind the titular event and the organizing principle of the main plot, he hastened to add a caveat: "It's not exactly a TVA novel."[1] Warren pointed out that he had tried to ensure this outcome by studiously avoiding recent releases with related subject matter. One of those works was Elia Kazan's *Wild River*. The other was *A Buried Land*, a 1963 novel by Madison Jones in which a past crime haunts a Tennessee lawyer: attempting to discard the body of a young woman in an area designated for a reservoir after she informed him that she was pregnant with his child and the back-alley abortion he arranged was fatally botched. Reading *Flood* suggests that Warren's stipulation amounts to a distinction without a difference. Nevertheless, his attempt to explain what his new novel was not raises the question: what is a TVA novel?

What follows is a discussion motivated by that prompt, with the focus set on two novels among several that might qualify as representative texts: Warren's *Flood* and Amy Greene's *Long Man*, published in 2014. The critical approach proceeds from the notion that "TVA novel" is a useful subgeneric designation for recovering works from relative obscurity for reevaluation, as is the case with *Flood*, or considering works that are worthy of critical attention they have not yet received, such as Greene's compelling novel. Other texts that fall under the category of relative obscurity include *A Buried Land* and the initial entries in the subgenre, William Bradford Huie's *Mud on the Stars* (1954) and Borden Deal's *Dunbar's Cove* (1957), both of which were the source material for *Wild River*, as noted in the previous chapter. *Long Man* is among a series of TVA novels starting at the turn of the new millennium: Norma Cole's *The Rising*, a YA novel published in 1999; Marianne Wiggins's *Evidence of Things Unseen* (2003), which uses the connections between the TVA and Oak Ridge, Tennessee, a Manhattan Project site, as material for historical fiction; Caleb Johnson's *Treeborne* (2018), a rich, evocative weave of familial and local history and magical realism set in northern Alabama that connects the arrival of the Conquistadors and the construction and later destruction of a dam by "the Authority" in a *longue durée* of exploitation and resistance; and *Watershed*, a 2019 novel by Mark Barr about a 1937 dam construction project that sets off a tumultuous mix of conflict, displacement, and opportunity in a small community in rural Tennessee.

A SENSE OF DISPLACEMENT

The material conditions that inform TVA novels are documented in *TVA and the Dispossessed*, in which Michael J. McDonald and John Muldowny use the construction of Norris Dam starting in 1933 as a case study. The authors describe the population of the Norris Basin as a "transitional society" in which the dual images of the transmission line and dynamo are presented as signifiers of modernization coming into contact and conflict with a traditional culture figured as "pre-modern."[2] McDonald and Muldowny explain that the first generation to experience rapid modernization, whether in a nation or a community, bears the brunt of disruption for subsequent generations. That was the case in the Norris Basin, an area "where rural communities bore the cost of disruption and dislocation in the short term so that deferred benefits could be gained."[3] Although upheaval was inevitable given the pace and scale of modernization, TVA officials and powerful advocates—foremost among them President Roosevelt—insisted that a plan was in place to minimize adverse effects as operations ran smoothly to deliver the promised benefits to the local communities, region, and nation. As evacuation and relocation began, the plan entailed assisting landowners in finding new properties, whether farms or not. The practice of not assisting tenants displaced from the land they were renting or farming on shares withstood legal challenges, continuing unabated as the agency cleared the path for construction. Overall, as McDonald and Muldowney document, TVA officials made decisions about land purchases under the provisions of eminent domain based on "the needs of the reservoir and watershed, and not on the basis of what would best suit the needs of agricultural communities of the Basin."[4]

In contrast to the abstract legalese and euphemisms prevalent in the discourse around land purchases, TVA novels often calculate the human toll in literary form by portraying the resulting hardship, upheaval, and grief experienced by those forced to move. At the same time, these novels account for complicated attitudes and feelings, depicting sharp divisions and mixed emotions within communities, families, and individuals that materialized as immediate and promised long-term benefits weakened firm opposition and neutralized efforts to mobilize local resistance. With these fundamental aspects in mind, it is possible to read TVA novels as imaginative responses to the official practice of delineating what Rob Nixon terms "unimagined communities."[5] Noting the centrality of imagined communities in defining and maintaining the terms of national identity and belonging, Nixon defines unimagined communities as formulations "internal to the space of the nation-state, communities whose vigorously unimagined condition becomes indispensable to maintaining a highly selective discourse of national development."[6] An irony is present in the case of the TVA's evacuation plan. The people and places of the Tennessee Valley have been vividly imagined in the American mythos and cultural narratives, as discussions of the vaunted pioneer figure or narratives steeped in settler colonial nostalgia in previous chapters demonstrate. Nevertheless, the specific communities designated for inundation and subject to mandatory evacuation and relocation plans become unimagined in the context of the bureaucratic mindset of the state that Nixon describes.

Narratives of national development strategically obscure such communities because they "inconvenience or disturb the implied trajectory of unitary national ascent."[7] This narrative strategy facilitates population displacement by performing a "rhetorical and visual evacuation," as government policies and official language create "the conditions for administered invisibility."[8] The result is a "spatial amnesia" that sets in after people and communities are "evacuated from place and time and thus uncoupled from the idea of both a national future and a national memory."[9] For authors of TVA novels, these empty spaces serve as sites for imaginative reckoning where elements of literature can be leveraged to recover and repopulate evacuated and submerged landscapes and communities. This mode of representation can give voice and visibility to localities omitted from national narratives of development and subsequently from public memory and history.

A profound sense of displacement pervades the atmosphere and mood of TVA novels, lending the subgenre an element of cohesion. This narrative effect is a corollary to the storied "sense of place" assigned to southern literature as a distinguishing feature by scholars invested in establishing and maintaining southern literary studies as a discipline in the post–World War II academy. A case in point is Frederick J. Hoffman's "The Sense of Place," one of several chapters in *South: Modern Southern Literature in its Cultural Setting* (1961) devoted to purportedly essential qualities of southern writing. Hoffman cites Eudora Welty's "Place in Fiction," occasioning what Martyn Bone aptly calls "an inadvertently auspicious moment" that "inaugurates a southern literary critical tradition" of citing Welty's essay, and her fiction in general, as exemplary of *the* (emphasis on Hoffman's preferred article) sense of place.[10] Welty's elucidation of an affective connection to place made her essay appealing to Hoffman and others looking to craft a working definition. Welty observes that the very nature of fiction binds it to the local because "*feelings* are bound up in place," broadening the implications to reiterate the elemental bond between location and emotion by making the point that "place in history partakes of feeling, as feeling about history partakes of place."[11] The ties Welty describes as binding are the very ones that TVA novels portray as severed by the sudden and painful ruptures attending large-scale infrastructure projects and the displacement it causes in the name of progress.

Although the cultural work TVA novels perform helps develop a more complete picture, it is important to stress that the view they afford is circumscribed. The tendency is to center the experiences of white people in the frame—usually small landowners or tenants who fit the yeoman farmer mold or, in the case of *Flood*, relatively affluent characters in a small rural town. Valorization of rural white southerners whose quasi-spiritual connection to the land and traditional folkways are imperiled echoes Southern Agrarian critiques of industrialization and technological advancement viewed as mechanisms for modernizing the region on a fast track. It stands to reason that Robert Penn Warren, notwithstanding his attempt to distinguish *Flood* from TVA novels, and Madison Jones, an Agrarian acolyte, found the subject matter compelling.

The prevailing whiteness makes for an uncanny Tennessee Valley when placed in a broader historical and cultural context. The recurring focus on the loss of land and mandatory relocation recalls historical narratives and cultural representations of Indian Removal. In this respect, TVA novels exhibit part of the cross-cultural influence that Melanie Benson Taylor cogently theorizes in mapping Native South studies as a field of critical inquiry concerned with detecting "indigenous traces in southern society."[12] In southern studies, this practice involves "smoking out the Indian ghosts and signifiers lurking in southern writing of the twentieth century" to understand how "the literature of the modern and contemporary South returns repeatedly and strategically to its Native analogues and perceived comrades in dispossession."[13] Indeed, as *Dunbar's Cove*, *Treeborne*, and *Long Man* demonstrate, TVA novels are open to this analytical framing since Indigenous traces inform the sense of displacement among descendants of white settlers forced to relinquish land to the federal government to make way for the TVA.

A counterintuitive pattern emerges when delving into the individual texts and the subgenre they inhabit: TVA novels do not tend to foreground the TVA. Rather, the emphasis is primarily on local people and communities as they experience the impacts of infrastructural development at a granular level. Components of infrastructure—dams, reservoirs, powerhouses, electrical grids, power lines, and nuclear facilities—function as mechanisms for defining stakes, enabling plot development and characterization, defining temporal scope and perception, and imbuing historical settings and perspectives with verisimilitude. Through these fictive designs, TVA novels often work to unsettle the dominant narrative of progress informing the TVA myth that state-sponsored cultural production of the New Deal era helped cement in the public imagination and historical record. This approach involves demystifying the technological sublime and interrogating the claim of modern marvels "built for the people" through a commitment to public works. Indeed, the project is to recover stories submerged over time in the material processes of infrastructural and economic development. In short, TVA novels often function as literary forms that pose counternarratives to the propagandistic yet aesthetically inventive cultural predecessors they draw from for formal inspiration, literary representation, and historical perspective.

DEEPLY UNSETTLED

Warren's attempt to distance *Flood* from fiction and film based explicitly on the TVA is evident in the fact that the agency is mentioned by name only once. There is a passing reference to TVA construction sites just across the border in Kentucky, where the protagonist, Bradwell Tolliver, would go during his post–Spanish Civil War, pre-Hollywood stint back home to get drunk and play poker with off-duty engineers and construction workers wanting to blow off steam.[14] The formation of the reservoir soon to erase Brad's hometown of Fiddlersburg, Tennessee, from the map is part of the TVA network—the massive infrastructure project unfolding in various stages of construction and expansion, from the standpoint of the novel's present-day setting in 1961, for nearly three decades. For Warren, the creative process took almost as long to unfold. Warren disclosed to Rubin that the actual writing went on for quite some time, deploying an apt pun given *Flood*'s primary setting: "I have been fiddling with it for eight years."[15] However, in an interview, Warren placed the novel's genesis in 1931, two years before Roosevelt's message to Congress calling for legislative action to establish the TVA. Warren recounts passing through southwest Tennessee, noting that it was the thirtieth anniversary of the Battle of Shiloh. He explains that he "saw the old house, hanging over the bluff of the river," that served as General Ulysses S. Grant's headquarters, adding that he did not pay a visit but "just saw it, drove past it, and the village was the germ of Fiddlersburg and that house was the germ of the Fiddler house."[16] The other fundamental part of the novel's premise took shape as TVA projects developed over time: "I've seen one or two flooded-out places in the TVA system in Tennessee. For years and years, I thought maybe somehow this was an image, this kind of doomsday to a community. Then, arbitrarily, BANG, the community is gone. What happens to human relations in that context? This was something vaguely in the back of my mind, a speculation, no reference to fiction."[17] Attempting to describe the intricate plot mechanics of *Flood* is quite an undertaking. For the purpose at hand, it suffices to say that the overarching storyline involves Brad Tolliver's return once again to his hometown; this time he arrives after working in Hollywood as an Oscar-winning screenwriter. He is accompanied by a renowned producer/director, Yasha Jones, to make a film that can portray Fiddlersburg as a microcosm of universal truth and thus achieve whatever measure of artistic immortality the silver screen can confer before the town is relegated to the depths of the new reservoir. Almost immediately, the assignment propels Brad into an identity crisis, worsened by the return of repressed historical and familial traumas rendered with Freudian inflections. Facing a deadline set according to standard infrastructural time, Brad suffers from a severe case of writer's block and a destabilizing uncertainty about what, if anything, it means to be from a place and where, for him, that place might be, whether in the past or from now on.

In defining the historical scope of *Flood*, Warren forges a time frame that encompasses and thematically draws together the Civil War and the establishment and expansion of the TVA. Historic national interventions in the region bookend this period of upheaval and rapid change. It is essentially the same temporal framing that Warren's erstwhile Southern Agrarian compatriot Donald Davidson used for the second volume of his sweeping historical narrative of the Tennessee Valley published sixteen years before *Flood*. For Davidson, the Civil War to the TVA is an epoch marred by defeat for the old southern "way of life." From military surrender and Reconstruction to the New Deal, Davidson traces in the Tennessee Valley what he views as part of a broader, ongoing effort by northeastern financial interests and the federal government to remove the last obstacles preventing industrial capitalism from supplanting agrarian life. Davidson describes the TVA as a force unleashed to bring about the self-fulfilling prophecy delivered by New Deal bureaucrats such as David Lilienthal: "that here in the Tennessee Valley, of all places, was emerging one of the marvels of the modern world."[18] Davidson's stance is grounded in sectionalism, insisting on an inherent animus dividing the nation along regional lines and pitting the rural South and West against the heavily urbanized and financially dominant Northeast. As Edward Shapiro observes, even accounting for the diversity of opinion that formed among the Southern Agrarians about the TVA, they commonly held that sectionalism was an essential deterrent: "The Agrarians argued that the only way to check the economic imperialism of the Northeast was through a revival of regional sentiment in the South and the West resulting in sectional economic self-determination."[19] This approach was fundamentally at odds with the conception of New Deal regional planning advocated by the TVA and promoted by *The River*, as discussed in chapter 2. The notion of overcoming sectional division also informed the idealized figuration of the electrical grid in the Federal Theatre Project Living Newspaper Unit's *Power*, as discussed in chapter 3. In these and other examples, thinking along regional lines served as a different kind of deterrent from what the Southern Agrarians envisioned—a means of using cooperation between the federal government and regions to keep divisive sectionalism at bay to serve national interests.

The influence of these oppositional models is a major force in the conflicted structure of feeling that Warren's TVA novel elucidates. The impending flood forces a reckoning for the protagonist and the place he has called home. By laying bare Brad Tolliver's state of mind, Warren depicts how persistent sectionalism surfaces in response to the state fantasy of national unity and progress through regional rehabilitation promoted by the TVA. In this scenario, competing forms of identification and belonging fail to deliver the satisfaction they promise. As Jacqueline Rose explains, "fantasy—far from being the antagonist of public, social being—plays a central, constructive role in the modern world of states and nations."[20] It does so by stimulating affective investments in the idea of the state such that fantasy is not an alternative to reality but a means of shaping it. For Rose, the conventional association of the state with the public sphere and fantasy with the private domain of individual consciousness needs rethinking. Rose draws on the alternative understanding of "state," meaning a psychic condition, to define how the nation-state works through fantasy to ensure that its ideological and political imperatives become internalized in citizens and expressed as individual desire for national belonging. In short, fantasy works to make citizens want the state they have. Jennifer Rae Greeson demonstrates that "the South" has long functioned as a regional "magnet" for such nation-building, a practice that "both exceeds and flattens the place; it is a term of the imagination, a site of national fantasy."[21] The formulation of the area apportioned to the TVA as a locus of state fantasy is part of an extensive historical pattern involving a regional imaginary providing ideological reinforcement over time.

Though a minor character in terms of appearances in the text, the engineer Digby, a Wisconsin native stationed in Tennessee, plays a significant role as the figure aligned with the state fantasy projected by the TVA. Through indirect discourse, the narrator describes Digby's reasoning as he appeals to local people to buy into the master plan. The enthusiastic booster holds that Fiddlersburg is "a natural place for a dam," implying that the new infrastructure will fit seamlessly into the contours of the landscape and that infrastructural time is merely an extension of geologic time running on a steady, inevitable course for millions of years (112). This appeal recalls *The River*'s opening section, in which the stentorian voice-over narration establishes the prehistoric formation of the Tennessee River as the genesis of a "natural" course with teleological progression leading to the arrival of the TVA in the 1930s. From his "reservoir of good nature," a phrase suggesting infrastructural embodiment, the engineer exudes optimism and enthusiasm, assuring Brad and Yasha that the dam will be "great," meaning impressive, functional, and beneficial (113). Like Chuck Glover in his initial appeal to Ella Garth in *Wild River*, Digby makes his pitch in the style of the Faustian dreamer promising the local people deliverance from a benighted existence: "A real skyline on the river, plant after plant. Getting shoes on the swamp rats too, teaching 'em to read and write and punch a time clock, and pull a switch. It was going to be a big industrial complex" (113). Digby's trust in modernity, evangelical fervor for public works, and investment in the TVA myth make him little more than a mouthpiece spouting the rhetoric employed for decades to gain public support.

Brad does not respond favorably to Digby's pitch. He resists the allure of the fantasy and doubts that the TVA can deliver on the promises it is making to the people on behalf of the state. A sticking point for Brad is Digby's scientism, which he expresses as a deep faith in the technological capacity of the dam project to save the region. Brad also takes issue with the notion of educating the "swamp rats" for the rat race of the "industrial complex," bristling not at the idea of educational opportunities for the rural poor per se but at the air of condescension toward them and the objective of turning them into proverbial cogs in the wheel of capitalism. This response makes sense in light of Brad's fascination with Frog-Eye, a swamp dweller living mostly off the grid. Brad views Frog-Eye as paradoxically bound by the freedom such a life allows in the modern era and yet enviable for the distance he can maintain from society. On another level, Frog-Eye stands in as a father figure, a surrogate for Brad's actual father, who was also a creature of the swamp. In the family lore stored in Brad's consciousness, his father was, as he tells Yasha, a hardscrabble, "true-born muskrat-skinner" who married into an aristocratic family in decline and needed drunken forays into the swamp to find refuge from a confining existence in town (53). Such a compulsion is ironic given that he died inebriated and face-down in the muck during what turned out to be his final swamp escape. This image of the father torments Brad and makes grappling with his patrilineal heritage an integral component of his identity formation. Faced with the impending flood, Brad's haunting memory of his father's death and his heightened interest in Frog-Eye turn the swamp into a highly charged symbolic site. As such, it represents a localized state of nature to which Brad feels deeply attached set against the overwhelming force of a state fantasy poised to relegate the swamp to watery depths and the realm of memory.

While Brad anticipates the inevitable losses that the flood will bring about, he is also keenly aware of the damage done to the local landscape and culture from the economic development that has already taken place. In the opening pages of the novel, as Brad nears Fiddlersburg, he spots a limestone bluff topped with cedars and sees a creek nearby, concluding that "[i]t was bound to be the place" that used to trigger shame (for reasons not yet disclosed) whenever he drove by (3). But the deductive reasoning is complicated by the fact that "new concrete" has replaced the old blacktop road and by the disappearance of a large sycamore tree, a cluster of willows, and a bluegrass meadow. "But the trouble was not so much what was not there," the narrator explains. "It was what was there" (4). In a small-scale allusion to the TVA's taming of the Tennessee River, the creek has been redirected to run between two constructed banks "where stones were mortised into the earth" and topped with kitschy figures: a cement frog and "a gnome, dwarf, brownie or some such improbability" (4). It is all part of a new roadside attraction, the name of which is emblazoned on a large billboard with unlit neon letters nevertheless glaring in their appeal to customers:

THE SEVEN DWARFS MOTEL
RELAX IN HAPPY DELL (4)

The name and location of the motel establish the site as a manifestation of Disneyfication. Moreover, the defining features of the setting that Brad remembers as bucolic have been either erased or repurposed in the development of an attraction advertised as bucolic to tourists from around the country.

The Seven Dwarfs complex resembles a Hollywood set, a venue for staging quotidian existence as a series of performances. When Brad stops at the gas station on site, he has a fraught encounter with a Black attendant whom he refers to in his interior voice as "Jingle Bells" due to the silly costume the man is required to wear as a work uniform. By instinct, Brad performs the role of the southern gentleman, affecting a syrupy southern accent that the attendant immediately clocks as fake. Meanwhile, the attendant, in a ploy to earn a good tip, parrots Stepin Fetchit in a live-action version of the minstrel cartoon figure painted on the billboard advertising the cottage where guests can enjoy a delicious, down-home breakfast of Tennessee smoked ham and red gravy. The minstrel figure's enthusiastic endorsement punctuates the guarantee: "YASSUH, BOSS!" (4). As he sits in his white Jaguar XK-150 waiting for the change from his payment, Brad's interior projector unfurls a montage of quaint scenes he envisions simultaneously taking place "somewhere" in the nearby rural environs: an old man by a picket fence gathering jonquils for his napping wife; a group of boys tossing a baseball and "uttering distant cries sad and sweet as killdees"; two young lovers walking hand in hand into a green grove of trees; and "an old Negro woman with a man's felt hat on her head" seated on the bank of a creek and casting her fishing line into the water (8–9). These overdetermined ruminations are no more "real" than the constructed creek bed, and they usher in Brad's increasing preoccupation with authenticity in reaction to the alienating effects of Disneyfication that he finds disorienting. Ironically, the marketing strategy is designed to have the opposite effect by attracting guests with the promise of leisure and enjoyment in a themed environment replete with familiar touchstones of American popular culture imposed on the local scene.

Brad later rehashes the encounter at the gas station in a conversation with Yasha as he tries to get a handle on the dramatic changes occurring in his native region. Even though the Seven Dwarfs is an eyesore, Brad recognizes that this "new Tennessee" pales in comparison to "the space-age vulgarities and Disneyland fantasia of L.A.," hastening to add that "this is the best a backward state can do" (36). Nevertheless, he views the motel as a harbinger of accelerated development once the new reservoir provides the infrastructure for an economy geared toward leisure and tourism. "As Fiddlersburg, with its wealth of Southern tradition, unassuming charm, homely virtue, and pellagra, sinks forevermore beneath the wave," Brad says to Yasha, "the Seven Dwarfs Motel will rise in spray, glimmering like a dream" (38). For Brad, conjuring the vision of the motel as a tourist destination springing into being from the surface of the reservoir is a bleak prophecy. It contains traces of the trademark postbellum southern declension narrative mourning the passing of a distinctive, traditional southern culture due to the flattening, homogenizing effects of modernization and development remaking the region. But the cynical tone and the reference to pellagra betray a lack of faith in the notion that an Old South golden age ever existed in Fiddlersburg. Moreover, the self-awareness and ironic detachment lacing Brad's remarks evoke a "postsouthern sense of place" that worsens his anxiety and informs the novel's engagement with questions of authenticity related to a broader conflict between tradition and modernity.[22]

Warren's attention to leisure and tourism as part of the larger infrastructure project in progress reveals a notable historical parallel between the publication of *Flood* and the start of a major new phase of development for the TVA. President Kennedy set aside a vast swath of land in Kentucky and Tennessee as a national recreation area in 1963. The project eventually became known as Land Between the Lakes; the name refers to an area between Kentucky Lake, a reservoir created by the TVA in 1944 as part of the Kentucky Dam project, and Lake Barkley, a reservoir formed in 1966 during the construction of Barkley Dam. Land Between the Lakes sparked another wave of "land acquisition" under eminent domain, forced relocations, and planned flooding along the lines of what transpired during the formation of the TVA three decades earlier and with the revival of the Tellico Project. Ronald A. Foresta convincingly argues that the narrative of the Land Between the Lakes should not be limited to a retelling of the story from the 1930s of "small people beset by a government that has grown too big, escaped the confines of democracy, and overstepped its authority."[23] Foresta's argument calls to mind the narrative staples of TVA novels and Kazan's *Wild River*. Instead of remaining in that mode, Foresta argues, it is useful to incorporate a second story about "concern for the future" or "futurity" that reveals Land Between the Lakes as a site for imagining where a new form of American leisure was supposed to come to pass but never did.[24] Indeed, as it turned out, the hope of turning an underdeveloped, impoverished region into an attractive tourist destination and an economic boon was never fulfilled. Land Between the Lakes was a product of state fantasy—an aspect of the larger vision of bringing progress to the region. *Flood* registers the deep-seated animosities rooted in sectionalism that this fantasy works to conceal. It does so by revealing a local landscape being leveled as new infrastructure takes shape and unity and progress take the form of homogenization driven by mass culture and the economics of leisure and tourism.

While Warren portrays the tourist trap in the valley as destructive to local history and culture, he does not hold up a nostalgic longing for a romanticized "old Tennessee" represented by Fiddlersburg as a viable alternative to the rise of the "new Tennessee."[25] As a result, the distance between the Warren of *Flood* and the Warren of "The Briar Patch," his regrettable contribution to the Southern Agrarian manifesto *I'll Take My Stand*, is apparent. A scene early in the novel, in the aftermath of Brad's stop at the Seven Dwarfs, illustrates this point. Brad and Yasha visit Brad's sister, Maggie Fiddler, "Mrs. Fiddler of Fiddlersburg," as he flippantly calls her (43). A local attorney and farmer, Blanding Cottshill, is also part of the group. Maggie lives in the Fiddler home with her ailing mother-in-law as her husband, a physician named Calvin Fiddler, serves a prison sentence in the penitentiary that sits conspicuously on a river bluff and repeatedly figures in the panoramic views Warren crafts. The scion of the town's founding family in decline was convicted of murdering a young engineer, presumably employed by the TVA, after word spread around town that he sexually assaulted Maggie during a drunken party at the Fiddler home he was attending with Brad. As the guests gather on the terrace overlooking the river, the evening is cast in moonlight, evoking what Maggie calls "kind illusions" despite the absence of the requisite magnolias that would complete the stereotypical combination (46). However, she immediately dispels that notion by pointing out that what Yasha will see in the harsh light of day is a river polluted with detritus. "By daylight," Maggie says, "you'll see, too that we're falling to pieces here. All Fiddlersburg has always been falling to pieces" (46). Brad adds that it has also fallen into obscurity: "'Fiddlersburg,' Brad said, 'it is as far as you can get outside of history and still feel that history exists. If,' he said, 'it does'" (46). Cottshill draws together these threads of space and time into a fatalistic declaration, "Let 'em flood us" (48), describing the town's demise in apocalyptic terms rather than striking the familiar melancholic notes of southern declension. For Cottshill, inundation is a fitting end to years of a steadily eroding sense of place traditionally defined.

The notion that the erasure of Fiddlersburg is a logical fate prompts even further historical contemplation steeped in anxiety and guilt. "Maybe [Fiddlersburg] was just some notion in the head of the first Fiddler who came here," Maggie proposes, citing the land grab and displacement of the Indigenous population that made the town possible (51). This moment marks the return of Indigenous history that TVA novels tend to repress, often by obscuring or erasing it altogether, as Michael Truscello points out when discussing Borden Deal's *Dunbar's Cove*.[26] Maggie's theory implies that the forced acquisition of land and population removal make the erasure of Fiddlersburg for economic development a faithful reenactment of its rapacious founding. Brad gets in on the act by assuming the role of a docent leading a tour of the historic Fiddler home. "Colonel Octavius Fiddler," he says, in the tone of an official announcement, "Virginia Revolutionary commission—militia, I regret—here by way of Kentucky, land-grabber, made last land grab here, built house and became a Tennessee aristocrat. Portrait, genuine oil painting, on left as you enter" (51). In this instance, Brad enacts a postsouthern parody of the tributes to pioneering self-made men such as David Dunbar in *Dunbar's Cove* and Woodbridge Garth in *Wild River*. While this scene dramatizes the persistence of sectionalism in the form of a preoccupation with local history, Warren resists the nostalgic turn that the conversation could take and exposes that option as no more edifying or meaningful than the state fantasy Digby espouses on behalf of the TVA. The veneration of the mythic pioneer, whether deployed in a whitewashed local origin story or repurposed to express TVA futurity, stands exposed as a means of diverting attention away from the material history and ongoing process of exploiting the natural resources and people of the region for profit.

For most of his adult life, Brad has been unable to connect with seemingly promising sources for achieving a sense of identity, purpose, and belonging. As a young writer in the 1930s, Brad was endorsed by the liberals and radicals in the leftist literary establishment advocating a resurgent social realism: they saw him as a thoughtful documentarian of southern social problems and an ally in the cultural politics of antifascism and progressive reform. In this respect, Brad was not unlike the writers and other artists who became part of the New Deal cultural apparatus, some of whom worked on TVA-related projects. Buoyed by this solidarity, Brad joined a *cause célèbre*, enlisting in one of the American volunteer brigades fighting for the Loyalists in the Spanish Civil War. Rather than documenting his experience, Brad was paralyzed with writer's block, the condition worsening after his editor sent an advance copy of *For Whom the Bell Tolls*. Brad heard in Hemingway's prose the voice of a generation he had aspired to express. The prospect of a civil war serving as ballast for identity formation is even less successful when Brad turns closer to home. His regional identity is split along the same fault line that demarcated Fiddlersburg according to divided loyalties between North and South during the US Civil War: the bottom land, Confederate; the swamps, "Blue-Belly" (121). "I'm mixed," Brad confesses to Yasha in a brief genealogy tracing Confederates in his maternal line and Unionists on the paternal side (121). This ambivalence resurfaces later as Brad wanders the deserted streets of downtown Fiddlersburg during a restless night; he imagines the floodwaters rising to engulf the town and wonders "what of himself—of Bradwell Tolliver—would not be here, or anywhere, when Fiddlersburg was not here any more" (254). Meeting Yasha at the base of the Confederate monument, Brad is unable to connect with the soldier's symbolic value such that he can identify as "southern." Instead, he recognizes the soldier as part of a symbolic infrastructure reinforcing another state fantasy by stimulating nationalistic desires for a lost cause that is as much a construction as the monument itself. "He is all that makes paranoid violence into philosophic virtue," Brad observes, eventually putting a finer point on it: "That lie which is the truth of the self" (256). This realization follows from Brad's earlier postsouthern meditation on the emptiness of "South" as a signifier, "a term without a referent" (166).

In his search for meaningful affiliation, Brad keeps trying to come home again: "What I believe in [. . .] is Fiddlersburg," he says (166). Still, when he tries to express this belief through his craft, Brad, the putative documentarian, loses sight of how to proceed. Leontine, a blind woman who seduces Brad (at the Seven Dwarfs Motel, no less) succinctly assesses his predicament: "*Being you's like being blind*" (242). Brad's ironic detachment, his personal dam constructed to regulate overwhelming feelings of pain and guilt associated with past familial traumas, makes him unable to render Fiddlersburg in distinctive rather than stereotypical terms. "It is expert," Yasha says, paying a backhanded compliment to a film treatment that Brad finally produces in a fleeting burst of dubious creative inspiration. "But [. . .] it is not you" (341). Yasha's verdict on the treatment, based on a painful incident involving Maggie, is that it comes across as "a parody of what happened" (342). The director insists that "what matters is the feeling. Where[] in this . . . is the feeling we want? Where is Fiddlersburg?" (342–43). Yasha's question points to the sharp affective turn that *Flood* takes, giving rise to a surfeit of desire and emotion that obscures the meaning of Fiddlersburg in advance of the impending flood.

At the end of the novel, Blanding Cottshill predicts that when Fiddlersburg is submerged, "God-A-Mighty will jerk our passports. We will be stateless persons. We will be DPs for eternity and thence forward.

We will have no identity" (423). Cottshill is overly dramatic in playing the part of a refugee, for the recently incorporated Lake Town is where he and other well-heeled displaced persons of Fiddlersburg will find refuge. Nevertheless, his performance suggests a reading of Fiddlersburg as a microcosm. Watching from a distance, Brad sees townspeople gathered for a farewell service and shares in the feeling of loss that belies a state fantasy of untold gains promoted to sell initiatives like the TVA. "For this was his country," the narrator intones, as Brad experiences "a sudden, unwilled, undecipherable, tearing, ripping gesture of his innermost being toward those people over yonder" (440). This moment of connection is only fleeting, though. In the end, Brad resists a full affective investment in Fiddlersburg, whether mourned in passing or submerged in the interest of progress. Although the issue of Brad's "country" is left unsettled, he remains open to the prospect of future affective investments. Ultimately, he tells himself the lie that is the truth where all nationalisms take hold: "*There is no country but the heart*" (440).

ABOUT DAM TIME

The premise of Warren's *Flood* is the most prominent feature among TVA novels that also qualify as "drowned town fiction," Truscello's designation for "a literary subgenre that portrays the deliberate flooding of towns and landscapes for the construction of hydroelectric assemblages."[27] In Amy Greene's *Long Man*, the small Tennessee town of Yuneetah and its surrounding environs face an imminent deluge because of a reservoir planned as part of a TVA dam construction project. The storyline involving a steely holdout resisting forced relocation to remain on the small farm that has been in her family for generations aligns Greene's novel more closely with *Dunbar's Cove* and *A Buried Land* than with Warren's novel of ideas centered on a cosmopolitan author and screenwriter having an identity crisis exacerbated by an impending flood. *Long Man* opens with an expansive setting of the scene: "In the summer of 1936 there was one woman left on the mountaintop where the river's headwaters formed in rocks ages old and shining with mica, the sediment washing down to tinge its shoals yellow-brown."[28] The timestamp of 1936 pinpoints this work of historical fiction in the initial phase of construction on the hydroelectric dams starting to appear along the Tennessee River and its tributaries. The woman in question is Silver Ledford, the aunt of Annie Clyde Dodson, whom we subsequently learn is down in the valley taking her stand against the mandatory evacuation order issued by the TVA. Annie Clyde understandably becomes even more defiant when her daughter goes missing after wandering away from the farm and falling through a patch of loose dirt into a limestone cave. Even though the mountaintop where Silver lives is not in the flood zone, all her neighbors, like most of the townspeople, have decided to leave—some for jobs on TVA construction sites and new homes in the surrounding planned communities, others to head north looking for work in manufacturing hubs.

The juxtaposition of the transformation of the valley under TVA auspices and its original formation in the past is reminiscent of the temporality in New Deal documentary projects commissioned to advance the TVA agenda. The photobook *The Valley and Its People: A Portrait of TVA* and the documentary film *The River* are cases in point. In those works, as previously discussed, the teleological framework creates the impression of a seamless transition from geologic time in one epoch to infrastructural time in another, as though the anthropogenic interventions underway in the valley were a matter of course in the flow of natural history. It was a visual and rhetorical means of framing the past as a prelude to the brand of futurity that the TVA was promoting in the present. The teleological path to the arrival of the TVA enabled the documentaries to forecast a brighter future for the region and tangible benefits to the nation. While *Long Man* sometimes evokes the temporality of pro-TVA documentaries produced during the novel's historical setting, the depiction of Yuneetah as representative of the displaced persons and inundated communities lost to history dictates significant alterations. This approach to time in *Long Man* involves reimagining connections between past and present through historical parallels, redefining the scope and meaning of futurity, and foregrounding the disruption of infrastructural time set by the TVA as the standard. In this respect, as in others, *Long Man* is an exemplary TVA novel.

A temporal perspective that pervades the novel involves prolepsis connected to Greene's use of infrastructure to frame events within the narrative structure. This feature is common among TVA novels that center on floods associated with dam and reservoir construction. In *About Time: Narrative, Fiction, and the Philosophy of Time*, Mark Currie observes that the tendency in narrative studies has been to concentrate on the present as a site where we subject stories of the past to constant revision while neglecting "the relationship between storytelling and the mode of continuous anticipation in which we attach significance to present moments."[29] Examining *Long Man* (or similar TVA novels) to redress such neglect means that the components of the infrastructure planned or in progress can be read as "protentions," which are elements "present as anticipatory expectation."[30] Such elements figure in "narratological prolepsis" as a defining aspect of the overarching temporal framework. Currie cites Peter Brooks and Gérard Genette among other theorists to define the concept as the "anticipation of, or flashforward to, events within the universe of narrated events."[31] In essence, narratological prolepsis facilitates the representation of a past in which the people leaving and lingering in Yuneetah were hyper-conscious of the flood as a mechanism of existential annihilation for the community and perceived infrastructural time accordingly.[32]

The opening section of *Long Man* shows how Greene establishes this perspective. As Silver peers into the valley, the narrator envisions what the future might hold in store for her: "This time next year if she came up here looking for a little more light she would see only miles of endless blue lake" (3). When Silver turns and spots the dam to the southeast, the perspective moves incrementally from panoramic to close, enacting a narrative adaptation of the alternating visual perspectives afforded in Pare Lorentz's *The River*. From the riverbank near the dam, where Silver would sometimes stand, "it was grand enough to steal her breath" (4). This instance of being overcome by the technological sublime in response to monumental infrastructure calls to mind the impression created in the photograph of David Lilienthal standing on the riverbank near Wilson Dam analyzed in chapter 1. Next, an abrupt shift in tone dispenses with the sublimity as the narrator makes an ominous pronouncement: "Behind the power company's concrete wall, on the upstream side of the river, the water was rising to form a reservoir that would drown the town of Yuneetah" (4). Faced with this reality, the townspeople speculate about how long they have left. With too many variables in the equation for them, it is up to the narrator to explain what transpired: "The reservoir would eventually reach sixteen miles wide, spilling across the lowlands the town had occupied since two brothers put up a lean-to shed along the riverbank to trade with the Cherokees and a settlement sprang up around it" (4). The description of the lake surface that Silver *would* see the following year if she returned to the same spot and the declarations that the reservoir forming *would* drown Yuneetah and *would* eventually cover an area comprising sixteen miles exemplify narratological prolepsis at work. Through such protentions, the narrative renders the anticipation of a past future by referencing in relative or conditional terms events that eventually took place or will likely transpire in the narrated world. Significantly, the narrator orients the reader to perceive the evacuation and the filling of the reservoir from the vantage point of the people experiencing displacement. This effect emphasizes the collective anxiety that formed because they knew what would happen based on the mandatory evacuation and the planned inundation. The version of futurity established in the opening paragraphs of *Long Man* stands in contrast to that on display in the pro-TVA documentary projects. Instead of the incremental rise of watermarks complementing the teleological progression to the arrival of the TVA and the final narrative gesture toward the promise of a better future, they measure the steady progression toward inevitable and profound losses for the people of Yuneetah with close ties to the land and community.

The title of the novel points to Greene's method of reimagining documentary tropes in crafting historical fiction. In *The River*, the relationship between the titular entity and the people living in dangerous flood zones is depicted as adversarial and potentially lethal. The heavy toll calculated in terms of lost lives and property is presented through compelling survivor testimony and dramatic footage of floodscapes, paving the way for the martial call at the film's end to conquer the river and harness its power through infrastructural development. Relations between the people of Yuneetah and the titular entity in Greene's novel are similarly defined by conflict, destruction, and loss. This local history and the meaning of the title come to light in the section introducing Amos, a Depression hobo whose peripatetic existence is interrupted by periodic returns to Yuneetah. The narrator explains that "Amos was the only one who always came back," describing him as "a force as sure and dangerous as the river" (65). The riparian connection is foundational to Amos's Dickensian upbringing: he was a foundling taken in at the age of four or five by Beulah Kesterson, a midwife and medicine woman, after he barely survived getting swept up in raging floodwaters and then deposited on a river bluff. While trying to impart knowledge to her de facto adopted son, Beulah told Amos that "Yuneetah was the white man's corruption of an Indian word for the spirit of the river" and that "the Cherokees who once lived on its shores had called it Long Man" (28). Although Amos is a loner, he is not alone in his traumatizing encounter with Long Man. Sam Washburn, the TVA agent tasked with convincing Annie Clyde Dodson to follow the evacuation order, also had a narrow escape as a young boy, running for his life after "he saw the river rushing out of its banks toward him like something seeking vengeance" (12). Annie Clyde's husband James still grieves the death of his father in the flood of 1925, the most severe on record to that point. This tragic loss compounds the difficulty of farming his wife's inherited land near the river: "As hard as he had labored to wrest a living from the ground of Yuneetah, there had been an enmity between him and the river since he was twelve years old" (78–79). This feeling contributes to the marital strife that worsens as the TVA's plans unfold. While Annie Clyde is steadfast in her opposition, her husband is open to the idea on the same logical grounds defined in *The River* to stake its pro-TVA claim: "After centuries of houses, livestock and bodies swept off in the floods, there had been a wall built to end them. James couldn't be against such a thing, not even for her sake" (79).

Despite the losses cataloged in the backstories of individual characters and the history of Yuneetah, the steady temporal flow of Long Man performs the archetypal function of representing historical continuity and serving as a source of communal identity. For James Dodson, the river is both traumatizing and comforting, giving back some semblance of what it took from him: "Sometimes it seemed James could hear his drowned father's voice in the water, as if it had kept Earl Dodson's spirit" (79). From a historical perspective informed by the river, Beulah takes stock of Yuneetah's losses as part of a steady decline, resembling what Fiddlersburg undergoes in *Flood*. Pondering the impending flood, Beulah has a stark realization: "The people of Yuneetah were losing more than their property" (92). But she understands the pain as part of a complex emotional brew: sorrow over having to leave tempered by the patriotic belief that "they were doing it for their country, the same reason they signed up to fight in wars" (92). Beulah draws some comfort from a hopeful view of the river, as articulated by the narrator: "All the electric lights in the world couldn't bind them enough to forget what they brought out and passed along to the babies she wouldn't birth. Wherever they ended up, they'd still hear Long Man rushing in their sleep" (92–93). This flashforward evinces what Currie, citing Peter Brooks, calls "anticipation of retrospection."[33] As such, it envisions a sense of futurity that counters the TVA myth by channeling a source of energy regarded as deeper and more sustaining than the hydroelectric power generated by infrastructural development. Nevertheless, as Beulah treks through a driving storm causing the floodwaters to rise ahead of schedule, she pauses for a bracing epiphany after glimpsing the river through the trees. She remembers annual visits to the shoals "to see the river unthawing, a ritual that meant winter was over" and recalls that she "thought the river might be speaking to her" as it did to the Cherokees (177). Beulah wonders if the collection of bones she has held on to for many years were remnants of a "strange fish" caught in the churning waters "[i]f it wasn't Long Man whispering to her about the people that lived along its shores, communicating in some way much older than hers, from before language" (177). The inevitable formation of the reservoir makes Beulah feel anticipatory grief about the passing of Long Man as a squandered resource for the people of Yuneetah. From this perspective, it is a largely untapped font of wisdom because "maybe they too could have heard the truths it told if they'd listened closer" (177).

The anxiety of displacement and the anticipation of loss assume a greater sense of urgency as narrative paths converge on the disappearance of Gracie Dodson against the backdrop of the mandatory evacuation. Just before her daughter goes missing, Annie Clyde's defiance of the order is tinged with resignation as she surveys the familiar surroundings and reflects on what will soon disappear underwater. This response comes in the wake of James's blunt reasoning in trying once again to convince her that the family should evacuate and move to Detroit so that he can find manufacturing work. "You can't stand against a flood, Annie Clyde," he insists (43). This reality check causes "a dead tiredness" and makes Annie Clyde acutely aware of abandoned and destroyed neighboring homes (44). She associates them with "the burial mounds on the riverbank, made by Indians that had lived in caves along the water longer ago than the Cherokees, destroyed by archaeologists from Knoxville and the workers they'd hired to do the digging" (44). Here, as in Beulah's ruminations about hearing whispers from the river, Indigenous traces evoke the presence of the past. The narrator notes that Annie Clyde and Gracie have "skin touched with Cherokee blood" (53). Later, in an encounter between Annie Clyde and Amos, he remembers that it was "common knowledge the Ledfords were Cherokees, the first to be run off this land," prompting speculation: "Maybe that loss, and not her father's farm, was Annie Clyde Dodson's inheritance" (127). Later, Amos picks up the thread again, pondering Gracie's strong resemblance to her mother, which he had noticed when they crossed paths in a cornfield before the little girl's disappearance:

> He had seen the Cherokee in her, as he did in her mother. They were remnants, shadows of those who first lived on this river and gave it a name. Gracie Dodson, one last child occupying the land that was taken from them all, standing in the corn with a drop or two of Indian blood coursing through the threads of her veins. About to be purged by the same government, unaware in her innocence that her birthright was being stolen. (245)

The depiction of the Ledford family in *Long Man* is like that of the Dunbar family in *Dunbar's Cove*, implying that the spiritual connection and material claim to the land gain added value from mixed blood comprising Indigenous and white settler ancestry. As in *Dunbar's Cove*, *Long Man* connects two points on the timeline to yield historical resonance. The forced evacuations enacted by the TVA's Reservoir Family Removal Section in the twentieth century read as a historical reenactment relative to the dispossession and displacement carried out by the federal government as part of Indian Removal in the nineteenth century. Such an implicit analogy is compelling but fraught since it risks "eras[ing] indigeneity" by committing the representational occlusion that Truscello identifies as common in *Dunbar's Cove* and other works of drowned town fiction.³⁴ In this case, the depiction of "Cherokee blood" as a trace barely detectable in descendants of white settler colonialism fails to acknowledge the experiences of Cherokees and other Indigenous people who would have been living in Tennessee and facing population removal in 1936.

Before Gracie's disappearance, the policies and practices of the Reservoir Family Removal Section were mainly abstract and officious, apart from Sam Washburn's personal touch in trying to convince Annie Clyde to evacuate. As the search for Gracie ensues and the designated date of the flood draws closer, the missing child adds a human dimension to the bureaucratic proceedings, symbolizing the collective sense of loss, displacement, and urgency felt by the people of Yuneetah. From Beulah's point of view, the narrator observes, "Soon the lake would reach the main road. There would be no getting in or out. It wasn't just the child slipping away. It was all of Yuneetah" (177). For the community, Gracie's disappearance calls to mind that of "the Deering boy," as he is collectively known, during the catastrophic 1925 flood. Along with his mother and two siblings, the boy was caught up in the turbulent floodwaters that dislodged the front porch of the family cabin and sent it careening through the valley. The sheriff recalls Wayne Deering stumbling around in shock in the wake of the flood and searching for his missing family members only to learn that his wife and daughter drowned while his infant child miraculously survived. Tragically, as Sheriff Ellard Moody recalls, "the third Deering child had seemed to vanish" (108). The historical parallel between children missing in flood zones—one resulting from a natural disaster, the other potentially from the reservoir—creates problems for the TVA because the argument for infrastructural development is that the scheduled inundation is essential for flood control and is thus a life-saving measure.

That history is repeating itself in the form of Gracie's disappearance threatens to disrupt the flow of infrastructural time the TVA wants to maintain to finish the reservoir on schedule. Sheriff Moody makes that clear when he visits the TVA headquarters, acting in the role of liaison he has reluctantly assumed because he is "determined not to let the big government machine forget they were dealing with individuals in Yuneetah" (132). Toward that end, the sheriff asks Clarence Harville, the chief of the Reservoir Family Removal Section, for a "drawdown" of the reservoir—a process of draining that would open more ground for the search parties to cover. The drawdown request is a tall order since Sheriff Moody makes it on August 1, just two days before the final evacuation deadline. Harville's reluctance to grant the request and his determination to stick with the original plan, despite the sheriff asking him what he would do if one of his children or grandchildren were missing under similar circumstances, makes his character come across as an unfeeling bureaucrat. In this respect, he resembles the disparaging portrait of TVA officials that critics held up as the norm when trying to mobilize opposition in local communities. After this exchange, the sheriff responds to Washburn's halfhearted attempt to defend his boss as "a decent person" with a firm rebuttal: "He don't care if that child's alive or dead" (139). It is a pivotal moment for Washburn, indicating that his idealism is starting to fade and prompting his decision to go to Yuneetah to join in the search rather than forcing the issue of evacuation with Annie Clyde.

The historical resonance between the missing children intensifies when Amos, considered a suspect because he encountered Gracie in the cornfield before her disappearance, takes the sheriff and James Dodson to a cave containing human remains he discovered. Amos allows the sheriff and James to believe they might be on the verge of recovering Gracie's body even though he has been aware of the bones for roughly a decade. After a forensic examination, an anthropology professor from the University of Tennessee determines that they must be the remains of the missing Deering child. The recovery from the past compounds the sense of urgency to find Gracie in the present—a feeling that goes beyond the confines of the family and the local authorities to reach members of the community, especially those who evacuated but have returned to join in the search. In retrospect, the recovery reads as a prefiguration since Gracie is found alive less than twenty-four hours later in a cave like the one that contained the Deering child's bones. The communal expression of joy over Gracie's recovery is not lost on Washburn when he returns to Yuneetah and goes to the hospital to find people lining the hallways and crowded into the waiting room. On the last day to comply with the mandatory evacuation order, a flood of displaced persons comes home searching for uplift. "They must have arrived by the car and truck load while he was gone," the narrator explains, "traveling from wherever the dam had scattered them to see proof of a resurrection from the graveyard of their drowning town" (255). The return of the townspeople to witness a veritable resurrection disrupts the timeline of evacuation set by the TVA and serves as a symbolic counterpoint to the material reality of the town's imminent submersion. The religious imagery and overtones liken this scene to the one near the end of *Flood* in which church congregants gather at the river to mark the end of Fiddlersburg as an act of communal tribute.

The reunion of Gracie and her mother is even more deeply affecting for Washburn than witnessing the townspeople gathered at the hospital. For the TVA agent, who "had wanted more than believed" when considering the prospect of the child's safe return, the sight of Gracie in her mother's embrace is life-altering, as revealed in a proleptic turn: "It would become his faith, that such things could and did happen" (259). As Washburn stares through the images of himself and the Dodsons cast onto a windowpane, he peers down at the "twinkling town" of Yuneetah two stories below, noticing that Gracie is entranced by the luminescence and realizing it is her first encounter with electricity (259). The vivid imagery accentuates Washburn's moment of reflection, as he considers the likelihood that Gracie will not remember "[h]ow black the night could get in Yuneetah" (259) in the time before rural electrification. This meditation on energy makes for a stark contrast between mother and daughter: Washburn surmises that the former "wasn't made for electric light" while the latter "would know nothing else" (259). These thoughts form the culmination of a conversion narrative, as Washburn envisions a sobering futurity that counteracts the TVA myth he formerly promoted as an idealistic advocate. Washburn's initial commitment to his work aligns him with Digby in Warren's *Flood*; however, the divided loyalties that make carrying out his assignment from the Reservoir Family Removal Section untenable show that he is cut from the same cloth as the conflicted agents depicted in TVA novels. Crawford Gates in *Dunbar's Cove*, the model for Chuck Glover in *Wild River*, is a prime example given that he, like Washburn, feels growing sympathy for the local people he is tasked with evicting.

As the novel concludes, the connection between Gracie's disappearance and safe return and Amos's reappearance becomes more pronounced, taking shape and meaning from infrastructural time. While Gracie's potential to disrupt the temporal flow regulated by the TVA comes from getting lost in the flood zone and inspiring a homecoming of the displaced when she is found, Amos's derives from his determination to act as a one-man force to strike a blow against infrastructural development. In recounting the character's backstory, the narrator reveals that Amos is no stranger to running on infrastructural time, having worked on road crews after the Federal-Aid Highway Act of 1925 led to a construction boom. Because he helped build highways, Amos feels implicated in the proliferation of "rest areas and filling stations and eyesore bridges of steel" and remorse for destroying mountainsides to make way for the new roads (122). As Amos witnessed firsthand the encroachment of cars and asphalt into backwoods areas, he was "sickened by what he saw" (122). The experience led to a form of radicalization. Although Amos has "no real ideology" and "no set convictions," he does have an anarchical disdain for "all forms of government and hierarchy and authority," which he directs toward the TVA and, more precisely, the dam (123). For Amos, it stands as a monumental expression of the state control he despises, drawing him back to Yuneetah after he came across a newspaper article about the planned inundation. "Soon enough he would find the dam," the narrator says in another instance of prolepsis. "He would stand before it and take its measure" (29). When the foreseen encounter between man and dam does come to pass, it makes sense that Amos first notices the two-lane highway "running across the top of the mammoth structure" to connect this part of the valley to US Highway 25 and Knoxville (119). He is piqued by the American flag and the TVA flag flying on a pole atop a concrete tower as though staking a claim to the valley. Amos recognizes that the modern architectural design of the facilities is supposed to be an appealing attribute; however, in an inversion of the technological sublime and an expression of his anti-government sentiment, it "reminded him of a penitentiary" (119).

The carceral analogy is fitting because Amos seems bound to the dam. While the coming flood leads him to perceive the dam as a monument to oppressive federal authority, it also gives him the sinking feeling that he has been living on borrowed time: "Yuneetah's passing only made him more certain that his own was coming" (30). As a result, and perhaps acting on the recognition that "he did have some attachment to Yuneetah, and its people, whether they knew it or not," Amos decides to use his experience with explosives from his road crew work to become a saboteur (27). Amos is realistic and fatalistic about the potential impact of his plan to steal dynamite from a TVA construction site and detonate it at a place in the foundation he deems vulnerable: "He knew the risk he was taking. As he knew that he couldn't stop the dam builders. They had plans to inundate hundreds of thousands of valley acres. His act was no more than an obstacle to their end result, but he wasn't meant to grow old anyway. If he died blowing up one of their dams, they'd have to admit he had once been alive" (245). In asserting that a single life has value and meaning, Amos's justification for disrupting the timeline of infrastructural development mirrors Ellard's argument that a drawdown is necessary to improve the odds of finding Gracie. As the plot unfolds, Amos has in mind planting the dynamite, lighting the fuse, and getting to a safe spot in time to watch the alternative inundation planned on his watch: "a torrent of silt and river roaring unleashed through the chasm" formed by his answer to the TVA's creative destruction (247). But the plan quickly goes awry when watchmen stationed on the spillway see his small boat headed for the dam. Wounded by gunshots after he fails to heed the watchmen's warnings, Amos once again gazes up at the flags flying atop the concrete tower. While using his chest to press the dynamite against the façade, his blood "flowed out in ribbons as the impounded waters of the river Long Man flowed back into him" (249). In effect, Amos's body becomes an improvised explosive device before detonation: "His eye was still open when the blast shot a glaring fireball along the wall but he didn't see it. His soul was released into the water a moment before his ashes" (250). It is a strangely intimate encounter between river, dam, and saboteur that counters the technological sublime with an instance of radical transcendence.

The outcome of Amos's fatal(istic) gambit to throw the TVA off schedule and force acknowledgment of his lone act of resistance as a proxy for the displaced persons of Yuneetah is telling. In "July 31, 1937," the final section of the novel, the narrator explains that Silver clocked the explosion from the mountaintop the previous year, looking into the valley at the smoke rising and listening to the rush of impounded water through the lone breech Amos was able to cause. The disruption of infrastructural time proved short-lived, however: "The freight trucks returned, the calling men on scaffolds, the clang of machinery. When the grit settled for the last time the lake went on spreading" (266). The restoration of order according to the TVA is evident in the Phoenix-like display Silver now sees in the valley at night: the bright lights on the dam "shining out of the charred and broken treetops with their own cold beauty to rival the stars and moon" (266). It turns out that Amos did get some posthumous satisfaction in his bid for recognition since news of "the man who blew a hole in the dam and the little girl resurrected from the ground" made national headlines (266). Notably, those intertwined stories have faded from the public sphere by the time the conditional moment in the future envisioned by the narrator in the opening section becomes actual. Once again, Silver stands on the mountainside, this time surveying the culmination of the reservoir's sixteen-mile expanse because she believes deeply that "somebody ought to bear witness" (271).

Rather than the panoramic view favored by producers of pro-TVA documentaries and replicated in the closing aerial shot in *Wild River*, *Long Man* affords a ground-level perspective on the flood. As the water spreads across fields and property lines, landmarks come into view briefly before disappearing. There is an emphasis on material structures and objects left behind—sheds, houses, hearths, and chimneys, even a pair of dirty work boots—as they are submerged in space and lost to infrastructural time. Eventually, the narrative frame centers Annie Clyde's farm, which she and her family finally abandoned for another plot of land in the valley outside the bounds of the reservoir. During her final visit to the farm, Silver learned that James was working in a steam plant generating hydroelectric power for the rapidly expanding grid and that Annie Clyde, hypervigilant in watching Gracie's every move, was pregnant. Although they seemed settled and relatively content, Silver detected notes of hardship that belied the relatively unburdened life of modern conveniences promised by the TVA: "Electricity couldn't put right everything wrong in this valley" (270). In the final passage, Silver sees the reservoir engulfing all forty acres her niece once held but still holds dear "[u]ntil there was nothing left to see but miles and miles of blue" (272). At this moment, the inundation becomes a narrative occasion for the reader to join Silver in bearing witness to the displaced and submerged and for *Long Man* to join *Flood* and other TVA novels in recovering some semblance of what was lost in the name of progress.

CODA

IN THE FALL SEMESTER OF 2021, AS THE COVID-19 PANDEMIC RAGED ON, I WAS TEACHING a group of masked students, most of whom were struggling with the combination of high stress and trouble concentrating that ran rampant in the wake of resuming in-person classes after months spent online. Suddenly, the power went out, and we waited for some time before a chorus of notification signals sounded. It was a Maroon Alert, the name for official messages sent through the university system, announcing a campuswide power outage and offering assurance that crews from the TVA had been dispatched to restore electricity as soon as possible. One student responded with a muffled query: "What's the TVA?" Another followed: "Like in *Loki*?" (more on that below). For the next ten minutes or so, we sat in the dark and talked about the agency responsible for keeping the lights on. At one point, I mentioned the large sign emblazoned with "TVA" on the slope outside the Mississippi Region office located near a busy intersection at one of the entrances to campus. Nobody recalled having seen it. When the lights flickered back on—power restored, mission accomplished—we returned to the actual course material and eventually to the default mode of taking electricity for granted. The impromptu lesson illustrated the disconnect between reliance on energy and indifference to the means of production that is possible from a relatively privileged position. It also demonstrated, albeit on a smaller scale than the pandemic, the axiom referenced in the preceding pages: that infrastructure can seem invisible until system failure draws attention to it out of necessity.

The student's question about *Loki* was based on awareness of the Time Variance Authority—"aka the other TVA," as a playful tweet from the Tennessee Valley Authority's Twitter account dubbed it.[1] The other TVA was featured in the Marvel Studios television series, the first season of which had aired on the Disney+ streaming service a few months earlier. *Loki* received generally positive reviews and, like most Marvel properties then, was a fixture in the cultural firmament during its run. The second, presumably final season aired in the fall of 2023. Most of my students had either watched the show or heard of it, and all of them were familiar with the titular character. In the first season, Loki, the Marvel version of the Norse God of Mischief and adopted brother of Thor, the hammer-wielding God of Thunder, becomes implicated in a complex plot with arcs involving the multiverse and the Time Variance Authority. Like its partner-in-acronym, this TVA has a designated coverage area, but one infinitely larger in scale than the Tennessee Valley. At the helm of the cosmic agency is He Who Remains, the last of the Time-Keepers, the omniscient founders. The TVA headquarters is in the Null-Time Zone, a realm outside time, occupying facilities that evoke the brutalism of real-world Tennessee Valley Authority architecture that emerged in the 1970s from the sleek modernist aesthetic of the initial phase of infrastructural development. The main purpose of the Time Variance Authority is to monitor and repair the machinations of the multiverse through a process that resembles flood control but with the manipulation of temporal rather than riparian currents.

Marvel's TVA originated in the comics, appearing in *The Mighty Thor* (Volume 1, #371, 1986) to restore the proper flow of realities after a major disruption. Donald Davidson likely did not think much of or even about comics, but I suspect he would have appreciated the depiction of TVA employees as clones bred to function solely as mindless bureaucrats. In the television series, one of the few breaks from the numbing monotony of the workplace comes from Miss Minutes, an anthropomorphized clock with an animated form and a faux chipper voice accented with southern inflections. The graphic design of Miss Minutes resembles that of cartoon mascots such as Reddy Kilowatt rendered as embodiments of electricity in promotional campaigns dating as far back as the 1920s. The use of such historical details reflects the inspiration behind the source material. The writer of the comic, Walter "Walt" Simonson, noted in an interview that the idea for the Time Variance Authority came from recollections of his childhood in Tennessee in the late 1940s. Simonson said that his father, a soil scientist, "was a fan of the Tennessee Valley Authority" because he felt it "leveled the playing field" by giving rural people access to electricity.[2] Based on Simonson's recollection, it seems his father's investment in the TVA enterprise became the son's inheritance in the form of creative inspiration. "So I've always loved the Tennessee Valley Authority," Simonson explained to the interviewer, "knowing nothing about it than what my dad told me."[3]

While my class was a small sample size, it was arguably consistent with American culture on the issue of name recognition. What does it mean that "the other TVA" likely surpassed the original by this measure just over two decades into the twenty-first century? The cultural history laid out in the preceding chapters suggests that several factors are in play: the elimination of government-funded cultural production in the post–New Deal era; the degraded TVA myth and dents in the agency's reputation due to the consequences of fossil-fuel dependence and unpopular development projects; and the general tendency toward infrastructural invisibility. The trend in which the largest public provider of electricity in the United States rarely makes national headlines unless something goes wrong has continued from the Tellico Project and Land Between the Lakes in the latter half of the twentieth century through the Kingston coal ash spill and implication in the severe flooding caused by strip mining in the twenty-first century. Compounding the problem were the rolling blackouts that dampened holiday spirits in December 2022—the first in the ninety-year history of the agency.[4]

While the blackouts were unprecedented, the scenario of the TVA facing the challenges of a global crisis is not. The agency formed amid the urgency and volatility of the Great Depression has been trying to figure out how to respond to the effects of climate change registering with increasing frequency and force. In recent years, TVA officials have pledged to "decarbonize" by exploring alternatives to coal. This decision came as the adoption of renewables gained momentum—even in some of the most conservative pockets of the country, albeit for economic rather than ecological reasons. In November 2022, the TVA blew up three cooling towers at the inaptly named TVA Paradise Fossil Plant as part of an incremental decommissioning and transitioning program. Officials have touted a 63 percent reduction in carbon emissions between 2005 and 2020, adding that hitting the 80 percent mark by

2030 is feasible.⁵ It is important to note that this plan fell short of the goal of achieving a carbon-free electric grid by 2035 set by the Biden administration at the time. The status as a federal corporation that the TVA has enjoyed since its inception in 1933 made the opt-out possible. Predictably, fossil-fuel interests—especially devotees of the oxymoronic notion of "clean coal"—have criticized the TVA for abandoning a longtime industry staple. Environmentalists charge that the mixed-bag approach of converting from coal to natural gas plants, restarting the mostly dormant nuclear program, and incrementally developing renewables (mainly solar) ensures unacceptable pollution levels for decades to come. For their part, TVA officials have responded that the agency will "build the energy system of the future, never compromising the low rates and high reliability that sustain the communities we serve."⁶ The pledge to deliver abundant, affordable, and clean energy while generating economic growth sounds familiar. This rhetorical throwback to the brief reign of hydropower creates the kind of historical rhyme that the Time Variance Authority would monitor closely to prevent convergent reality flows.

What is in store for energy production and consumption on the domestic front is a point of contention, speculation, and, for too many stakeholders, willful denial. Robert Kunzig raises the question of the "right road to net-zero" carbon emissions before pointing in a familiar direction for exploring energy options: "The Tennessee Valley is an illuminating microcosm of a national debate, in which the imperative of addressing climate change is pitted against the enormous practical challenge of not only maintaining a reliable electric supply but dramatically expanding it to meet the needs of a decarbonizing economy."⁷ Despite talk about abundant opportunities and perpetual economic growth in a green energy economy, the specter of scarcity is a haunting presence. After all, the controversial development of natural gas plants and the nuclear component are included in the TVA's long-term plan because of concerns that relying too heavily on renewables might leave customers under-serviced and in the dark.⁸ Kunzig's framing was accurate in 2023, but the terms of debate have since changed under the second Trump administration. After assuming power, officials made climate change denial and robust support for fossil fuels as the future of energy production core tenets of federal energy policy. While the need to address climate change will remain, the prospect of the TVA effectively *recarbonizing* would not be a surprising turn of events.

The question of the "right road" to take calls to mind another TVA-adjacent cultural property attuned to possible futures: Cormac McCarthy's *The Road*. McCarthy's novel, a 2006 work of postapocalyptic speculative fiction, is obviously in a much different register than *Thor #371* or *Loki*, but the origin stories have something in common. Like Simonson, McCarthy had a TVA connection through his father. Charles Joseph McCarthy was a lawyer stationed at the TVA headquarters in Knoxville from 1934 to 1967. Early in *The Road*, the unnamed father and son at the center of the narrative take a brief respite from walking the highway, which no longer accommodates automobiles but courses through a scorched, barren landscape in which the air is thick with ash. Various markers suggest the Tennessee Valley as the likely location. After taking a path through the woods, father and son emerge to find a bench positioned at a vantage point affording a panoramic view. A large lake and dam are visible in the valley despite "the gritty fog."[9] The area appears to be an overlook like the ones created at Norris Dam and other sites to entice and impress visitors empowered by automobility with the allure of technologically sublime encounters with TVA monumentality. However, in this instance, it becomes the setting for a teachable moment tailored to someone whose lack of infrastructural awareness stems from deprivation rather than privileged indifference. "The dam used the water that ran through it to turn big fans called turbines that would generate electricity," the father explains. "To make lights," the son says. "Yes. To make lights," answers the father, completing an exchange that evokes the divine command in the Genesis creation story only to underscore the loss of power and the reign of darkness in a horrific wasteland.[10]

The brevity of the encounter with the dam does not diminish the profundity of the lessons to be learned. "Will the dam be there for a long time?" the son asks. The father speculates that it will endure for "hundreds of years. Thousands even."[11] In McCarthy's deft hands, the air of inevitability and longevity projected with optimism and confidence in TVA cultural production gets an Ozymandian revision that unsettles the signature brand of futurity. The unease intensifies as the brief episode ends on a sharp note. When the son asks whether fish might live in the lake, the father's answer is definitive: "There's nothing in the lake."[12]

The laconic response is a sort of death sentence—a postapocalyptic corollary to the passage from Patrick McCully's *Silenced Rivers* cited in the introduction in which he describes dams taming rivers to the point of stagnation and ecological harm. When contemplating the scene at the dam—the entire novel, for that matter—Patricia Yaeger's query, also cited in the introduction, bears repeating: "What is it like to be stuck, night and day, dreaming of infrastructure?" There is a growing recognition that we are indeed stuck with infrastructure. As a conduit for many of the problems the world faces at this moment of crisis, infrastructure "also promises the solution to these problems" by providing the technologies and mechanisms necessary to render fossil-fuel dependence and its harmful effects obsolete.[13] At this juncture, this outcome seems farther down the road than it was even a year ago, perhaps existing only as a faint mirage. From this vantage point, McCarthy's dam fits into the extensive pattern of monumental designs as symbolic expressions examined in this study, standing as a cautionary ruin projecting through ominous implication the urgent need for powerhouses such as the Tennessee Valley Authority to imagine and strive to bring about a sustainable infrastructural and energy future.

NOTES

INTRODUCTION

1. Franklin Delano Roosevelt, "Inaugural Address," edited by Gerhard Peters and John T. Woolley. *The American Presidency Project*, accessed October 25, 2024, https://www.presidency.ucsb.edu/documents/inaugural-address-8.

2. TVA cultural production is the focus of Tim Culvahouse, ed., *The Tennessee Valley Authority: Design and Persuasion* (New York: Princeton Architectural Press, 2007). This edited volume includes essays on architectural design, landscape architecture, and visual arts (photography, murals, and graphic design). Official TVA photography is featured in two collections compiled and edited by Patricia Bernard Ezzell: *TVA Photography: Thirty Years of Life in the Tennessee Valley* (Jackson: University Press of Mississippi, 2003) and *TVA Photography, 1963–2008* (Jackson: University Press of Mississippi, 2008). As of this writing, the most recent addition to the field is Avigail Sachs, *The Garden in the Machine: Planning and Democracy in the Tennessee Valley Authority* (Charlottesville: University of Virginia Press, 2023). Sachs's book delves into TVA regional planning, architecture, and landscape architecture to demonstrate important contributions to American architectural and landscape design during the Great Depression and World War II. There are journal articles and chapters in edited collections—many of which are cited hereafter—that engage in individual or comparative analysis of cultural works related to the TVA. *Monumental Designs* affords a more comprehensive view, mainly by extending the focus beyond the 1930s and 1940s.

3. Michael Kreyling, *Inventing Southern Literature* (Jackson: University Press of Mississippi, 1998). See also C. Hugh Holman, "No More Monoliths Please: Continuities in the Multi Souths," in *Southern Literature in Transition: Heritage and Promise*, ed. Philip Castille and William Osborn (Memphis: Memphis State University Press, 1983), xiii–xxiv. Holman's proposal in the early 1980s to replace "the South" with "Multi-Souths," thus enabling the field to adapt to "a profoundly pluralistic world," was an early challenge to the traditional regional paradigm (xviii).

4. Houston Baker Jr., *Turning South Again: Re-thinking Modernism/Re-reading Booker T.* (Durham, NC: Duke University Press, 2001), 9.

5. See, for example, Leigh Anne Duck, *The Nation's Region: Southern Modernism, Segregation, and U.S. Nationalism* (Athens: University of Georgia Press, 2006); Jennifer Rae Greeson, *Our South: Geographic Fantasy and the Rise of National Literature* (Cambridge, MA: Harvard University Press, 2010); Houston Baker Jr. and Dana D. Nelson, eds., "Violence, the Body and 'The South,'" special issue, *American Literature* 73, no. 2 (June 2001): 231–44, JSTOR. While the label "new southern studies" has been used mostly in literary and cultural studies, southern historians have worked along similar lines: Matthew D. Lassiter and Joseph Crespino, eds., *The Myth of Southern Exceptionalism* (New York: Oxford University Press, 2009); Natalie J. Ring, *The Problem South: Region, Empire, and the New Liberal State, 1880–1930* (Athens: University of Georgia Press, 2012).

6. Representative texts include Jon Smith and Deborah Cohn, eds., *Look Away!: The U.S. South in New World Studies* (Durham, NC: Duke University Press, 2004); Kathryn McKee and Annette Trefzer, eds., "Global Contexts, Local Literatures: The New Southern Studies," *American Literature* 78, no. 4 (December 2006), JSTOR. For a set of comparable work in other disciplines, albeit not overtly aligned with the new southern studies, see James L. Peacock, Harry L. Watson, and Carrie R. Matthews, eds., *The American South in a Global World* (Chapel Hill: University of North Carolina Press, 2005).

7. Jon Smith, "Toward a Postpostpolitical Southern Studies: On the Limits of the 'Creating and Consuming' Paradigm," in Martyn Bone, Brian E. Ward, and William A. Link, *Creating and Consuming the American South* (Gainesville: University Press of Florida, 2015), 75.

8. Leigh Anne Duck, "Southern Nonidentity," *Safundi* 9, no. 3 (2008): 329, Taylor & Francis Online.

9. Martyn Bone, *Where the New World Is: Literature About the U.S. South at Global Scales* (Athens: University of Georgia Press, 2018), 25.

10. Patricia Yaeger, "Introduction: Dreaming of Infrastructure," *PMLA* 122, no. 1 (2007): 15, JSTOR.

11. My use of "infrastructure" is informed by Michael Rubenstein, *Public Works: Infrastructure, Irish Modernism, and the Postcolonial* (Notre Dame, IN: University of Notre Dame Press, 2010), 6–7. Like Rubenstein, I apply the term as an anachronism—in this case, within the historical and cultural contexts of the New Deal and the Great Depression—to convey that the scale and pace of construction and development was so novel that the specific language to describe it was not yet available.

12. Michael Rubenstein, Bruce Robbins, and Sophia Beal, "Infrastructuralism: An Introduction," *Modern Fiction Studies* 61, no. 4 (Winter 2015): 576, JSTOR.

13. Brian Larkin, "The Politics and Poetics of Infrastructure," *Annual Review of Anthropology* 42 (2013): 328, JSTOR.

14. Larkin, "The Politics and Poetics of Infrastructure," 328.

15. Susan Leigh Star, "The Ethnography of Infrastructure," *American Behavioral Scientist* 43, no. 3 (1999): 380.

16. Larkin, "The Politics and Poetics of Infrastructure," 336.

17. Rubenstein, Robbins, and Beal, "Infrastructuralism," 576.

18. Jessica Hurley and Jeffrey Insko, "Introduction: The Infrastructure of Emergency," in "The Infrastructure of Emergency," special issue, *American Literature* 93, no. 3 (2021): 351, MLA International Bibliography.

19. Hurley and Insko, "Introduction: The Infrastructure of Emergency," 351.

20. Rubenstein, *Public Works*, 3.

21. Rubenstein, *Public Works*, 3–4.

22. Jeff Diamanti, "Infrastructure," in *Fueling Culture: 101 Words for Energy and Environment*, ed. Imre Szeman, Jennifer Wenzel, and Patricia Yaeger (New York: Fordham University Press, 2017), 198.

23. Patrick McCully, *Silenced Rivers: The Ecology and Politics of Large Dams* (Atlantic Highlands, NJ: Zeb Books, 1996), 10.

24. Sharon Ann Musher, *Democratic Art: The New Deal's Influence on American Culture* (Chicago: University of Chicago Press, 2015), 5.

25. McCully, *Silenced Rivers*, 1.

26. Frederick Buell, "A Short History of Oil Cultures: Or, the Marriage of Catastrophe and Exuberance," *Journal of American Studies* 46, no. 2 (May 2012): 273, JSTOR.

27. Patricia Yaeger, "Editor's Column: Literature in the Ages of Wood, Tallow, Coal, Whale Oil, Gasoline, Atomic Power and Other Energy Sources," *PMLA* 126, no. 2 (March 2011): 308, JSTOR.

28. A notable exception is the fictional representation of the historic role the TVA played in supporting the facilities in Oak Ridge, Tennessee, one of the three "secret cities" involved in the development of the atomic bomb under the auspices of the Manhattan Project. Notable texts include Marianne Wiggins, *Evidence of Things Unseen: A Novel* (New York: Simon & Schuster, 2004), and Janet Beard, *The Atomic City Girls* (New York: HarperCollins, 2018).

29. Yaeger, "Editor's Column," 305.

30. Imre Szeman, "Literature and Energy Futures," in Yaeger, "Editor's Column," 324.

31. Szeman, "Literature and Energy Futures," 325.

32. Robert S. McElvaine, *The Great Depression: America, 1929–1941* (New York: Times Books, 1984), 155–56.

33. Richard A. Colignon, *Power Plays: Critical Events in the Institutionalization of the Tennessee Valley Authority* (Albany: State University of New York Press, 1997), 104–6.

34. William U. Chandler, *The Myth of TVA: Conservation and Development in the Tennessee Valley, 1933–1983* (Cambridge, MA: Ballinger, 1984), 47.

35. Franklin Delano Roosevelt, "Message to Congress Suggesting the Tennessee Valley Authority," April 10, 1933, edited by Gerhard Peters and John T. Woolley, *The American Presidency Project*, University of California, Santa Barbara, accessed October 25, 2024, https://www.presidency.ucsb.edu/node/208057.

36. Roosevelt, "Message to Congress Suggesting the Tennessee Valley Authority."

37. Chandler, *The Myth of TVA*, 1. Chandler's study offers an unflinching view, disrupting the established pattern in retrospective accounts of reinforcing official histories and dominant narratives. A case in point is Roscoe C. Martin, ed., *TVA: The First Twenty Years* (Tuscaloosa: University of Alabama Press and Knoxville: University of Tennessee Press, 1956), a collection of essays by members of the TVA staff. The introduction, "The Meaning of the TVA," concludes with the recognition that "the Tennessee Valley Authority means different things to different people" (14). Tellingly, the different meanings attributed to various segments of the valley population all have positive connotations. A perfunctory recognition of opposition is noted, with the insistence that it amounts to "few within in the region, to be sure" (15).

38. Erwin C. Hargrove, *Prisoners of Myth: The Leadership of the TVA, 1933-1990* (Princeton, NJ: Princeton University Press, 1994), 4.

39. Hargrove, *Prisoners of Myth*, 4.

40. Hargrove, *Prisoners of Myth*, 5-6. For the material Hargrove condenses, see Philip Selznick, *TVA and the Grass Roots: A Study in the Sociology of Formal Organization* (Berkeley and Los Angeles: University of California Press, 1953), 19-84. It is important to note that Hargrove, like Selznick, is concerned with an organizational culture within the structure and operations of the TVA. *Monumental Designs* extends this focus to consider how the organizational environment facilitated cultural production in the Tennessee Valley.

41. I use the term "cultural region" (variants include "culture area" or "cultural area") as it is generally applied in the fields of anthropology and human geography, that is, to denote a geographical area with predominant traits (language, history, religion, and so on) that contribute to the formation of a discernable culture.

42. Rupert B. Vance, *Human Geography of the South: A Study in Regional Resources and Human Adequacy*, 2nd ed. (Chapel Hill: University of North Carolina Press, 1935), 482. Vance cites George Perkins Marsh's *The Earth as Modified by Human Action* as the original source for this line of thinking. Vance notes that Marsh's argument laid the groundwork for turning away from geographic determinism.

43. Vance, *Human Geography of the South*, ix.

44. Howard W. Odum, *Southern Regions of the United States* (Chapel Hill: University of North Carolina Press, 1936).

45. Vance, *Human Geography of the South*, 483.

46. Vance, *Human Geography of the South*, 483.

47. The three men comprised an administrative triumvirate, with Arthur Morgan serving as chairman and Harcourt Morgan as vice chairman. That was the case until Arthur Morgan's resignation in 1941, at which point Lilienthal became chairman, remaining in the post until 1946. It is commonly held that Lilienthal was the most influential of the three, chiefly because of his impassioned articulation of the TVA vision and promotion of its agenda.

48. David E. Lilienthal, *TVA: Democracy on the March* (New York: Pocket Books, 1944), 156. See Arthur E. Morgan, *The Making of the TVA* (Buffalo, NY: Prometheus Books, 1974) for another chronicle of the formative years from within the trio of top administrators.

49. Lilienthal, *TVA: Democracy on the March*, 157.

50. Lilienthal, *TVA: Democracy on the March*, 157-58.

51. Lilienthal, *TVA: Democracy on the March*, 158.

52. Colignon, *Power Plays*, 166.

53. Roosevelt, "Message to Congress Suggesting the Tennessee Valley Authority."

54. Roosevelt, "Message to Congress Suggesting the Tennessee Valley Authority."

55. James Agee, "Tennessee Valley Authority," in *Complete Journalism, Articles, Book Reviews, and Manuscripts*, ed. Paul Ashdown (Knoxville: University of Tennessee Press, 2013), 77-90. See also, in the same volume, "T.V.A.: Work in the Valley," 197-222, which appeared in the May 1935 issue of *Fortune*.

56. Agee, "Tennessee Valley Authority," 81.

57. Agee, "Tennessee Valley Authority," 82.

58. Agee, "Tennessee Valley Authority," 82.

59. David E. Whisnant, *Modernizing the Mountaineer: People, Power, and Planning in Appalachia* (Boone, NC: Appalachian Consortium Press, 1980), 43.

60. Donald Davidson, *The Attack on Leviathan* (Chapel Hill: University of North Carolina Press, 1938). The publication of Davidson's book shows that the University of North Carolina Press was a prominent venue for competing models of regionalism held on one hand by the Southern Agrarians and on the other by the scholars affiliated with the Institute for Research in Social Science. See Michael O'Brien, *The Idea of the American South, 1920–1941* (Baltimore: Johns Hopkins University Press, 1979) for an extensive treatment of what he describes in a usefully encapsulated form as "the conservative aestheticism of Nashville" set against "the liberal sociology of Chapel Hill" (xv).

61. Donald Davidson, *The Tennessee*, vol. 2, *The New River: Civil War to TVA* (New York: Rinehart, 1948), 224.

62. Davidson, *The Attack on Leviathan*, 224.

63. Davidson, *The Attack on Leviathan*, 225.

64. Harry M. Caudill, "The Rape of the Appalachians," *Atlantic Monthly*, April 1962, 41. See also Caudill, *Night Comes to the Cumberlands: A Biography of a Depressed Region* (Boston: Little, Brown, 1962), in which the author incorporates material from the magazine article into a broader focus.

65. Caudill, "The Rape of the Appalachians," 42.

66. John Egerton, *The Americanization of Dixie: The Southernization of America* (New York: Harper & Row, 1974), 52.

67. National Emergency Council, *Report on Economic Conditions of the South* (Washington, DC: Government Printing Office, 1938): 1, Internet Archive, Open Library, https://archive.org/details/reportoneconomicoonati.

68. James Branscome, "Commentary: TVA Owes Eastern Kentucky Reparations for Strip Mining's Role in Flooding," *Daily Yonder*, August 15, 2022, https://dailyyonder.com/commentary-unprecedented-and-unnecessary-kentuckys-flooding-and-its-mining-history/2022/08/15/.

CHAPTER 1. A DAM SITE MORE MODERN: DEVELOPING TVA MONUMENTALITY IN VISUAL CULTURE

1. Franklin Delano Roosevelt, "Informal Extemporaneous Remarks at Sheffield, Alabama on Muscle Shoals Inspection Trip," *The American Presidency Project*, University of California, Santa Barbara, accessed October 25, 2024, https://www.presidency.ucsb.edu/documents/informal-extemporaneous-remarks-sheffield-alabama-muscle-shoals-inspection-trip.

2. Roosevelt, "Informal Extemporaneous Remarks."

3. Roosevelt, "Informal Extemporaneous Remarks."

4. Rob Nixon, *Slow Violence and the Environmentalism of the Poor* (Cambridge, MA: Harvard University Press, 2013), 167.

5. Nixon, *Slow Violence*, 167.

6. Nixon, *Slow Violence*, 167.

7. Kiran Klaus Patel, *The New Deal: A Global History* (Princeton, NJ: Princeton University Press, 2016), 99.

8. Patel, *The New Deal: A Global History*, 99.

9. Nixon, *Slow Violence*, 156.

10. Patel, *The New Deal*, 98.

11. Nixon, *Slow Violence*, 156.

12. "Wilson," Tennessee Valley Authority, accessed May 16, 2023, https://www.tva.com/energy/our-power-system/hydroelectric/wilson.

13. *Mr. Smith Goes to Washington*, directed by Frank Capra (1939; Sony Pictures Home Entertainment, 2018), Blu-ray Disc.

14. Robert A.M. Stern, *Modern Classicism* (New York: Rizzoli, 1988), 46.

15. Stern, *Modern Classicism*, 7.

16. Christine Macy and Sarah Bonnemaison, *Architecture and Nature: Creating the American Landscape* (New York: Routledge, 2003), 145. The book includes a chapter on the TVA; see the section titled "The Making of Norris Dam," 146–52, for a more detailed account of Wank's renegade campaign for his modernist blueprint.

17. Chandler, *The Myth of TVA*, 87.

18. Stern, *Modern Classicism*, 51.

19. *TVA Architecture, as Shown at the Museum of Modern Art* (Knoxville: Tennessee Valley Authority, 1941). The material in the book first appeared in a periodical format: Frederick A. Gutheim, "Tennessee Valley Authority: A New Phase in Architecture," *Magazine of Art* 33 (September 1940): 516–31.

20. Franklin Delano Roosevelt, "Radio Address of the President, Dedication of the Museum of Modern Art, N.Y. City, May 10, 1939," Franklin Delano Roosevelt Day by Day, Pare Lorentz Center at the FDR Presidential Library, Master Speech File, FDR Library, 2011, http://www.fdrlibrary.marist.edu/daybyday/resource/may-1939-2/. Subsequent references to Roosevelt's remarks in the paragraph come from this source.

21. Roosevelt, "Radio Address of the President."

22. Roosevelt, "Radio Address of the President."

23. Roosevelt, "Radio Address of the President."

24. "David E. Lilienthal, Director of TVA, Opens Exhibition of TVA Architecture and Design at Museum of Modern Art," Museum of Modern Art, accessed September 29, 2024, https://assets.moma.org/documents/moma_press-release_325220.pdf, 1.

25. "David E. Lilienthal, Director of TVA," 2.

26. "David E. Lilienthal, Director of TVA," 2.

27. Lilienthal documented an encounter with a sculptor, Jo Davidson, who crashed a party so that he could pitch his idea for a "monumental figure" of a man on the Norris Dam spillway appearing to hold back the water. According to Lilienthal, Wank "violently differed with him on the aesthetics of the thing," making the case that a dam's beauty derived from functional design elements rather than ornamentation. David E. Lilienthal, *The Journals of David E. Lilienthal*, vol. 1, *The TVA Years, 1939–1945* (New York: Harper & Row, 1964), 48.

28. Museum of Modern Art records available in a digital format include a master checklist of items as well as photographs of the installation. It is possible to glean from the archival materials a sense of how the curatorial hand guided the public appeal of the exhibition. "T.V.A. Architecture and Design," Museum of Modern Art, accessed September 29, 2024, https://www.moma.org/calendar/exhibitions/2087.

29. "The Artist With a Camera," Tennessee Valley Authority, accessed September 29, 2024, https://www.tva.com/about-tva/our-history/tva-heritage/the-artist-with-a-camera. See also Ezzell, *TVA Photography: Thirty Years of Life in the Tennessee Valley*. In addition to photographs by Krutch, *TVA Photography* features work by the noted photographer Lewis Hine, who was employed by the TVA for less than a month but was nevertheless able to capture some indelible images of the early phase of construction on Norris Dam.

30. "The Artist With a Camera."

31. Beaumont Newhall, ed., *Photography, 1839–1937* (New York: Museum of Modern Art, 1937). After receiving a Guggenheim fellowship in 1947, Newhall revised and expanded the book, which was published as *The History of Photography, 1839 to the Present*. He continued to work on new editions over the next several years, and it became a standard text for the history of photography among academics and the general reading public alike. For more on the significance of Newhall's contributions, see Allison Bertrand, "Beaumont Newhall's 'Photography: 1839–1937' Making History," *History of Photography* 21, no. 2 (1997): 137–46.

32. Margaret Bourke-White, Photographs of the Fort Peck Dam Project, *Life*, November 23, 1936.

33. Stephen Bennett Phillips, *Margaret Bourke-White: Photography of Design, 1927–1936* (New York: Rizzoli, 2003) examines the photographer's interest in industrial forms and other aspects of the Machine Age.

34. Theodor Adorno, "Functionalism Today," in *Rethinking Architecture: A Reader in Cultural Theory*, ed. Neil Leach, 4–18 (New York: Routledge, 1997), 7.

35. Adorno, "Functionalism Today," 10.

36. Adorno, "Functionalism Today," 14.

37. "David E. Lilienthal, Director of TVA," 3.

38. "David E. Lilienthal, Director of TVA," 4.

39. "David E. Lilienthal, Director of TVA," 4.

40. "David E. Lilienthal, Director of TVA," 4.

41. Lewis Mumford, "The Architecture of Power," *New Yorker*, June 7, 1941, NewYorker.com, accessed September 29, 2024, https://archives.newyorker.com/newyorker/1941-06-07/flipbook/058/, 58.

42. Mumford, "The Architecture of Power," 58.

43. "David E. Lilienthal, Director of TVA," 2.

44. Walter Benjamin, "The Work of Art in the Age of Its Technological Reproducibility," in *The Work of Art in the Age of Its Technological Reproducibility, and Other Writings on Media*, ed. Brigid Doherty, Michael William Jennings, and Thomas Y. Levin, trans. E. F. N. Jephcott, Howard Eiland, and Rodney Livingstone (Cambridge, MA: Harvard University Press, 2008), 23.

45. Benjamin, "The Work of Art," 23.

46. Benjamin, "The Work of Art," 23.

47. I use the term "photobooks," but the genre also falls under the category of "photo-texts" or "documentary books." See John Puckett, *Five Photo-Textual Documentaries* (Ann Arbor: UMI Research Press, 1984), an influential study that established a representative set of texts for subsequent studies: Jefferson Hunter's *Image and Word: The Interaction of*

Twentieth-Century Photographs and Texts (Cambridge, MA: Harvard University Press, 1987); Carol Shloss, *In Visible Light: Photography and the American Writer, 1840–1940* (New York: Oxford University Press, 1987); Patrizia Di Bello, Colette Wilson, and Shamoon Zamir, eds., *The Photobook: From Talbot to Ruscha and Beyond* (New York: Routledge, 2020). See also Joseph R. Millichap, *These Vivid American Documents: Walker Evans, Dorothea Lange, and FSA Photography* (Knoxville: University of Tennessee Press, 2024).

48. Walter Benjamin, *The Arcades Project*, trans. Howard Eiland and Kevin McLaughlin (Cambridge, MA: Belknap Press, 1999), 5.

49. Benjamin, *The Arcades Project*, 5.

50. R. L. Duffus and Charles Krutch, *The Valley and Its People: A Portrait of TVA* (New York: Knopf, 1946), 11. Subsequent references appear in parentheses within the main body of the text.

51. Benjamin, "The Work of Art," 27.

52. Benjamin, "The Work of Art," 27.

53. Andrew Higgott and Timothy Wray, introduction to *Camera Constructs: Photography, Architecture and the Modern City*, ed. Higgott and Wray (Burlington, VT: Ashgate, 2012), 5.

54. Walter Benjamin, "The Author as Producer," in *Walter Benjamin: Selected Writings, Volume 2, Part 2, 1931–1934*, ed. Michael W. Jennings, Howard Eiland, and Gary Smith, trans. Rodney Livingstone et al., 769–82 (Cambridge, MA: Harvard University Press, 1999), 774.

55. Benjamin, "The Author as Producer," 775.

56. Benjamin, "The Author as Producer," 775.

57. Brian Larkin, "The Politics and Poetics of Infrastructure," 334.

58. During a tour of the powerhouse on November 15, 2022, Patricia Bernard Ezzell, Senior Specialist (History), Communications for the Tennessee Valley Authority, told me she thought the artist was one of the architects from the original design team who worked on plans for Norris Dam.

59. "Art for the People," TVA: Tennessee Valley Authority, accessed December 8, 2022, https://www.tva.com/about-tva/our-history/built-for-the-people/art-for-the-people.

60. "Art for the People."

61. At some point, the mural was completely covered by a large carpet mounted on plywood, with numerous holes bored into the wall to attach the frame. In 2016 the forgotten mural was uncovered as preparations began for an event marking the eightieth anniversary of Norris Dam. The TVA secured funding for repairs and restoration and held an unveiling in 2018. For further details, see Chris Salvemini, "Hidden Knoxville Native's Mural Found, Restored in Norris Dam," *Knox News*, October 21, 2018, https://www.knoxnews.com/story/news/2018/10/17/norris-dam-mural-robert-birdwell-restored/1661684002/.

62. Holger Cahill, "American Folk Art," in *American Folk Art: The Art of the Common Man in America, 1750–1900* (1932; repr., New York: Arno Press for the Museum of Modern Art, 1969), 27.

63. Todd Smith, "Almost Fully Modern: The TVA's Visual Art Campaign," in Culvahouse, *The Tennessee Valley Authority*, 108.

64. "Art for the People."

65. Jean Baudrillard, "The Precession of Simulacra," in *Simulacra and Simulation*, trans. Sheila Faria Glaser (Ann Arbor: University of Michigan Press, 1994), 1.

66. Caroll Van West, *Tennessee's New Deal Landscape: A Guidebook* (Knoxville: University of Tennessee Press, 2001), 221.

67. See Sachs, *The Garden in the Machine*, 94–104, for analysis of the overlooks at Norris Dam and other sites.

68. Davidson, *The Tennessee*, 229.

69. "Norris Dam State Park, Tennessee: Lenoir Museum—Rice Grist Mill—Crosby Threshing Barn" (Nashville: Tennessee Department of Environment and Conservation, 2021), https://tnstateparks.com/assets/pdf/additional-content/norris_dam_museum_brochure.pdf.

70. Davidson, *The Tennessee*, 231.

71. "Norris Dam State Park."

CHAPTER 2. DOCUMENTARY FORMS: INFRASTRUCTURAL INEVITABILITY IN *THE RIVER* AND *THE VALLEY OF THE TENNESSEE*

1. Paula Rabinowitz, "1930s Documentary and Visual Culture," in *The Wiley-Blackwell History of American Film*, eds. Cynthia Lucia, Roy Grundmann, and Art Simon (Malden, MA: Blackwell Publishing, 2012), 142.

2. Rabinowitz, "1930s Documentary and Visual Culture," 142.

3. *The Valley of the Tennessee*, directed by Alexander Hammid (Washington, DC: Office of War Information, 1944), National Archives, YouTube, https://youtu.be/SfJt-W7fwTY?feature=shared.

4. Pare Lorentz, *FDR's Moviemaker: Memoirs & Scripts* (Reno: University of Nevada Press, 1992), 35.

5. Michael Denning, *The Cultural Front: The Laboring of American Culture in the Twentieth Century* (New York: Verso, 1997), 265.

6. Denning, *The Cultural Front*, 266.

7. Denning, *The Cultural Front*, 266–67.

8. Hannah Appel, "Infrastructural Time," in *The Promise of Infrastructure*, ed. Nikhil Anand, Akhil Gupta, and Appel (Durham, NC: Duke University Press, 2018), Location 1045 of 6102, Kindle.

9. Appel, "Infrastructural Time," Location 1068 of 6102.

10. Appel, "Infrastructural Time," Location 1086 of 6102.

11. Rabinowitz, "1930s Documentary and Visual Culture," 146.

12. Marijke de Valck, *Film Festivals: From European Geopolitics to Global Cinephilia* (Amsterdam: Amsterdam University Press, 2007), 48.

13. For a concise and instructive comparison, see Astrid Böger, *People's Lives, Public Images: The New Deal Documentary Aesthetic* (Tübingen, Germany: Gunter Narr Verlag, 2001), 210.

14. The most glaring example of this approach came in the 1970s, prompting Susan Sontag to issue a pointed rebuke: "Fascinating Fascism," *New York Review of Books*, February 6, 1975, 25–30, accessed November 25, 2022, https://www.nybooks.com/articles/1975/02/06/fascinating-fascism/.

15. Jeremy Hicks, *Dziga Vertov: Defining Documentary* (London: I.B. Tauris, 2007), 50.

16. Hicks, *Dziga Vertov*, 57.

17. Hicks, *Dziga Vertov*, 59.

18. Lorentz, *FDR's Moviemaker*, 63. Subsequent references to this source are cited with parenthetical documentation in the main text.

19. Anna Lawton, "Rhythmic Montage in the Films of Dziga Vertov: A Poetic Use of the Language of Cinema," *Pacific Coast Philology* 13 (1978): 44, JSTOR.

20. Lawton, "Rhythmic Montage in the Films of Dziga Vertov," 49.

21. Peter C. Rollins, "Ideology and Film Rhetoric: Three Documentaries of the New Deal Era (1936–1941)," in *Hollywood as Historian: American Film in A Cultural Context*, rev. ed., ed. Rollins (Lexington: University Press of Kentucky, 1983), 41.

22. Rollins, "Ideology and Film Rhetoric," 42.

23. Larkin, "The Politics and Poetics of Infrastructure," 329.

24. Larkin, "The Politics and Poetics of Infrastructure," 329.

25. Larkin, "The Politics and Poetics of Infrastructure," 335.

26. William L. White, "Pare Lorentz," *Scribner's*, January 1939, 11.

27. Robert L. Snyder, *Pare Lorentz and the Documentary Film* (Reno: University of Nevada Press, 1994), 184.

28. See Finis Dunaway, *Natural Visions: The Power of Images in American Environmental Reform* (Chicago: University of Chicago Press, 2008), 73–77, for a helpful summary of critical responses that consider *The River* in relation to Whitman's poetry in general and *Leaves of Grass* in particular. Dunaway also takes up the comparison, adding Stephen Vincent Benét's poem "Ode to Walt Whitman" (1935) to the discussion as a mediating device.

29. Sven Beckert, *Empire of Cotton: A Global History* (New York: Vintage Books, 2014), 221.

30. Frederick Jackson Turner, *The Frontier in American History* (New York: Henry Holt, 1953; New York: Dover, 1996), 190. The citation is from the Dover edition.

31. Walter Johnson, *River of Dark Dreams: Slavery and Empire in the Cotton Kingdom* (Cambridge, MA: Harvard University Press, 2013), 3.

32. Lorentz notes the concern that arose when he pointed out the necessity of addressing the Civil War in the film. His supervisors were wary of offending lawmakers from the South. The decision to cast Lee in the glowing light of Lost Cause mythology suggests an attempt to guard against severe pushback that might undermine the pro–New Deal, pro-TVA aims of the film. For a fuller account, see Lorentz, *FDR's Moviemaker*, 58–59.

33. Lilienthal, *TVA: Democracy on the March*, 157.

34. Lilienthal, *TVA: Democracy on the March*, 157.

35. See Howard W. Odum, "Regionalism vs. Sectionalism in the South's Place in the National Economy," *Journal of Social Forces* 12 (March 1934): 338–54. Odum's article had a significant impact on the thinking of officials in the Roosevelt administration as they shaped New Deal policies and programs and served as the foundation for his influential 1936 study, *Southern Regions of the United States*.

36. Ring, *The Problem South*, 15.

37. Duck, *The Nation's Region*, 1–16.

38. National Emergency Council, *Report on Economic Conditions of the South*.

39. Böger, *People's Lives*, 207.

40. Walter Benjamin, "On the Concept of History," in *Selected Writings*, ed. Howard Eiland and Michael W. Jennings, trans. Edmund Jephcott, vol. 4, *1938–1940* (Cambridge, MA: Belknap, 2006), 392.

41. John M. Barry, *Rising Tide: The Great Mississippi River Flood of 1927 and How It Changed America* (New York: Simon and Schuster, 1997), 16. Barry's book is an indispensable resource for understanding the scale of the flood, from the experiences of those who suffered the devastation firsthand to the local, state, and national efforts to provide relief in the face of an overwhelming emergency. For a contemporaneous narrative of the flood, see Saxon, *Father Mississippi: The Story of the Great Flood of 1927* (Gretna, LA: Pelican Publishing, [1927] 2006).

42. African American newspapers outside the South reported these abuses at the time. It became part of a contested narrative, as public officials and prominent citizens, mainly Delta planters, tried to justify these practices. See William Alexander Percy, *Lanterns on the Levee: Recollections of a Planter's Son* (Baton Rouge: Louisiana State University Press, [1941] 2004), especially the chapter titled "The Flood of 1927." Percy, who led the relief and recovery effort in Washington County, Mississippi, exhibits trademark paternalism in characterizing the Black community as ungrateful for the care he provided for them.

43. Susan Scott Parish, *The Flood Year 1927: A Cultural History* (Princeton, NJ: Princeton University Press, 2017), 8.

44. Parrish, *The Flood Year 1927*, 9.

45. Parrish, *The Flood Year 1927*, 9.

46. Parrish, *The Flood Year 1927*, 9.

47. Giorgio Agamben, *Homo Sacer: Sovereign Power and Bare Life*, in *The Omnibus Homo Sacer* (Stanford, CA: Stanford University Press, 2017), 99–100.

48. Hicks, *Dziga Vertov*, 60.

49. Appel, "Infrastructural Time," Location 1303 of 6102.

50. In addition to directing films, Hammid (born Alexander Siegfried George Hackenschmied in Linz, Austria-Hungary) worked as a cinematographer and editor; he was also an accomplished photographer. He immigrated to the United States from Czechoslovakia as the German occupation began with the annexation of the Sudetenland in 1938. The occupation was the subject of his highly regarded documentary film *Crisis* (1939). For a discussion of Hammid's biography and filmography, see Thomas E. Valasek, "Alexander Hammid: A Survey of His Film-Making Career," *Film Culture* 67–69 (1979): 250–322.

51. Lilienthal, *TVA: Democracy on the March*, 203.

52. Lilienthal, *TVA: Democracy on the March*, 204.

53. Lilienthal, *TVA: Democracy on the March*, 204–5.

54. Lilienthal, *TVA: Democracy on the March*, 206.

55. Ian Scott, *In Capra's Shadow: The Life and Career of Screenwriter Robert Riskin* (Lexington: University Press of Kentucky, 2006), 175.

56. Clayton R. Koppes and Gregory D. Black, "What to Show the World: The Office of War Information and Hollywood, 1942–1945," *Journal of American History* 64, no. 1 (June 1977): 88, JSTOR.

57. Koppes and Black, "What to Show the World," 89. It is beyond the scope of this chapter but nevertheless worth noting that the view of film as a powerful instrument of

mass persuasion is relevant to the critique of the "culture industry" in Theodor Adorno and Max Horkheimer, "The Culture Industry: Enlightenment as Mass Deception," in *Dialectic of Enlightenment*, trans. John Cumming (New York: Verso, 2008): 120–67. In this landmark essay, Hollywood movies produced on virtual assembly lines figure prominently as one of the mass-produced forms of popular entertainment serving state interests and maintaining the status quo of capitalism. This critique first appeared in 1944, the same year that *The Valley of the Tennessee* was produced and started screening in liberated parts of Western Europe.

58. Dean J. Kotlowski, "Selling America to the World: The Office of War Information's 'The Town' (1945) and the 'American Scene' Series," *Australasian Journal of American Studies* 35, no. 1 (July 2016): 80, JSTOR.

59. Kotlowski, "Selling America to the World," 84.

60. Kotlowski, "Selling America to the World," 80.

61. Marja Roholl, "An Invasion of a Different Kind: The Office of War Information and 'The Projection of America' Propaganda in the Netherlands, 1944–1945," in Hans Bak, Frank Mehring, and Mathilde Roza, eds., *Politics and Cultures of Liberation: Media, Memory, and Projections of Democracy* (Boston: Brill, 2018), 17.

62. Speaking for subjects, especially the poor and marginalized, was common in 1930s documentary projects. A case in point is the dialogue by Erskine Caldwell that serves as captions for Margaret Bourke-White's photographs in *You Have Seen Their Faces* (New York: Modern Age Books, 1937; Athens: University of Georgia Press, 1995).

63. McElvaine, *The Great Depression*, 201–2.

64. McElvaine, *The Great Depression*, 219.

65. McElvaine, *The Great Depression*, 221.

CHAPTER 3. *POWER* TO THE PEOPLE: THE SPECTACULAR DRAMA OF RURAL ELECTRIFICATION

1. Kurt Eisen, "Circulating *Power*: National Theatre as Public Utility in the Federal Theatre Project," *Theatre Symposium: A Journal of the Southeastern Theatre Conference* 9 (2001): 39, ProQuest.

2. Hallie Flanagan, *Arena: The History of the Federal Theatre* (New York: Benjamin Blom, 1940), 6.

3. The challenges to the Tennessee Valley Authority Act created a complex web of legal maneuvers. In 1936 the US Supreme Court issued a ruling in *Ashwander v. TVA* that was considered a resounding victory for the TVA. But nineteen companies doing business in nine states quickly filed a new complaint; the plaintiffs sought an injunction on the grounds that the Supreme Court decision applied to the Wilson Dam, not to all TVA dam projects. This was the unresolved legal matter influencing the production of *Power*. For a more detailed summary of the legal issues, see C. Herman Pritchett, *The Tennessee Valley Authority: A Study in Public Administration* (Chapel Hill: University of North Carolina Press, [1943] 2014), 60–65.

4. Records show that casting was a challenge for all the productions of *Power* mounted in various parts of the country. In the production bulletin for the 1937 Seattle run, the FTP state director, Guy Williams, explains that "a frenzied amount of doubling" was necessary to simplify the casting specifications provided by the New York company. The bulletin for

the 1938 production in Portland, Oregon, shows that producers relied heavily on assigning multiple roles to actors. Casting correspondence for the New York revival at the 49th Street Theatre in 1938 includes a steady stream of urgent messages about settling for novice actors to replace cast members who had bowed out to take better jobs or canceling performances if one actor fell ill. Container 1057, Federal Theatre Project Collection, Music Division, Library of Congress, Washington, DC.

    5. Jane DeHart Mathews, *The Federal Theatre, 1935–1939: Plays, Relief, and Politics* (Princeton, NJ: Princeton University Press, 1967), 114.

    6. Laura Browder, *Rousing the Nation: Radical Culture in Depression America* (Amherst: University of Massachusetts Press, 1998), 118.

    7. Browder, *Rousing the Nation*, 118.

    8. Ilka Saal, *New Deal Theater: The Vernacular Tradition in American Public Theater* (New York: Palgrave Macmillan, 2007), 2.

    9. Flanagan, *Arena*, 65.

    10. For a detailed account of the ill-fated production history of *Ethiopia*, see Susan Quinn, *A Furious Improvisation: How the WPA and a Cast of Thousands Made High Art out of Desperate Times* (New York: Bloomsbury, 2011), 60, 66–70.

    11. Mathews, *The Federal Theatre, 1935–1939*, 109–10.

    12. Mathews, *The Federal Theatre*, 110, 111.

    13. Quinn, *A Furious Improvisation*, 119.

    14. Lynn Mally, "The Americanization of the Soviet Living Newspaper," *The Carl Beck Papers in Russian and East European Studies*, no. 1903 (2008): 3, https://doi.org/10.5195/cbp.2008.140.

    15. Flanagan, *Arena*, 73.

    16. Arthur Arent, "Technique of the Living Newspaper," *Theatre Quarterly* 1, no. 4 (1971): 57.

    17. Arnold Goldman, "Life and Death of the Living Newspaper Unit," *Theatre Quarterly* 3, no. 9 (1973): 69.

    18. Arthur Arent, *Power*, in *Federal Theatre Plays*, edited by Pierre De Rohan (New York: De Capo Press, 1973), 10. Subsequent references to this source are cited with parenthetical documentation in the main text.

    19. Accounts of Flanagan's HUAC testimony appear in various sources. For a recent discussion, see Mally, "The Americanization of the Soviet Living Newspaper," 25–27. Flanagan recalls the experience in a chapter of her memoir in which she describes the demise of the WPA and its subsidiary agencies, in part due to the political machinations of Dies and HUAC. Flanagan, "Blasting Work: Suspended," *Arena*, 333–73.

    20. Denning, *The Cultural Front*.

    21. Edmund Wilson, "The Literary Class War: I," *New Republic*, May 4, 1932, 320–23, and "The Literary Class War: II," *New Republic*, May 11, 1932.

    22. For a study in this vein, see Andreas Huyssen, *After the Divide: Modernism, Mass Culture, Postmodernism* (Bloomington: Indiana University Press, 1987). See Fredric Jameson, *The Antinomies of Realism* (New York: Verso, 2015) on relations between realism and modernism.

    23. Brooks Atkinson, "'Power' Produced by the Living Newspaper Under Federal Theatre Auspices," *New York Times*, February 24, 1937, 18, *TimesMachine*, accessed October 26, 2024, https://timesmachine.nytimes.com/browser/.

24. Atkinson, "'Power' Produced by the Living Newspaper," 18.

25. Mathews, *The Federal Theatre, 1935–1939*, 113.

26. Flanagan, *Arena*, 185.

27. Flanagan, *Arena*, 185.

28. Production bulletin for *Power*, Federal Theatre Project Regional Company, Seattle, WA, Container 1057, Federal Theatre Project Collection, Music Division, Library of Congress, Washington, DC.

29. Production bulletin. All subsequent quotations in the paragraph come from this source.

30. Eisen, "Circulating *Power*," 41.

31. Arent, *Power*, 60. Subsequent references to this edition of the play are cited in parentheses in the main text.

32. Ira Katznelson, *Fear Itself: The New Deal and the Origins of Our Time* (New York: Liveright, 2013), 22.

33. Katznelson, *Fear Itself*, 23.

34. David E. Nye, "The Great White Way," in *Energy Humanities: An Anthology*, ed. Imres Szeman and Dominic Boyer (Baltimore: Johns Hopkins University Press, 2017), 71.

35. Nye, "The Great White Way," 71.

36. Container 1192j, Federal Theatre Project Collection.

37. David E. Nye, *American Technological Sublime* (Cambridge, MA: MIT Press, 1994), 143.

38. Nye, *American Technological Sublime*, 143.

39. Nye, *American Technological Sublime*, 144.

40. Nye, *American Technological Sublime*, 145.

41. Nye, *American Technological Sublime*, 145.

42. Ring, *The Problem South*, 15.

43. Wolfgang Schivelbusch, *The Three New Deals: Reflections on Roosevelt's America, Mussolini's Italy, and Hitler's Germany, 1933–1939* (New York: Henry Holt, 2006), 142–44. The comparison between the TVA and the Agro Pontino is most pointed, but the chapter on public works also discusses the construction of the autobahn in Germany. Schivelbusch prefaces the comparative analysis by making the case that the Western nations in question were motivated to take up large-scale construction by the boom in public works projects in the Soviet Union in the late 1920s, which undermined capitalist superiority in technology and innovation and became an even more serious challenge as the global economic crisis erupted.

44. Arent, "Techniques of the Living Newspaper," 58.

45. Arent, "Techniques of the Living Newspaper," 59.

46. I am drawing from Benedict Anderson's discussion of the role of newspapers (and novels) in shaping nations as imagined communities. Anderson describes a ceremonial function for newspapers, as readers participate in the act of reading together and develop a sense of national belonging. Benedict Anderson, *Imagined Communities: Reflections on the Origin and Spread of Nationalism* (New York: Verso, 1991), 25–36.

47. Nye, *American Technological Sublime*, 38.

48. Saal, *New Deal Theater*, 133.

49. Saal, *New Deal Theater*, 133.

50. Davidson, *The Tennessee*, 237.

51. Davidson, *The Tennessee*, 237.

52. The public criticism of the TVA by Davidson and others associated with the Southern Agrarians as an intellectual movement led to a critical consensus that there was a united front in opposition to the federal enterprise. In letters and even in some of their published writing, however, the responses were not uniformly negative. For an overview of the consensus point of view and for compelling evidence for a more nuanced understanding that accounts for divisions within the Agrarian ranks, see Edward Shapiro, "The Southern Agrarians and the Tennessee Valley Authority," *American Quarterly* 22, no. 4 (Winter 1970): 791–806.

53. Schivelbusch, *The Three New Deals*, 114.

54. For an extensive treatment of the visit, see Mardges Bacon, "Le Corbusier and Postwar America: The TVA and *Béton Brut*," *Journal of the Society of Architectural Historians* 74, no. 1 (2015): 13–40, https://doi.org/10.1525/jsah.2015.74.1.13.

55. Schivelbusch, *The Three New Deals*, 117–18.

56. On a trip to Norris Dam, I spoke with Frank Laszlo, who was on desk at the visitor's center. Retired from the TVA's engineering operations, Laszlo was working on a history of Norris Dam. He told me Jean Thomas documented "The TVA Song," which was written and performed by a local man named Jilson Setters, a pseudonym for James William (J. W.) Day. Laszlo said "The TVA Song" was originally a folk song. That would make the Sousa-style rendition in *Power* a notable departure from the original.

57. Metropolitan Playhouse, "Power," accessed October 26, 2024, https://metropolitanplayhouse.org/powerinfo.htm.

58. Metropolitan Playhouse, "Power."

59. The lines from reviews come from a compendium on the Metropolitan's website. Metropolitan Playhouse, "Reviews—Power," accessed October 26, 2024, https://metropolitanplayhouse.org/powerreview. Attempts to find the full reviews turned up empty since they were originally posted online and then eventually disappeared, even eluding Internet Archive's Wayback Machine. While the curated list of positive responses indicates a marketing strategy at work, these reviews are still helpful for making the point that the production and reception of the revival centered on the connections between past and present that it evoked.

60. Metropolitan Playhouse, "Reviews—Power."

61. Metropolitan Playhouse, "Reviews—Power."

62. Metropolitan Playhouse, "Reviews—Power."

63. Alex Soloski, "Metropolitan Playhouse Revives a 1937 'Living Newspaper,'" *Village Voice*, March 25, 2009, https://www.villagevoice.com/2009/03/25/metropolitan-playhouse-revives-1937-living-newspaper/.

64. Soloski, "Metropolitan Playhouse Revives a 1937 'Living Newspaper.'"

65. A byproduct of burning coal—in this case, to generate electricity—coal fly ash concentrates in smokestacks as a grainy substance that forms a thick, mud-like texture when mixed with water. Scientific studies have shown that it contains a high level of toxins and carcinogens. A capture method was developed to prevent coal ash residue from circulating freely in the atmosphere but finding sufficient storage space for the waste poses logistical and financial challenges. In the case of the Kingston facility, as with other sites where spills

have occurred, the stockpile exceeded capacity to the point that a coal ash pond breach occurred. See Mark Guarino, "Tennessee Spill Revives Coal Ash Controversy," *Christian Science Monitor*, December 31, 2008, https://www.csmonitor.com/Environment/2008/1231/tennessee-spill-revives-coal-ash-controversy; Shaila Dewan, "Coal Ash Spill Revives Issue of Its Hazards," *New York Times*, December 24, 2008, ProQuest.

66. Gregory Button, *Disaster Culture: Knowledge and Uncertainty in the Wake of Human and Environmental Catastrophe* (Walnut Creek, CA: Left Coast Press, 2010), 127.

67. Joel K. Bourne Jr., "Coal's Other Dark Side: Toxic Ash That Can Poison Water and People," *National Geographic*, February 19, 2019, https://www.nationalgeographic.com/environment/article/coal-other-dark-side-toxic-ash.

68. Button, *Disaster Culture*, 137.

69. Coal ash was a source of intense controversy before the Kingston spill drew attention to it. Questions about toxicity levels, official EPA designations, and removal fueled disputes involving the federal government (primarily the EPA), environmental organizations such as the Natural Resources Defense Council (NRDC), and the coal industry. For more on the science, politics, and economics of this issue in the context of Kingston, see Button, *Disaster Culture*, 132–35; and Bourne, "Coal's Other Dark Side."

70. Lilienthal, *TVA: Democracy on the March*, 209.

71. Lilienthal, *TVA: Democracy on the March*, 209.

72. David Lilienthal, "Author's Note to the Edition of 1953," *TVA: Democracy on the March*, Twentieth Anniversary ed. (New York: Harper & Row, 1953), x.

73. Bourne, "Coal's Other Dark Side."

CHAPTER 4. BACK TO THE FUTURE: CROSSCURRENTS OF DEVELOPMENT IN ELIA KAZAN'S *WILD RIVER*

1. For a concise overview of this transition, see Barbara A. Miller and Richard B. Reidinger, eds., *Comprehensive River Basin Development: The Tennessee Valley Authority*, World Bank Technical Paper, No. 416 (Washington, DC: World Bank, 1998), 61–64. See also David A. Tillman, *Coal-Fired Electricity and Emissions Control: Efficiency and Effectiveness* (Cambridge, MA: Butterworth-Heinemann, 2018), 101–4. On the nuclear front, the TVA played an instrumental role in the development of the atomic bomb. The main contribution was supplying electricity to facilities at Oak Ridge, Tennessee, one of three sites with the "Secret City" designation within the Manhattan Project.

2. John F. Kennedy, "Remarks on 30th Anniversary of Tennessee Valley Authority, Muscle Shoals, Alabama, 18 May 1963," John F. Kennedy Presidential Library and Museum, *jfklibrary.org*, accessed October 25, 2024, https://www.jfklibrary.org/Asset-Viewer/Archives/JFKPOF-044-021.aspx. All subsequent quotations in the paragraph come from this source.

3. "Eisenhower Points to the T.V.A. as 'Creeping Socialism,'" *New York Times*, June 8, 1953, *TimesMachine*, accessed October 26, 2024, https://timesmachine.nytimes.com/timesmachine/1953/06/18/83725405.html.

4. Kennedy, "Remarks on 30th Anniversary of Tennessee Valley Authority."

5. *Wild River*, directed by Elia Kazan (1960; Los Angeles: 20th Century Fox Home Video, 2013), DVD.

6. Kazan initially employed Ben Maddow, a formerly blacklisted screenwriter, to write the script. Unsatisfied with the final product, Kazan tried his hand at writing the screenplay himself with input from Huie. The script went through several drafts and title changes before Kazan enlisted Osborn, who made substantial revisions in producing the shooting script. For more on the production history, see Brian Neve, *Elia Kazan: The Cinema of an American Outsider* (New York: I.B. Tauris, 2009), 126–30.

7. Laura Beth Daws and Susan L. Brinson, *Greater Good: Media, Family Removal, and Dam Construction in Northern Alabama* (Tuscaloosa: University of Alabama Press, 2019), 52.

8. In discussing *Wild River*, I reference Deal's *Dunbar's Cove* in more detail than Huie's *Mud on the Stars* to note parallels and significant revisions and omissions during the adaptation process. A brief description of Deal's novel is in order. The plot centers on the Dunbar family as they contend with an order from the TVA under eminent domain to relinquish land held by the family since patriarch David Dunbar first staked his claim under settler colonialism. The seizure of land for the planned Chickasaw Dam and a reservoir prompts the current proprietor, Matthew Dunbar, to take a stand against the federal government. Deal deepens the emotional stakes by connecting the Dunbars to the land through traces of Indigenous ancestry, often in terms that read as racist. Matthew refuses to comply with the order despite efforts by Crawford Gates, a local man hired by the TVA and enthralled by its mythic vision, to convince him that doing so will serve a greater good and that resistance is futile. The standoff splits the extended family, as some members leave due to the enticement of TVA jobs and others stay behind to join Matthew in resisting the federal government. A further complication develops when Matthew's daughter Arlis falls in love with Crawford Gates and marries him. Eventually, Matthew backs down, resulting in a peaceful resolution. But this outcome is undermined by the lingering sadness over the loss of a cherished home. The final scene in the novel depicts the TVA crew at work and the rising floodwaters about to engulf the stone remnants of the Dunbar house, which was burned in preparation.

9. Elia Kazan, *Elia Kazan: A Life* (New York: Knopf, 1988), 596.

10. Kazan, *Elia Kazan: A Life*, 597.

11. Kazan, *Elia Kazan: A Life*, 597.

12. Donald Chase, "Watershed: Elia Kazan's *Wild River*," *Film Comment* 32, no. 6 (November–December 1996): 11, JSTOR. The question of where the film stands is a matter of debate. See Brian Black, "Authority in the Valley: TVA in *Wild River* and the Popular Media, 1930–1940," *Journal of American Culture* 8, no. 2 (1995): 1–14, Wiley Online Library. Where Chase finds ambivalence, Black sees clarity, arguing that *Wild River* "is not objective. [Kazan's] work dramatically states that any forced regional progression is accomplished only at the cost of regional culture" (4).

13. Kazan saw parallels between Kennedy and Roosevelt. Regarding Kennedy's assassination in 1963, Kazan says that it struck Hollywood with a force not felt since FDR's death. Although Kazan claims that he "stayed close" to Kennedy after two visits to the White House, a note of wariness is noticeable in his recollection of qualities that made the young president appealing. Kazan describes Kennedy as a "leading man" who was "media made, much like Roosevelt had been, but with more clout since the equipment he used was better" (*Elia Kazan: A Life*, 669–70).

14. Fredric Jameson, *Postmodernism, or, The Cultural Logic of Late Capitalism* (Durham, NC: Duke University Press, 1991), 19.

15. Jameson, *Postmodernism*, 19.

16. Jameson, *Postmodernism*, 19.

17. In taking a nostalgic turn to the 1930s, *Wild River* became part of a minor trend in film and television of the 1960s and 1970s. *Bonnie and Clyde* (1967), *They Shoot Horses, Don't They?* (1969), *Paper Moon* (1973), and *The Sting* (1973) are examples from the big screen. *The Waltons* television series, which premiered in 1973 and ran until 1982, covered a period from 1933 to 1946.

18. *People of the Cumberland*, directed by Sidney Meyers and Jay Leyda (New York: Frontier Films, 1937), National Film Preservation Foundation, https://www.filmpreservation.org/sponsored-films/screening-room/people-of-the-cumberland-1937.

19. For more on the early history of the Highlander Folk School, which shifted its main emphasis from labor issues to race relations and civil rights activism in the early 1950s, see John M. Glen, *Highlander: No Ordinary School, 1932–1962* (Lexington: University Press of Kentucky, 2021); and Frank Adams and Myles Horton, *Unearthing Seeds of Fire: The Idea of Highlander* (Winston-Salem, NC: J. F. Blair, 1975).

20. Indelible images from the Farm Security Administration (FSA) trove of photographs define the Depression era in public consciousness. With the invention of Kodachrome film, color photography was possible by the late 1930s. Nevertheless, because the process was cost-prohibitive on a large scale, relatively few color pictures were taken for the government. But a stash of some 1,600 color slides was discovered by a historian in the 1970s. Those images were made public in *Bound for Glory: America in Color, 1939–1943*, the title of a 2004 book and a 2006 exhibition at the Library of Congress. From my perspective, the experience of watching Kazan's Depression in Technicolor in *Wild River* is analogous to viewing the period color photographs.

21. At one point, Kazan considered not limiting the setting to 1935 so that the film could address the issue of anti-federal sentiment in response to the *Brown v. Board of Education* decision in 1954 and the Civil Rights Act of 1957, the first of its kind since Reconstruction (Neve, *Elia Kazan*, 126–27).

22. Marshall Berman, *All That Is Solid Melts Into Air: The Experience of Modernity* (New York: Penguin, 1988), 39.

23. Berman, *All That Is Solid Melts Into Air*, 39–40.

24. Berman, *All That Is Solid Melts Into Air*, 74.

25. Berman, *All That Is Solid Melts Into Air*, 74.

26. Berman, *All That Is Solid Melts Into Air*, 74. See also Barry M. Katz, "Ideology and Engineering in the Tennessee Valley," in Culvahouse, *The Tennessee Valley Authority: Design and Persuasion*. Katz posits that "[t]he fortunes of Faust provide a striking parable for the vast undertakings of the TVA" (80). Citing the burgeoning programs of the New Deal, the mounting threat of world war, and resistance among locals, Katz asserts that "the ambitions of the TVA were Faustian both in ideology and engineering. The bridge between them—then, as now—was design" (80).

27. Berman, *All That Is Solid Melts Into Air*, 43.

28. Berman, *All That Is Solid Melts Into Air*, 40.

29. Robin L. Murray and Joseph K. Heumann, *Ecology and Popular Film: Cinema on the Edge* (Albany: State University of New York Press, 2009), 46.

30. Duck, *The Nation's Region*, 8.

31. Matt Wray, *Not Quite White: White Trash and the Boundaries of Whiteness* (Durham, NC: Duke University Press, 2006), 57. See also Sylvia Jenkins Cook, *From Tobacco Road to Route 66: The Southern Poor White in Fiction* (Chapel Hill: University of North Carolina Press, [1976] 2012) and Nancy Isenberg, *White Trash: The 400-Year Untold History of Class in America* (New York: Penguin, 2017). For analysis of cinematic representations, see Allison Graham, *Framing the South: Hollywood, Television, and Race During the Civil Rights Struggle* (Baltimore: Johns Hopkins University Press, 2001).

32. Wray, *Not Quite White*, 57.

33. For a historical account of this response, see Barry, *Rising Tide*, 303–35.

34. For more information, including digitized primary documents, see "The TVA and the Relocation of Mattie Randolph," National Archive, Educator Resources, Washington, DC, August 15, 2016, https://www.archives.gov/education/lessons/tva-relocation.html.

35. Murray and Heumann, *Ecology and Popular Film*, 39.

36. Michael Truscello, *Infrastructural Brutalism: Art and the Necropolitics of Infrastructure* (Cambridge, MA: MIT Press, 2020), 58.

37. Truscello, *Infrastructural Brutalism*, 58–59.

38. Borden Deal, *Dunbar's Cove* (New York: Scribner's, 1957), 1–2.

39. Deal, *Dunbar's Cove*, 2.

40. Deal, *Dunbar's Cove*, 2.

41. Berman, *All That Is Solid Melts Into Air*, 51.

42. Berman, *All That Is Solid Melts Into Air*, 51.

43. Berman, *All That Is Solid Melts Into Air*, 51.

44. Berman, *All That Is Solid Melts Into Air*, 65.

45. Berman, *All That Is Solid Melts Into Air*, 66.

46. Berman, *All That Is Solid Melts Into Air*, 67.

47. Nancy L. Grant, *TVA and Black Americans: Planning for the Status Quo* (Philadelphia: Temple University Press, 1990), 14, 17.

48. Grant, *TVA and Black Americans*, 19.

49. Grant, *TVA and Black Americans*, 19.

50. Yaeger, "Editor's Column," 309.

51. Berman, *All That Is Solid Melts Into Air*, 69.

52. Berman, *All That Is Solid Melts Into Air*, 68.

53. Berman, *All That Is Solid Melts Into Air*, 68.

54. Isabel Duarte-Gray, "Tennessee Valley Authority," Poetry Foundation, accessed July 25, 2023, https://www.poetryfoundation.org/poems/156607/tennesse-valley-authority.

55. William Bruce Wheeler and Michael J. McDonald, *TVA and the Tellico Dam, 1936–1979: A Bureaucratic Crisis in Post-Industrial America* (Knoxville: University of Tennessee Press, 1986), 3–4.

56. Wheeler and McDonald, *TVA and the Tellico Dam*, 44.

57. In *TVA and the Tellico Dam*, Wheeler and McDonald offer a detailed historical account. See also Michael R. Fitzgerald and Stephen J. Rechichar, *The Consequences of Administrative Decision: TVA's Economic Development Mission and Intragovernment Regulation* (Knoxville: Bureau of Public Administration, University of Tennessee, 1983).

58. Marilou Awiakta, *Selu: Seeking the Corn-Mother's Wisdom* (Golden, CO: Fulcrum Publishing, 1993). For an insightful examination of Awiaktu's work, including *Selu*, see the fifth chapter of Melanie R. Benson, *Disturbing Calculations: The Economics of Identity in Postcolonial Southern Literature, 1912–2002* (Athens: University of Georgia Press, 2008), 164–201.

59. Awiakta, *Selu*, 44.

60. Awiakta, *Selu*, 46.

61. Awiakta, *Selu*, 47.

62. Awiakta, *Selu*, 47.

63. The survey findings were first published in Jefferson Chapman, *Tellico Archaeology: 12,000 Years of Native American History* (Knoxville: University of Tennessee Press, 1985). Revised editions have been published since then.

64. Awiakta, *Selu*, 50.

65. Awiakta, *Selu*, 59.

66. Awiakta, *Selu*, 61.

CHAPTER 5. FROM *FLOOD* TO *LONG MAN*: THE RISE OF THE TVA NOVEL

1. Robert Penn Warren to Louis Rubin Jr., July 6, 1963, in *Selected Letters of Robert Penn Warren*, Vol. 4, *New Beginnings and New Directions, 1953–1968*, ed. Randy Hendricks and James A. Perkins (Baton Rouge: Louisiana State University Press, 2008), 378.

2. Michael J. McDonald and John Muldowny, *TVA and the Dispossessed: The Resettlement of Population in the Norris Dam Area* (Knoxville: University of Tennessee Press, 1982), 25.

3. McDonald and Muldowney, *TVA and the Dispossessed*, 25–26.

4. McDonald and Muldowney, *TVA and the Dispossessed*, 267.

5. Nixon, *Slow Violence*, 150.

6. Nixon, *Slow Violence*, 150.

7. Nixon, *Slow Violence*, 150.

8. Nixon, *Slow Violence*, 150.

9. Nixon, *Slow Violence*, 151.

10. Frederick J. Hoffman, "The Sense of Place," in *South: Modern Southern Literature in its Cultural Setting*, ed. Louis D. Rubin Jr. and Robert D. Jacobs (Garden City, NY: Dolphin Books, 1961); Martyn Bone, *The Postsouthern Sense of Place in Contemporary Fiction* (Baton Rouge: Louisiana State University Press, 2005), 38.

11. Eudora Welty, "Place in Fiction," in *Eudora Welty: Stories, Essays, and Memoir* (New York: Library of America, 1998), 787. It is worth noting that Welty wrote her essay in response to what she perceived as a practice in literary criticism of using "regional" as code for "provincial." Ironically, Welty's ardent defense of the local as grounds for exploring indelible themes with appeal beyond the confines of a given region became an instrument in the hands of Hoffman and others for asserting that literature of "the South"—defined in monolithic terms—is unique and exceptional.

12. Melanie Benson Taylor, *Reconstructing the Native South: American Indian Literature and the Lost Cause* (Athens: University of Georgia Press, 2011), 2.

13. Taylor, *Reconstructing the Native South*, 2–3.

14. Robert Penn Warren, *Flood: A Romance of Our Time* (New York: Random House, 1964; Baton Rouge: Louisiana State University Press, 2003), 249. Citations refer to the 2003 edition and will subsequently appear parenthetically in the main text.

15. Warren to Rubin, 378.

16. Robert Penn Warren, "An Interview in New Haven with Robert Penn Warren," interview by Richard B. Sale, in *Critical Essays on Robert Penn Warren*, ed. William Bedford Clark (Boston: G. K. Hall, 1981), 82. See also Joseph Blotner, *Robert Penn Warren: A Biography* (New York: Random House, 1977), 354.

17. Warren, "An Interview in New Haven with Robert Penn Warren," 82.

18. Davidson, *The Tennessee*, 251.

19. Shapiro, "The Southern Agrarians and the Tennessee Valley Authority," 795–96. In a footnote, Shapiro references an interview he conducted with Warren in 1965, disclosing that the author expressed his support for the TVA (791). This stance is at odds with the skepticism and cynicism about the TVA project that pervades *Flood*, which is a product of the disillusionment that Brad feels when faced with the recognition that "progress" in the form of development is irreversible and that nostalgic investment in an idealized past is a futile endeavor.

20. Jacqueline Rose, *States of Fantasy* (Oxford: Clarendon Press, 1996), 4.

21. Greeson, *Our South*, 1.

22. See Lewis P. Simpson, "The Closure of History in Postsouthern America," in *The Brazen Face of History: Studies in the Literary Consciousness of America* (Baton Rouge: Louisiana State University Press, 1980), 255–72, for the original conception of "postsouthern" as a critical concept. Simpson identifies the emergence of "a postsouthern America" in the last quarter of the twentieth century and sounds the death knell for the regional artistic mindset that enabled the "Southern Renascence" in literature (269). For Simpson, Walker Percy's fiction is emblematic of this dramatic shift in sensibilities. My understanding of how Warren portrays Brad Tolliver's anxious response to Disneyfication and accelerated development is influenced by Stephen Flinn Young, "Post-southernism: The Southern Sensibility in Postmodern Sculpture," *Southern Quarterly* 27, no. 1 (1989): 41–60, Humanities International Complete. Young contends that postsouthern art questions the "sense of place" often deemed elemental to the "southern sensibility" defined in terms of regional distinctiveness, and he considers whether "we may have even become prisoners of our own fascination" with "sense of place" given that "when change overtakes us and place, even the place we call the South, is not the place it used to be, anxiety strikes" (41). The efficacy of deploying "postsouthern" to add a regional inflection to the postmodern has been a topic of critical debate. See, for example, Michael Kreyling, "Parody and Postsouthernness," in *Inventing Southern Literature*, 148–66, and Martyn Bone, *The Postsouthern Sense of Place in Contemporary Fiction*. Bone's book includes a chapter titled "Toward a Postsouthern Sense of Place: Robert Penn Warren's *A Place to Come To* and Walker Percy's *The Moviegoer*," 55–74, in which he argues that Warren's last novel, published in 1977, amounts to a postsouthern parody calling into question

foundational concepts such as "the South," "southern literature," and "sense of place" and signaling a breakdown of meaning for terms associated with a Southern Agrarian aesthetics of place rooted in opposition to development. I contend that Warren's *Flood* shows the author moving "toward a postsouthern sense of place" at an even earlier stage.

23. Ronald A. Foresta, *The Land Between the Lakes: A Geography of the Forgotten Future* (Knoxville: University of Tennessee Press, 2013), 1.

24. Foresta, *The Land Between the Lakes*, 2.

25. Zackary Vernon, in "A Yearning for the Mud: Metafiction, Metafilm, and Bioregionalism in Robert Penn Warren's *Flood*," *Mississippi Quarterly* 76, no. 4 (2024): 371, ProjectMuse, notes a tendency among critics who have responded unfavorably to *Flood* to read the novel as putting agrarianism and industrialization into binary opposition. I agree with Vernon that "such a reading is reductive" and that instead "Warren creates a complex interrogation of both agrarianism and industrialization."

26. Truscello, *Infrastructural Brutalism*, 63.

27. Truscello, *Infrastructural Brutalism*, 42.

28. Amy Greene, *Long Man* (New York: Knopf, 2014), 3. Subsequent citations are to this edition and will appear parenthetically in the main text.

29. Mark Currie, *About Time: Narrative, Fiction, and the Philosophy of Time* (Edinburgh: Edinburgh University Press, 2007), 6.

30. Currie, *About Time*, 13.

31. Currie, *About Time*, 29, 31.

32. Narratological prolepsis is one of three forms that Currie defines in "Prolepsis," the third chapter of his book; the others are structural prolepsis and rhetorical prolepsis (Currie, *About Time*, 31). While I recognize the critical potential for applying the latter concepts to *Long Man*, the nature of this chapter requires a streamlined approach. Since the focus is on narratological prolepsis and the characters' perception of time within the narrated world, I am using the present tense to discuss the events unfolding in the primary historical setting as the evacuation deadline and the deluge loomed. The rationale is that these events seem present to the reader learning about them for the first time even though the narrator recounts them in the preterite (or simple past) tense as already having taken place.

33. Currie, *About Time*, 29–30.

34. Truscello, *Infrastructural Brutalism*, 58.

CODA

1. Tennessee Valley Authority (@TVANews). "We have checked our records, and it doesn't appear the [sic] Loki has been spotted at any of our facilities. If we spot him we will reach out to the Time Variance Authority (aka the other TVA). @Marvel @LokiOfficial #loki." Twitter, April 5, 2021. https://twitter.com/TVAnews/status/1379078898013573121.

2. "Walter Simonson on the Time Variance Authority," The Comics Cube, June 8, 2021, YouTube video, 3:06, https://youtu.be/DURfbGa6GHo.

3. "Walter Simonson on the Time Variance Authority."

4. Jamie McGee and Clifford Krauss, "Tennessee Residents Endure Blackouts and Are Warned to Save Power," *New York Times*, December 23, 2022, ProQuest.

5. Tennessee Valley Authority, "Leadership and Innovation on a Path to Net-Zero: TVA and the Energy System of the Future," May 6, 2021, https://tva-azr-eastus-cdn-ep-tvawcm-prd.azureedge.net/cdn-tvawcma/docs/default-source/environment/carbon-report.pdf?sfvrsn=4971bcca_2, 4.

6. Tennessee Valley Authority, "Leadership and Innovation on a Path to Net-Zero," 4.

7. Robert Kunzig, "A Controversial Model for America's Climate Future," *The Atlantic*, July 25, 2023, https://www.theatlantic.com/science/archive/2023/07/tennessee-valley-authority-energy-transition-nuclear/674729/.

8. Kunzig, "A Controversial Model for America's Climate Future."

9. Cormac McCarthy, *The Road* (New York: Vintage, 2006), 19.

10. McCarthy, *The Road*, 20.

11. McCarthy, *The Road*, 20.

12. McCarthy, *The Road*, 20.

13. Hurley and Insko, "Introduction: The Infrastructure of Emergency," 348.

BIBLIOGRAPHY

Adams, Frank, and Myles Horton. *Unearthing Seeds of Fire: The Idea of Highlander*. Winston-Salem, NC: J. F. Blair, 1975.

Adorno, Theodor. "Functionalism Today." In *Rethinking Architecture: A Reader in Cultural Theory*, edited by Neil Leach, 4–18. New York: Routledge, 1997.

Adorno, Theodor, and Max Horkheimer. "The Culture Industry: Enlightenment as Mass Deception." In *Dialectic of Enlightenment*, translated by John Cumming, 120–67. New York: Verso, 2008.

Agamben, Giorgio. *Homo Sacer: Sovereign Power and Bare Life*. In *The Omnibus Homo Sacer*, 1–159. Stanford, CA: Stanford University Press, 2017.

Agee, James. *Complete Journalism, Articles, Book Reviews, and Manuscripts*, edited by Paul Ashdown. Knoxville: University of Tennessee Press, 2013.

Agee, James. "Tennessee Valley Authority." In Agee, *Complete Journalism*, 77–90.

Agee, James. "T.V.A.: Work in the Valley." In Agee, *Complete Journalism*, 197–222.

Anderson, Benedict. *Imagined Communities: Reflections on the Origin and Spread of Nationalism*. New York: Verso, 1991.

Appel, Hannah. "Infrastructural Time." In *The Promise of Infrastructure*, edited by Nikhil Anand, Akhil Gupta, and Hannah Appel, Location 974–1390. Durham, NC: Duke University Press, 2018. Kindle.

Arent, Arthur. *Power*. In *Federal Theatre Plays*, edited by Pierre De Rohan, 3–91. New York: Da Capo Press, 1973.

Arent, Arthur. "The Technique of the Living Newspaper." *Theatre Quarterly* 1, no. 4 (1971): 57–59.

"Art for the People." TVA: Tennessee Valley Authority. Accessed December 8, 2022. https://www.tva.com/about-tva/our-history/built-for-the-people/art-for-the-people.

"The Artist with a Camera." TVA: Tennessee Valley Authority. Accessed November 22, 2022. https://www.tva.gov/About-TVA/Our-History/heritage/The-Artist-With-a-Camera.

Atkinson, Brooks. "'Power' Produced by the Living Newspaper Under Federal Theatre Auspices." *New York Times*, February 24, 1937. TimesMachine. Accessed October 26, 2024. https://timesmachine.nytimes.com/browser/.

Awiakta, Marilou. *Selu: Seeking the Corn-Mother's Wisdom*. Golden, CO: Fulcrum Publishing, 1993.

Bacon, Mardges. "Le Corbusier and Postwar America: The TVA and *Béton Brut.*" *Journal of the Society of Architectural Historians* 74, no. 1 (2015): 13–40, https://doi.org/10.1525/jsah.2015.74.1.13.

Baker, Houston, Jr. *Turning South Again: Re-thinking Modernism/Re-reading Booker T.* Durham, NC: Duke University Press, 2001.

Baker, Houston, Jr., and Dana D. Nelson, eds. "Violence, the Body and 'The South.'" Special issue, *American Literature* 73, no. 2 (June 2001): 231–44, JSTOR.

Barry, John M. *Rising Tide: The Great Mississippi Flood of 1927.* New York: Simon and Schuster, 1997.

Baudrillard, Jean. "The Precession of Simulacra." In *Simulacra and Simulation,* translated by Sheila Faria Glaser, 1–42. Ann Arbor: University of Michigan Press, 1994.

Beard, Janet. *The Atomic City Girls.* New York: HarperCollins, 2018.

Beckert, Sven. *Empire of Cotton: A Global History.* New York: Vintage Books, 2014.

Benjamin, Walter. *The Arcades Project.* Translated by Howard Eiland and Kevin McLaughlin. Cambridge, MA: Belknap Press, 1999.

Benjamin, Walter. "The Author as Producer." In *Walter Benjamin: Selected Writings,* edited by Michael W. Jennings, Howard Eiland, and Gary Smith, translated by Rodney Livingstone et al., vol. 2, part 2, *1931–1934,* 768–82. Cambridge, MA: Harvard University Press, 1999.

Benjamin, Walter. "On the Concept of History." In *Walter Benjamin: Selected Writings,* edited by Howard Eiland and Michael W. Jennings, translated by Edmund Jephcott, vol. 4, *1938–1940,* 389–400. Cambridge, MA: Harvard University Press, 2006.

Benjamin, Walter. "The Work of Art in the Age of Its Technological Reproducibility." In *The Work of Art in the Age of Its Technological Reproducibility, and Other Writings on Media,* edited by Michael W. Jennings, Brigid Doherty, and Thomas Y. Levin, translated by E. F. N. Jephcott, Howard Eiland, and Rodney Livingstone, 19–55. Cambridge, MA: Harvard University Press, 2008.

Benson, Melanie R. *Disturbing Calculations: The Economics of Identity in Postcolonial Southern Literature, 1912–2002.* Athens: University of Georgia Press, 2008.

Berman, Marshall. *All That Is Solid Melts into Air: The Experience of Modernity.* New York: Penguin, 1988.

Black, Brian. "Authority in the Valley: TVA in *Wild River* and the Popular Media, 1930–1940." *Journal of American Culture* 8, no. 2 (1995): 1–14, Wiley Online Library.

Blotner, Joseph. *Robert Penn Warren: A Biography.* New York: Random House, 1977.

Böger, Astrid. *People's Lives, Public Images: The New Deal Documentary Aesthetic.* Tübingen, Germany: Gunter Narr Verlag, 2001.

Bone, Martyn. *The Postsouthern Sense of Place in Contemporary Fiction.* Baton Rouge: Louisiana State University Press, 2005.

Bone, Martyn. *Where the New World Is: Literature About the U.S. South at Global Scales.* Athens: University of Georgia Press, 2018.

Bourke-White, Margaret. Photographs of Fort Peck Dam Project. *Life,* November 23, 1936.

Bourne, Joel K., Jr. "Coal's Other Dark Side: Toxic Ash That Can Poison Water and People," *National Geographic.* February 19, 2019, https://www.nationalgeographic.com/environment/article/coal-other-dark-side-toxic-ash.

Branscome, James. "Commentary: TVA Owes Eastern Kentucky Reparations for Strip Mining's Role in Flooding." Accessed October 25, 2024. *Daily Yonder*, August 15, 2022, https://dailyyonder.com/commentary-unprecedented-and-unnecessary-kentuckys-flooding-and-its-mining-history/2022/08/15/.

Browder, Laura. *Rousing the Nation: Radical Culture in Depression America*. Amherst: University of Massachusetts Press, 1998.

Buell, Frederick. "A Short History of Oil Cultures: Or, the Marriage of Catastrophe and Exuberance." *Journal of American Studies* 46, no. 2 (May 2012): 273–93.

Button, Gregory. *Disaster Culture: Knowledge and Uncertainty in the Wake of Human and Environmental Catastrophe*. Walnut Creek, CA: Left Coast Press, 2010.

Cahill, Holger. "American Folk Art." In *American Folk Art: The Art of the Common Man: The Art of the Common Man in America, 1750–1900*. 1932. New York: Arno Press for the Museum of Modern Art, 1969.

Caldwell, Erskine, and Margaret Bourke-White. *You Have Seen Their Faces*. New York: Modern Age Books, 1937. Reprinted with a foreword by Alan Trachtenberg. Athens: University of Georgia Press, 1995.

Capra, Frank, dir. *Mr. Smith Goes to Washington*. 1939; Sony Pictures Home Entertainment, 2018. Blu-ray Disc.

Caudill, Harry M. *Night Comes to the Cumberlands: A Biography of a Depressed Area*. Boston: Little, Brown, 1962.

Caudill, Harry M. "The Rape of the Appalachians." *Atlantic Monthly*, April 1962.

Chandler, William U. *The Myth of TVA: Conservation and Development in the Tennessee Valley, 1933–1983*. Cambridge, MA: Ballinger Publishing, 1984.

Chapman, Jefferson. *Tellico Archaeology: 12,000 Years of Native American History*. Knoxville: University of Tennessee Press, 1985.

Chase, Donald. "Watershed: Elia Kazan's *Wild River*." *Film Comment* 32, no. 6 (November–December 1996): 10–15, JSTOR.

Chase, Stuart. *A New Deal*. New York: Macmillan, 1932.

Colignon, Richard A. *Power Plays: Critical Events in the Institutionalization of the Tennessee Valley Authority*. Albany: State University of New York Press, 1997.

Cook, Sylvia Jenkins. *From Tobacco Road to Route 66: The Southern Poor White in Fiction*. Chapel Hill: University of North Carolina Press, [1976] 2012.

Culvahouse, Tim, ed. *The Tennessee Valley Authority: Design and Persuasion*. New York: Princeton Architectural Press, 2007.

Currie, Mark. *About Time: Narrative, Fiction, and the Philosophy of Time*. Edinburgh: Edinburgh University Press, 2006.

"David E. Lilienthal, Director of TVA, Opens Exhibition of TVA Architecture and Design at Museum of Modern Art." Accessed September 29, 2024, https://assets.moma.org/documents/moma_press-release_325220.pdf. Museum of Modern Art. New York, NY.

Davidson, Donald. "The Artist as Southerner." *Saturday Review of Literature*, May 15, 1926.

Davidson, Donald. *The Attack on Leviathan: Regionalism and Nationalism in the United States*. Chapel Hill: University of North Carolina Press, 1938.

Davidson, Donald. *The Tennessee*. Vol. 2, *The New River: Civil War to TVA*. New York: Rinehart, 1948.

Daws, Laura Beth, and Susan L. Brinson. *The Greater Good: Media, Family Removal, and Dam Construction in Northern Alabama*. Tuscaloosa: University of Alabama Press, 2019.

Deal, Borden. *Dunbar's Cove*. New York: Scribner's, 1957.

Denning, Michael. *The Cultural Front: The Laboring of American Culture in the Twentieth Century*. New York: Verso, 1997.

De Valck, Marijke. *Film Festivals: From European Geopolitics to Global Cinephilia*. Amsterdam: Amsterdam University Press, 2007.

Dewan, Shaila. "Coal Ash Spill Revives Issue of Its Hazards." *New York Times*, December 24, 2008, ProQuest.

Diamanti, Jeff. "Infrastructure." In *Fueling Culture: 101 Words for Energy and Environment*, edited by Imre Szeman, Jennifer Wenzel, and Patricia Yaeger, 198–201. New York: Fordham University Press, 2017.

Di Bello, Patrizia, Colette Wilson, and Shamoon Zamir, eds. *The Photobook: From Talbot to Ruscha and Beyond*. New York: Routledge, 2020.

Duarte-Gray, Isabel. "Tennessee Valley Authority." Poetry Foundation. Accessed July 25, 2023, https://www.poetryfoundation.org/poems/156607/tennesse-valley-authority.

Duck, Leigh Anne. *The Nation's Regions: Southern Modernism, Segregation, and U.S. Nationalism*. Athens: University of Georgia Press, 2006.

Duck, Leigh Anne. "Southern Nonidentity." *Safundi* 9, no. 3 (July 2008): 319–30, Scopus.

Duffus, R. L., and Charles Krutch. *The Valley and Its People: A Portrait of TVA*. New York: Knopf, 1946.

Dunaway, Finis. *Natural Visions: The Power of Images in American Environmental Reform*. Chicago: University of Chicago Press, 2016.

Egerton, John. *The Americanization of Dixie: The Southernization of America*. New York: Harper & Row, 1974.

Eisen, Kurt. "Circulating *Power*: National Theatre as Public Utility in the Federal Theatre Project." *Theatre Symposium: A Journal of the Southeastern Theatre Conference* 9 (2001): 38–44, ProQuest.

"Eisenhower Points to the T.V.A. as 'Creeping Socialism.'" *New York Times*, June 8, 1953. TimesMachine. Accessed October 26, 2024, https://timesmachine.nytimes.com/timesmachine/1953/06/18/83725405.html.

Ekbladh, David. "'Mr. TVA': Grass-Roots Development, David Lilienthal, and the Rise and Fall of the Tennessee Valley Authority as a Symbol for U.S. Overseas Development, 1933–1973." *Diplomatic History* 26, no. 1 (July 2002): 335–74.

Ezzell, Patricia Bernard. *TVA Photography, 1963–2008*. Jackson: University Press of Mississippi, 2008.

Ezzell, Patricia Bernard. *TVA Photography: Thirty Years of Life in the Tennessee Valley*. Jackson: University Press of Mississippi, 2003.

Federal Theatre Project Collection. Music Division, Library of Congress, Washington, DC.

Fitzgerald, Michael R., and Stephen J. Rechichar. *The Consequences of Administrative Decision: TVA's Economic Development Mission and Intragovernment Regulation*. Knoxville: Bureau of Public Administration, University of Tennessee, 1983.

Flanagan, Hallie. *Arena: The History of the Federal Theatre.* New York: B. Blom, [1940] 1965.
Foresta, Ronald A. *The Land Between the Lakes: A Geography of the Forgotten Future.* Knoxville: University of Tennessee Press, 2013.
Glen, John M. *Highlander: No Ordinary School, 1932–1962.* Lexington: University Press of Kentucky, 2021.
Goldman, Arnold. "Life and Death of the Living Newspaper Unit." *Theatre Quarterly* 3, no. 9 (1973): 69–89.
Graham, Allison. *Framing the South: Hollywood, Television, and Race during the Civil Rights Struggle.* Baltimore: Johns Hopkins University Press, 2001.
Grant, Nancy L. *TVA and Black Americans: Planning for the Status Quo.* Philadelphia: Temple University Press, 1990.
Greene, Amy. *Long Man.* New York: Knopf, 2014.
Greeson, Jennifer Rae. *Our South: Geographic Fantasy and the Rise of National Literature.* Cambridge, MA: Harvard University Press, 2010.
Guarino, Mark. "Tennessee Spill Revives Coal Ash Controversy." *Christian Science Monitor*, December 31, 2008. *CSMonitor.com*. Accessed August 16, 2022, https://www.csmonitor.com/Environment/2008/1231/tennessee-spill-revives-coal-ash-controversy.
Gutheim, Frederick A. "Tennessee Valley Authority: A New Phase in Architecture." *Magazine of Art* 33 (September 1940): 516–31.
Hammid, Alexander, dir. *The Valley of the Tennessee.* Washington, DC: Office of War Information, 1944. National Archives. YouTube, https://youtu.be/SfJt-W7fwTY?feature=shared.
Hargrove, Erwin C. *Prisoners of Myth: The Leadership of the TVA, 1933–1990.* Princeton, NJ: Princeton University Press, 1994.
Hendrickson, Paul. *Bound for Glory: America in Color, 1939–43.* New York: Harry N. Abrams, 2004.
Hicks, Jeremy. *Dziga Vertov: Defining Documentary.* London: I.B. Tauris, 2007.
Higgott, Andrew, and Timothy Wray. Introduction to *Camera Constructs: Photography, Architecture and the Modern City*, edited by Higgott and Wray, 1–22. Burlington, VT: Ashgate, 2012.
Hoffman, Frederick J. "The Sense of Place." In *South: Modern Southern Literature in Its Cultural Setting*, edited by Louis D. Rubin Jr. and Robert D. Jacobs. Garden City, NY: Dolphin Books, 1961. 60–75.
Holman, C. Hugh. "No More Monoliths, Please: Continuities in the Multi-Souths." In *Southern Literature in Transition: Heritage and Promise*, edited by Philip Castille and William Osborne, xiii–xxiv. Memphis: Memphis State University Press, 1983.
Hunter, Jefferson. *Image and Word: The Interaction of Twentieth-Century Photographs and Texts.* Cambridge, MA: Harvard University Press, 1987.
Hurley, Jessica, and Jeffrey Insko. "Introduction: The Infrastructure of Emergency." In "The Infrastructure of Emergency." Special issue, *American Literature* 93, no. 3 (2021): 345–59, MLA International Bibliography.
Huyssen, Andreas. *After the Great Divide: Modernism, Mass Culture, Postmodernism.* Bloomington: Indiana University Press, 1987.

Isenberg, Nancy. *White Trash: The 400-Year Untold History of Class in America*. New York: Penguin, 2017.

Jameson, Fredric. *The Antinomies of Realism*. New York: Verso, 2015.

Jameson, Fredric. *Postmodernism, or, The Cultural Logic of Late Capitalism*. Durham, NC: Duke University Press, 1991.

Johnson, Walter. *River of Dark Dreams: Slavery and Empire in the Cotton Kingdom*. Cambridge, MA: Harvard University Press, 2013.

Katz, Barry M. "Ideology and Engineering in the Tennessee Valley." In Culvahouse, *The Tennessee Valley Authority*, 80–95.

Katznelson, Ira. *Fear Itself: The New Deal and the Origins of Our Time*. New York: Liveright, 2013.

Kazan, Elia. *Elia Kazan: A Life*. New York: Knopf, 1988.

Kazan, Elia, dir. *Wild River*. 1960; Los Angeles, CA: 20th Century Fox Home Video, 2013. DVD.

Kennedy, John F. "Remarks on 30th Anniversary of Tennessee Valley Authority, Muscle Shoals, Alabama, 18 May 1963," John F. Kennedy Presidential Library and Museum. Accessed October 25, 2024. https://www.jfklibrary.org/Asset-Viewer/Archives/JFKPOF-044-021.aspx.

Koppes, Clayton R., and Gregory D. Black. "What to Show the World: The Office of War Information and Hollywood, 1942–1945." *Journal of American History* 64, no. 1 (June 1977): 87–105, JSTOR.

Kotlowski, Dean J. "Selling America to the World: The Office of War Information's 'The Town' (1945) and the 'American Scene' Series." *Australasian Journal of American Studies* 35, no. 1 (July 2016): 80, JSTOR.

Kreyling, Michael. *Inventing Southern Literature*. Jackson: University Press of Mississippi, 1998.

Kunzig, Robert. "A Controversial Model for America's Climate Future." *The Atlantic*, July 25, 2023. https://www.theatlantic.com/science/archive/2023/07/tennessee-valley-authority-energy-transition-nuclear/674729/.

Larkin, Brian. "The Politics and Poetics of Infrastructure." *Annual Review of Anthropology* 42 (2013): 327–43, JSTOR.

Lassiter, Matthew D., and Joseph Crespino, eds. *The Myth of Southern Exceptionalism*. New York: Oxford University Press, 2009.

Lawton, Anna. "Rhythmic Montage in the Films of Dziga Vertov: A Poetic Use of the Language of Cinema." *Pacific Coast Philology* 13 (1978): 44–50, JSTOR.

Lilienthal, David E. "Author's Preface to the Edition of 1953." *TVA: Democracy on the March*. Twentieth Anniversary edition, ix–xix. New York: Harper & Row, 1953.

Lilienthal, David E. *The Journals of David E. Lilienthal*. Vol. 1, *The TVA Years, 1939–1945*. New York: Harper & Row, 1964.

Lilienthal, David E. *TVA: Democracy on the March*. New York: Pocket Books, 1944.

Lilienthal, David E. *TVA: Democracy on the March: Twentieth Anniversary Edition*. New York: Harper & Row, 1953.

Lorentz, Pare. *FDR's Moviemaker: Memoirs & Scripts*. Reno: University of Nevada Press, 1992.

Lorentz, Pare, dir. *The River*. Our Daily Bread *and Other Films of the Great Depression*. Chatsworth, CA: Image Entertainment, [1937] 1999.

Macy, Christine, and Sarah Bonnemaison. *Architecture and Nature: Creating the American Landscape*. New York: Routledge, 2003.

Mally, Lynn. "The Americanization of the Soviet Living Newspaper." *The Carl Beck Papers in Russian and East European Studies*, no. 1903 (2008): 1–40, https://doi.org/10.5195/cbp.2008.140.

Martin, Roscoe C. *TVA: The First Twenty Years*. Tuscaloosa: University of Alabama Press and Knoxville: University of Tennessee Press, 1956.

Mathews, Jane DeHart. *The Federal Theatre, 1935–1939: Plays, Relief, and Politics*. Princeton, NJ: Princeton University Press, 1967.

McCarthy, Cormac. *The Road*. New York: Vintage, 2006.

McCully, Patrick. *Silenced Rivers: The Ecology and Politics of Large Dams*. Atlantic Highlands, NJ: Zeb Books, 1996.

McDonald, Michael J., and John Muldowny. *TVA and the Dispossessed: The Resettlement of Population in the Norris Dam Area*. Knoxville: University of Tennessee Press, 1982.

McElvaine, Robert S. *The Great Depression: America, 1929–1941*. New York: Times Books, 1984.

McGee, Jamie, and Clifford Krauss. "Tennessee Residents Endure Blackouts and Are Warned to Save Power." *New York Times*, December 23, 2022, ProQuest.

McKee, Kathryn, and Annette Trefzer, eds. "Global Contexts, Local Literatures: The New Southern Studies." Special issue, *American Literature* 78, no. 4 (December 2006), JSTOR.

Metropolitan Playhouse. "Power." Accessed October 26, 2024, https://metropolitanplayhouse.org/powerinfo.htm.

Meyers, Sidney, and Jay Leyda, dir. *People of the Cumberland*. New York: Frontier Films, 1937. National Film Preservation Foundation, https://www.filmpreservation.org/sponsored-films/screening-room/people-of-the-cumberland-1937.

Miller, Barbara A., and Richard B. Reidinger. *Comprehensive River Basin Development: The Tennessee Valley Authority*, World Bank Technical Paper, No. 416. Washington, DC: World Bank, 1998.

Millichap, Joseph R. *These Vivid American Documents: Walker Evans, Dorothea Lange, and FSA Photography*. Knoxville: University of Tennessee Press, 2024.

Morgan, Arthur E. *The Making of the TVA*. Buffalo, NY: Prometheus Books, 1974.

Mumford, Lewis. "The Architecture of Power." *New Yorker*, June 7, 1941. *New Yorker.com*. Accessed September 29, 2024, https://archives.newyorker.com/newyorker/1941-06-07/flipbook/058/.

Murray, Robin L., and Joseph K. Heumann. *Ecology and Popular Film: Cinema on the Edge*. Albany: State University of New York Press, 2009.

Musher, Sharon Ann. *Democratic Art: The New Deal's Influence on American Culture*. Chicago: University of Chicago Press, 2015.

National Emergency Council. *Report on Economic Conditions of the South.* Washington, DC: Government Printing Office, 1938. Internet Archive. Open Library. https://archive.org/details/reportoneconomicoonati.

National Resources Committee. *Regional Factors in National Planning and Development.* Washington, DC: US Government Printing Office, 1935. New York: Creative Media Partners, 2018.

Neve, Brian. *Elia Kazan: The Cinema of an American Outsider.* New York: I.B. Tauris, 2009.

Nixon, Rob. *Slow Violence and the Environmentalism of the Poor.* Cambridge, MA: Harvard University Press, 2013.

"Norris Dam State Park, Tennessee: Lenoir Museum—Rice Grist Mill—Crosby Threshing Barn." Nashville: Tennessee Department of Environment and Conservation. November 22, 2021. https://tnstateparks.com/assets/pdf/additional-content/norris_dam_museum_brochure.pdf.

Nye, David E. *American Technological Sublime.* Cambridge, MA: MIT Press, 1994.

Nye, David E. "The Great White Way." In *Energy Humanities: An Anthology,* edited by Imre Szeman and Dominic Boyer, 71–79. Baltimore: Johns Hopkins University Press, 2017.

O'Brien, Michael. *The Idea of the American South, 1920–1941.* Baltimore: Johns Hopkins University Press, 1979.

Odum, Howard W. "Regionalism vs. Sectionalism in the South's Place in the National Economy." *Journal of Social Forces* 12 (March 1934): 338–54.

Odum, Howard W. *Southern Regions of the United States.* Chapel Hill: University of North Carolina Press, 1936.

Parrish, Susan Scott. *The Flood Year 1927: A Cultural History.* Princeton, NJ: Princeton University Press, 2017.

Patel, Kiran Klaus. *The New Deal: A Global History.* Princeton, NJ: Princeton University Press, 2016.

Peacock, James L., Harry L. Watson, and Carrie R. Matthews, eds. *The American South in a Global World.* Chapel Hill: University of North Carolina Press, 2005.

Percy, William Alexander. *Lanterns on the Levee: Recollections of a Planter's Son.* Baton Rouge: Louisiana State University Press, [1941] 2004.

Phillips, Stephen Bennett. *Margaret Bourke-White: Photography of Design, 1927–1936.* New York: Rizzoli, 2003.

Pritchett, C. Herman. *The Tennessee Valley Authority: A Study in Public Administration.* Chapel Hill: University of North Carolina Press, [1943] 2014.

Puckett, John. *Five Photo-Textual Documentaries.* Ann Arbor: UMI Research Press, 1984.

Quinn, Susan. *Furious Improvisation: How the WPA and a Cast of Thousands Made High Art out of Desperate Times.* New York: Bloomsbury, 2011.

Rabinowitz, Paula. "1930s Documentary and Visual Culture." In *The Wiley-Blackwell History of American Film,* edited by Cynthia Lucia, Roy Grundemann, and Art Simon, 133–55. Malden, MA: Blackwell Publishing, 2012.

"Reviews—Power." Metropolitan Playhouse. Accessed October 26, 2024. https://metropolitanplayhouse.org/powerreview.

Ring, Natalie J. *The Problem South: Region, Empire, and the New Liberal State, 1880–1930.* Athens: University of Georgia Press, 2012.

Roholl, Marja. "An Invasion of a Different Kind: The Office of War Information and 'The Projection of America' Propaganda in the Netherlands, 1944–1945." In Hans Bak, Frank Mehring, and Mathilde Roza, eds., *Politics and Cultures of Liberation: Media, Memory, and Projections of Democracy*, 17–38. Boston: Brill, 2018.

Rollins, Peter C. "Ideology and Film Rhetoric: Three Documentaries of the New Deal Era (1936–1941)." In *Hollywood as Historian: American Film in A Cultural Context*, 32–48. Revised ed., edited by Rollins. Lexington: University Press of Kentucky, 1983.

Roosevelt, Franklin Delano. "Inaugural Address," edited by Gerhard Peters and John T. Woolley. *The American Presidency Project*. University of California, Santa Barbara. Accessed October 25, 2024. https://www.presidency.ucsb.edu/documents/inaugural-address-8.

Roosevelt, Franklin Delano. "Informal Extemporaneous Remarks at Sheffield, Alabama on Muscle Shoals Inspection Trip," edited by Gerhard Peters and John T. Woolley. *The American Presidency Project*. University of California, Santa Barbara. Accessed October 25, 2024. https://www.presidency.ucsb.edu/documents/informal-extemporaneous-remarks-sheffield-alabama-muscle-shoals-inspection-trip.

Roosevelt, Franklin Delano. "Message to Congress Suggesting the Tennessee Valley Authority," April 10, 1933, edited by Gerhard Peters and John T. Woolley. *The American Presidency Project*. University of California, Santa Barbara. Accessed October 25, 2024. https://www.presidency.ucsb.edu/node/208057.

Rose, Jacqueline. *States of Fantasy*. Oxford: Clarendon Press, 1996.

Rubenstein, Michael, Bruce Robbins, and Sophia Beal. "Infrastructuralism: An Introduction." *Modern Fiction Studies* 61, no. 4 (Winter 2013): 575–86, JSTOR.

Rubenstein, Michael. *Public Works: Infrastructure, Irish Modernism, and the Postcolonial*. Notre Dame, IN: University of Notre Dame Press, 2010.

Saal, Ilka. *New Deal Theater: The Vernacular Tradition in American Political Theater*. New York: Palgrave Macmillan, 2007.

Sachs, Avigail. *The Garden in the Machine: Planning and Democracy in the Tennessee Valley Authority*. Charlottesville: University of Virginia Press, 2023.

Salvemini, Chris. "Hidden Knoxville Native's Mural Found, Restored in Norris Dam." *Knox News*. October 21, 2018. https://www.knoxnews.com/story/news/2018/10/17/norris-dam-mural-robert-birdwell-restored/1661684002/.

Saxon, Lyle. *Father Mississippi: The Story of the Great Flood of 1927*. Gretna, LA: Pelican Publishing, [1927] 2006.

Schivelbusch, Wolfgang. *The Three New Deals: Reflections on Roosevelt's America, Mussolini's Italy, and Hitler's Germany, 1933–1939*. New York: Henry Holt, 2006.

Scott, Ian. *In Capra's Shadow: The Life and Career of Screenwriter Robert Riskin*. Lexington: University Press of Kentucky, 2006.

Selznick, Philip. *TVA and the Grass Roots: A Study in the Sociology of Formal Organization*. Berkeley and Los Angeles: University of California Press, 1953.

Shapiro, Edward. "The Southern Agrarians and the Tennessee Valley Authority." *American Quarterly* 22, no. 4 (Winter 1970): 791–806.

Shloss, Carol. *In Visible Light: Photography and the American Writer, 1840–1940*. New York: Oxford University Press, 1987.

Simpson, Lewis P. "The Closure of History in Postsouthern America." In *The Brazen Face of History: Studies in the Literary Consciousness of America*, 255–72. Baton Rouge: Louisiana State University Press, 1980.

Smith, Jon. "Toward a Postpostpolitical Southern Studies: On the Limits of the 'Creating and Consuming' Paradigm." In *Creating and Consuming the American South*, edited by Martyn Bone, Brian Ward, and William A. Link, 72–96. Gainesville: University Press of Florida, 2015.

Smith, Jon, and Deborah Cohn, eds. *Look Away!: The U.S. South in the New World Studies*. Durham, NC: Duke University Press, 2004.

Smith, Todd. "Almost Fully Modern: The TVA's Visual Art Campaign." In Culvahouse, *The Tennessee Valley Authority*, 104–19.

Snyder, Robert L. *Pare Lorentz and the Documentary Film*. Reno: University of Nevada Press, 1994.

Soloski, Alex. "Metropolitan Playhouse Revives a 1937 'Living Newspaper.'" *Village Voice*, March 25, 2009. http://www.villagevoice.com/2009/03/25/metropolitan-playhouse-revives-1937-living-newspaper/.

Sontag, Susan. "Fascinating Fascism." *New York Review of Books*, February 6, 1975. 23–30. Accessed November 25, 2022, https://www.nybooks.com/articles/1975/02/06/fascinating-fascism/.

Star, Susan Leigh. "The Ethnography of Infrastructure." *American Behavioral Scientist* 43, no. 3 (1999): 377–91.

Stern, Robert A. M. *Modern Classicism*. New York: Rizzoli, 1988.

Szeman, Imre. "Literature and Energy Futures." In Yaeger, "Editor's Column: Literature in the Ages of Wood, Tallow, Coal, Whale Oil, Gasoline, and Other Energy Sources," 323–25.

Taylor, Melanie Benson. *Reconstructing the Native South: American Indian Literature and the Lost Cause*. Athens: University of Georgia Press, 2011.

Tennessee Valley Authority. "Leadership & Innovation on a Path to Net-Zero: TVA and the Energy System of the Future." May 6, 2021. https://www.tva.com/environment/environmental-stewardship/sustainability/carbon-report.

Tillman, David A. *Coal-Fired Electricity and Emissions Control: Efficiency and Effectiveness*. Cambridge, MA: Butterworth-Heinemann, 2018.

Truscello, Michael. *Infrastructural Brutalism: Art and the Necropolitics of Infrastructure*. Cambridge, MA: MIT Press, 2020.

Turner, Frederick Jackson. *The Frontier in American History*. New York: Henry Holt, 1953. Reprint, New York: Dover, 1996.

TVA Architecture, as Shown at the Museum of Modern Art. Knoxville: Tennessee Valley Authority, 1941.

"T.V.A. Architecture and Design." Museum of Modern Art. Accessed September 29, 2024. https://www.moma.org/calendar/exhibitions/2087.

"The TVA and the Relocation of Mattie Randolph." Educator Resources. National Archives, Washington, DC. August 15, 2016. https://www.archives.gov/education/lessons/tva-relocation.html.

Valasek, Thomas E. "Alexander Hammid: A Survey of His Film-Making Career." *Film Culture* 67–69 (1979): 250–322.
Vance, Rupert B. *Human Geography of the South: A Study in Regional Resources and Human Adequacy*. Chapel Hill: University of North Carolina Press, 1935.
Vernon, Zackary. "A Yearning for the Mud: Metafiction, Metafilm, and Bioregionalism in Robert Penn Warren's *Flood*." *Mississippi Quarterly* 76, no. 4 (2024): 360–86, Project Muse.
"Walter Simonson on the Time Variance Authority." The Comics Cube. June 8, 2021. YouTube video, https://youtu.be/DURfbGa6GHo.
Warren, Robert Penn. *Flood: A Romance of Our Time*. Baton Rouge: Louisiana State University Press, 2003. First published 1964 by Random House (New York).
Warren, Robert Penn. "An Interview in New Haven with Robert Penn Warren." In *Critical Essays on Robert Penn Warren*, edited by William Bedford Clark, 81–107. Boston: G. K. Hall, 1981.
Warren, Robert Penn. Robert Penn Warren to Louis Rubin Jr., July 6, 1963. In *Selected Letters of Robert Penn Warren*, Vol. 4, *New Beginnings and New Directions*, edited by Randy Hendricks and James A. Perkins, 378–79. Baton Rouge: Louisiana State University Press, 2008.
Welty, Eudora. "Place in Fiction." In *Eudora Welty: Stories, Essays, and Memoir*. New York: Library of America, 1998. 781–96.
West, Carroll Van. *Tennessee's New Deal Landscape: A Guidebook*. Knoxville: University of Tennessee Press, 2001.
Wheeler, William Bruce, and Michael J. McDonald. *TVA and the Tellico Dam, 1936–1979: A Bureaucratic Crisis in Post-Industrial America*. Knoxville: University of Tennessee Press, 1986.
Whisnant, David E. *Modernizing the Mountaineer: People, Power, and Planning in Appalachia*. Boone, NC: Appalachian Consortium Press, 1980.
White, William L. "Pare Lorentz." *Scribner's*, January 1939.
Wiggins, Marianne. *Evidence of Things Unseen: A Novel*. New York: Simon & Schuster, 2004.
"Wilson." TVA: Tennessee Valley Authority. Accessed May 16, 2023. https://www.tva.gov/Energy/Our-Power-System/Hydroelectric/Wilson-Reservoir.
Wilson, Edmund. "The Literary Class War: I." *New Republic*, May 4, 1932.
Wilson, Edmund. "The Literary Class War: II." *New Republic*, May 11, 1932.
Wray, Matt. *Not Quite White: White Trash and the Boundaries of Whiteness*. Durham, NC: Duke University Press, 2006.
Yaeger, Patricia. "Editor's Column: Literature in the Ages of Wood, Tallow, Coal, Whale Oil, Gasoline, and Other Energy Sources." *PMLA* 126, no. 2 (March 2011): 305–26. JSTOR.
Yaeger, Patricia. "Introduction: Dreaming of Infrastructure." *PMLA* 122, no. 1 (2007): 9–26, JSTOR.
Young, Stephen Flinn. "Post-southernism: The Southern Sensibility in Postmodern Sculpture." *Southern Quarterly* 27, no. 1 (1989): 41–60. Humanities International Complete.

INDEX

Page numbers in *italics* indicate illustrations.

About Time (Currie), 168, 206n32
Abstract Expressionism, 51
Adorno, Theodor, 37–38
African Americans. *See* Black Americans
Agamben, Giorgio, 74
Agee, James, 19–20, 41
Agricultural Adjustment Act (AAA), 92
agriculture: agrarian ideals, 20, 45, 162; demonstration farms, 85–86; monoculture crop production, 43, 70; sharecropping, 131, 141–42; test demonstration farmers, 84–85. *See also* Southern Agrarians
Agro Pontino project, Italy, 105, 198n43
"American Folk Art" (MoMA exhibition), 53
American Graffiti (film), 123
Americanization of Dixie, The (Egerton), 22
American Progress (Gast), 71–72
American Scene film series, 58, 80
Anderson, Benedict, 9, 198n46
Angelus Novus (Klee), 72
animal magnetism, 103
Appel, Hannah, 60–61, 78
architecture: of dams, 38–40; design elements, 5, 39, 43–44; functionalism, 34, 37–38; Greco-Roman design, 28–29; harmony in design, 37, 44, 47–48; modernism, 29–30, 33–34; monumentalism, 29, 31; neoclassical design, 28–29; and power, symbolism of, 39–41; "stripped classicism," 28–29, 30, 33, 37
Arendt, Hannah, 74
Arent, Arthur, 80, 89, 93, 94, 101, 105, 106
Arts Biennale (1932), 62
Atkinson, Brooks, 96–97
Atlantic Monthly, Caudill article, 21–22
atomic bomb, 8
Attack on Leviathan, The (Davidson), 20, 189n60
Awiakta, Marilou, 146–49

"back to the land" ideals, 109
Baker, Houston, Jr., 9
Barkley Dam, 162
Barr, Mark, 151
Barry, John M., 72–73, 195n41
Battle of Shiloh, 155–56
Baudrillard, Jean, 54
Bauhaus School, 30
Beal, Sophia, 11
Beckert, Sven, 67–68
Benjamin, Walter, 41–42, 44, 48, 72
Benton, Thomas Hart, 52
Berman, Marshall, 126, 127, 136–37, 139–40, 143, 144

Bess, Big Jeff, 130
Best Years of Our Lives, The (film), 81
Birdwell, Robert, 51–52, 54
Black Americans: agricultural laborers, 125, 129; exodus of during Great Flood, 131–32; flood relief in Mississippi Delta, 73–74, 195n42; labor in South, 129; and segregation, 140–41
blackouts, electrical (2022), 181
Blaine, Richard, 123
body, human, and infrastructure, 62–63, 158
Böger, Astrid, 71
Bone, Martyn, 10, 153
Bonnemaison, Sarah, 30
Boone Dam, 52
Boulder Canyon Project, 25
Bourke-White, Margaret, 36–37, 41, 130, 196n62
Brady, Mathew, 70
Branscome, James, 22
Brecht, Bertolt, 94
Brinson, Susan L., 121
Brooks, Peter, 167
Browder, Laura, 90
Browns Ferry nuclear facility, 52
Buell, Frederick, 14
Buried Land, A (Jones), 150, 151, 166
Button, Gregory, 116

Cahill, Holger, 53
Caldwell, Erskine, 41, 123, 130, 196n62
capitalism: and economic crisis, 115–16; free-market economy, 60; and materialism, 65, 72; and public works, 12; and regulation, 91, 112
Capra, Frank, 29
carbon emissions, 119, 181–82
Caudill, Harry M., 21–22
Chalmers, Thomas Hardie, 64, 66–67, 70, 77
Chandler, William U., 16, 31, 187n37
Chaplin, Charlie, 37
Chase, Donald, 122, 201n12
Chase, Stuart, 38, 39–40, 110, 119
Cherokee Dam, 34
Cherokee Nation, 146–49

Chickamauga Dam, 31, 34, 44
City Light (Columbia River Valley), 97–98
Civilian Conservation Corps (CCC), 54, 55, 73, 76
civil rights movement, 125
Civil War, Spanish, 155, 164
Civil War, US, 68, 70, 164–65, 194n32
Clark, Henry, 83–86
Clarke, Richard, 51
classical design, 28–29
Clift, Montgomery, 121, 132
climate change, 8, 181, 182–83
coal-fired power, 8, 142; alternatives to/shift away from, 181–82; pollution, 199n65, 200n69; transition to, 6, 14, 91, 119–20. *See also* energy industry
Cole, Norma, 151
Columbia River Valley, 97–98
Communist Party USA, 93–94
Confederate States of America, 68–69
Congress of Industrial Organizations (CIO), 92
conservation movements: energy, 111; and natural wonders, 31; soil, 14, 52, 76–77
consumerism, 106, 107–8
"Contemporary Unknown American Painters" (MoMA exhibition), 53
Coolidge, Calvin, 25
Copland, Aaron, 80
cotton production, 67–68; portrayed in *The River*, 74–75; westward expansion of, 71–72
COVID-19 pandemic, 179
Currie, Mark, 168, 206n32

Dadaism, 48
dams: architecture, 39–40; balance and control, 44; construction of, 25–26; environmental/geologic impact, 12–13, 184; functionalism vs. decoration, 33–34, 190n27; megadams, 25–26; symbolism of, 13–14, 25–26, 76, 86–87
Davidson, Donald, 20–21, 36, 47, 54–56, 108–9, 156–57, 189n60
Davis, Elmer, 80

Daws, Laura Beth, 121
Deal, Borden, 121, 132, 151, 163, 180, 201n8
decarbonization, 181–82
deforestation, 4, 43, 71–72, 75–76
Denning, Michael, 60, 86, 96
Denton, Martin, 115
De Valck, Marijke, 62
Diamanti, Jeff, 12
Dies, Martin, 95, 197n19
displacement, sense of, 153, 154, 171–72. *See also* relocation, forced
Dixie Flyer, The (newspaper), 147
Dneprostroi Dam, 26
Dnieper River Valley, Ukraine, 26, 63–64; Dnieper Dam, 63
documentary film, 57–87; hybrid journalistic forms, 63; montage technique, 65; New Deal aesthetic influence, 57–58; poetic technique, 66–67; *The River*, techniques used, 59–61; *Wild River*, techniques used, 123–25
Dombrowski, Jim, 123
Duarte-Gray, Isabel, 144
Duck, Leigh Anne, 9–10, 70, 128
Duffus, R. L., 42–45, 48
Dunbar's Cove (Deal), 121, 127, 132, 133, 135, 136, 151, 163–64, 172–73, 175, 201n8
Dunne, Philip, 80
Dust Bowl, 59, 60

Edison, Thomas, 24–25, 102
Egerton, John, 22
Eisen, Kurt, 89, 99
Eisenhower, Dwight D., 120
Eisenstein, Sergei, 65, 94
electric power: commodity vs. entitlement, 115; "electrical sublime," 102; *The Eleventh Year*, 63–64, 77, 133; grid, symbolism of, 91, 111, 157; *Power*, 88–95; supply and demand, 91, 99–100, 104, 106; transformative power of, 100–102
electrification: impact of, 117–18; legal frameworks, 99–100; rural, 24, 88; symbolism of, 102–3
Elia Kazan: A Life (Kazan), 121–22

eminent domain, 121, 137, 146–48, 152, 162
Emory River, 116
Endangered Species Act, 146
energy: conservation, 111; "dirty energy," reliance on, 15; fossil-fuel dependency, 8; green, 182–83; hydroelectric power, 4, 14, 16, 48, 78, 117–18; nuclear power, 8, 52, 120; power, symbolism of, 39–41; and profit motive, 43, 106, 111; rates, fair and affordable, 15–16; renewable, 8, 181, 182; service denial and price manipulation, 111–12. *See also* coal-fired power
environmental damage, 123–24
Environmental Protection Agency (EPA), 22, 200n69
erosion, 4, 43–44, 58, 74–75, 82, 83
"eternal present" (Giedion), 30
Ethiopia (drama), 93, 106
"Ethnography of Infrastructure, The" (Star), 11
Evans, Walker, 41
Evidence of Things Unseen (Wiggins), 151
Ewing, Charles Kermit "Buck," 51
exceptionalism, American/southern, 7

Farm Security Administration (FSA), 57–58, 77, 202n20
Faust (Goethe), 126
Faustian model of development, 125–36
Federal-Aid Highway Act (1925), 176
Federal Art Project (FAP), 51, 53, 88
federal corporation, TVA status 12, 15–16, 182
Federal Music Project (FMP), 88
Federal Project One, 114
Federal Theatre Project (FTP), 88–89, 92–97, 114
Federal Writers' Project (FWP), 88
financial crisis (2008), 115–16
Flanagan, Hallie, 88–89, 92, 93, 94, 95, 97, 114, 197n19
Flippen, Jay C., 129
Flood: A Romance of Our Time (Warren), 150, 155–66

flooding, 4, 58; Eastern Kentucky, 22; Great Flood (1927), 59, 72, 73–74, 131–32, 195n41; perspectives in *Long Man* (Greene), 178; in *The River*, 72–78
folk art, 52, 53
Ford, Henry, 16, 24–25
Ford, John, 60, 85
Foresta, Ronald A., 162
Fort Loudon Dam, 34
Fort Patrick Henry Dam, 52
Fort Peck Dam, 36
Frontier Films, 121, 123, 145
functionalism, 33–34, 37–38
"Functionalism Today" (Adorno), 37–38

Gast, John, 71–72
Giedion, Sigfried, 30
Goethe, Johann Wolfgang von, 126
Gold, Michael, 96
Goldman, Arnold, 94
Grant, Nancy L., 141
Grant, Ulysses S., 156
Grapes of Wrath, The (film), 60, 85
Grapes of Wrath, The (Steinbeck), 60
Great Leviathan, The (Davidson), 36–37
Great Recession (2008), 115–16
Great Smoky Mountains National Park, 45
Greene, Amy, 150, 166–78
Green New Deal, 8
Greeson, Jennifer Rae, 158
Gropius, Walter, 30
Guntersville Dam, 34

Hammid, Alexander, 58, 78–80, 84, 195n50
Harborth, Mark, 114
Hargrove, Erwin C., 16–17, 21, 188n40
Heimatstil (native style), 109
Heumann, Joseph K., 127, 134
Hicks, Jeremy, 63, 64, 77
Higgins, Horace, 83–86
Higgins, Joanne, 51
Highlander Folk School, 123, 124, 202n19
Historical Preservation Act, 147
Hitler, Adolf, 26, 29

Hiwassee Dam, 31, 34; Krutch's photography, 38, *39*
Hoffman, Frederick J., 153
Homo Sacer (Agamben), 74
Hoover, Herbert, 3, 25
Hoover Dam, 25–26
Hopkins, Harry, 97
Horton, Myles, 123
House Un-American Activities Committee (HUAC), 81, 95, 114, 197n19
Huie, William Bradford, 121, 151, 201n6
Human Geography in the South (Vance), 17
Hurley, Jessica, 11–12
"Hydraulic Generator Scroll Casing, 1936" (Krutch), 36–37, *37*

I'll Take My Stand (Twelve Southerners), 20, 45, 162
"imagined community" (Anderson), 9, 198n46
Indian Removal, 106, 107, 148–49, 154, 172–73
Indigenous peoples, 106–7; Cherokee sacred sites, 146–48; removal of, 134–35; traces of, in southern culture, 154
individualism, 76–77, 85, 127; acquisitive vs. cooperative, 85–86
industrial disasters, 116–17
"infrastructural time," 60–61
infrastructure: definitions, 11, 186n11; global trends, 26; and human bodies, 62–63, 158; studies, 10–11; symbolic aspects, 12; visibility/invisibility, 11–12
Injunction Granted (drama), 92–93, 107
Insko, Jeffrey, 11–12
Inventing Southern Literature (Kreyling), 9

Jackson, Andrew, 106–7
Jameson, Fredric, 122–23, 142, 144
Janis, Sidney, 53
Jefferson, Thomas, 69
Jeffersonian ideals, 20, 83
Johnson, Caleb, 151
Johnson, Walter, 69
Jones, Madison, 150, 154

INDEX

Jones, Robert Earl, 132
Joyce, James, 66

Katznelson, Ira, 99
Kazan, Elia, 120, 121–22, 141–42, 144, 201n13. See also *Wild River* (film)
Kennedy, John F., 120, 201n13; Land Between the Lakes project, 162
Kentucky Dam, 34, 162
Kingston disaster, 116–18, 181, 199–200n13
Klee, Paul, 72
Knoxville Seven, 51
Kreyling, Michael, 9
Krutch, Charles, 35–36; Hiwassee Dam photography, 39; portrayals of people, 46–47; TVA photography, 36–37; *The Valley and Its People*, 41–48
Kunzig, Robert, 182

labor movement, 92, 107, 124
Land Between the Lakes project, 21, 162, 181
land seizure, 121, 146–48. See also relocation, forced
Lange, Dorothea, 35, 75
Larkin, Brian, 11, 49, 65
Laszlo, Frank, 199n56
Lawton, Anna, 65
Leaves of Grass (Whitman), 194n28
Le Corbusier, 109–10
Lee, Robert E., 68–69
Lehman Brothers, 115
Leopold, Aldo, 45
Lerner, Irving, 80
Let Us Now Praise Famous Men (Evans and Agee), 41
Levett, Karl, 115
Life magazine, 36
Lilienthal, David E., 18–19, 188n47; as Faustian developer, 126; meeting with Le Corbusier, 110; MoMA reception address (1939), 38, 41, 49; on sectionalism, 69; on transition to coal-fired power, 117–18; *TVA: Democracy on the March*, 33, 78–79, 117–18; at Wilson Dam, 27–29, 28, 168

"living newspapers," 89, 90–91, 92, 94–96, 105–6
Living Newspaper Unit, 92, 93, 96, 106, 107–8, 114
Loki (television series), 179–80
Long Man (Greene), 150, 166–78; documentary tropes in, 169–70; temporal frameworks, 167–68
Loos, Alfred, 34, 38
Lorentz, Pare, 58, 121, 123, 194n32; innovative techniques, 62–63; poetic technique, 66; on regionalism of TVA, 70; *The River* production, 59–61
Losey, Joseph, 92–93, 94, 96
Lost Cause, myth of, 7, 69, 165, 194n32
Louisiana Purchase, 67
Lucas, George, 123
Luce, Henry, 36

Machine in the Garden, The (Marx), 45
MacLeish, Archibald, 80
Macy, Christine, 30
Maddow, Ben, 201n6
malaria, 4
Manhattan Project, 8
Manifest Destiny, 19, 43, 71–72, 77, 82, 134–35
March, Fredric, 80, 82–83, 86
Marx, Leo, 45
"Masters of Popular Painting" (MoMA exhibition), 53
Mathews, Jane de Hart, 90, 93
McCall, Nellie, 148
McCarthy, Charles Joseph, 183
McCarthy, Cormac, 183–84
McCully, Patrick, 13, 184
McDonald, Michael J., 151–52
McElvaine, Robert S., 85
Mesmer, Franz Friedrich Anton, 103
Metropolitan Playhouse, New York City, 114–15, 199n59
Mexico: A Study of Two Americas (Chase), 110
Meyerhold, Vsevelo, 94
Mies van der Rohe, Ludwig, 30
Mighty Thor, The (comic), 180

Mississippi Valley: freedom and democracy in region, 68–69; Mississippi River tributaries, 58, 61
Modern Classicism (Stern), 29
modernist architecture, 29–30
modernization: accelerated pace of, 128–29, 139, 151–52; global initiatives, 25, 26, 61; push for, in rural US, 4, 9, 91, 120, 127
Modern Times (film), 37
montage cinematic technique, 29, 65, 68, 75, 82, 123–24
monumentality, 5, 31, 49–56, 75–76; Lilienthal photographed at Wilson Dam, 27–29, 28; and natural wonders, 31
Morgan, Arthur E., 18, 27, 53, 188n47
Morgan, Harcourt A., 18, 27, 83, 188n47
"mountaineer" figure, mythology of, 20
Mr. Smith Goes to Washington (film), 29
Mud on the Stars (Huie), 121, 128, 136, 151
Muldowny, John, 151–52
Mumford, Lewis, 40–41
murals, 27, 42, 51–54, 192n61
Murray, Robin L., 127, 134
Muscle Shoals, Alabama, 16, 24–25, 120, 146
Museum of Modern Art (MoMA): "American Folk Art" (1932 exhibition), 53; "Contemporary Unknown American Painters," 53; "Masters of Popular Painting," 53; "Photography: 1839–1937," 35–36; "T.V.A. Architecture and Design" exhibition (1941), 31–32, 33–35, 38–41, 49–51
Musher, Sharon Ann, 13
Mussolini, Benito, 26, 29
Mussolini, Vittorio, 62
Mussolini Cup, 62

nationalism, 29, 39, 78, 41, 48, 91
National Recovery Act (NRA), 124–25
Native South studies, 154
natural disasters, 60
nature: imitation of, 42; and invasiveness of technology, 45–46; majesty of, 44–45; temporal patterns, 64

Nazism, 62
neoclassical design, 28–29
Neve, Brian, 125
Newark, New Jersey, blackout (1936), 101
New Deal, 3–4, 38, 57–58, 60, 76–77, 130–31; economic strategies, 107; influence of regional scholarship, 17–18; liberalism, 4, 85, 86, 121, 122; and New Frontier, 120–21; regional planning, 32, 69, 74, 98–99; and southern modernism, 128
New Deal, The (Patel), 26–27
New Frontier, 120, 145
Newhall, Beaumont, 35, 191n31
New Objectivity (*Neue Sachlichkeit*), 47
New Photography movement, 47–48
Newspaper Guild of America, 88
New Theatre League, 90
Nichols, Philip, 51
Niebuhr, Reinhold, 123
Nixon, Rob, 25–26, 152
Norris, George, 15, 24, 83
Norris Dam, 30, 31, 34, 45, 49–50, 50, 76, 77–78, 132, 151–52, 199n56; Davidson's criticism of, 55; functionalism, 34; mural, 52, 53–54; presentation of, 54–56; Rice Grist Mill, 55; *TVA and the Dispossessed*, 151–52
Norris Village (planned community), 54–55
nostalgia: New Deal, 122, 124, 125, 131; films, 122–25, 202n17; white settler, 135, 152
Not Quite White (Wray), 129
novels. *See* fiction
nuclear power, 8, 52, 120
Nye, David E., 100, 102–3

Oak Ridge, Tennessee, 151, 187n28; Manhattan Project, 8
Odum, Howard W., 17, 69, 194n35
Office of Facts and Figures (OFF), 80
Office of War Information (OWI), 58, 79–80
Off Off Line (website), 115
Olympia (documentary film), 62
"Ornament and Crime" (Loos), 34

INDEX   227

Osborn, Paul, 121, 122, 201n6
Overton, Frank, 138

Paradise Fossil Plant, 181
Parrish, Susan Scott, 73–74
Patel, Kiran Klaus, 26–27
People of the Cumberland (film), 121, 123, 125, 144
photobook genre, 41–42, 57–58, 167, 191n47
photography: Bourke-White's photojournalism, 36–37; Charles Krutch and TVA, 35–37, 41–42, 44–48, 51; cult value vs. exhibition value, 44; influence on documentary film, 57; New Photography movement, 47–48
"Photography: 1839–1937" (MoMA exhibition), 35–36
Pickwick Dam, 34, 47
Pilot (documentary film), 62
pioneer, mythos of, 19, 20, 43, 81–82, 152, 164
Plow That Broke the Plains, The (documentary film), 59, 64
Pontine Marshes, Italy, 105, 198n43
Popular Front, 91, 96, 107, 121
populism, 106, 107–8, 112, 131
poverty: childhood, 82; poor whites, 129–30; portrayed in *The River*, 74–75; sharecropping, 131, 141–42
Power (drama), 88–95; casting, 196n4; electrical grid symbolism, 157; historical consciousness of, 106–7, 115; lighting as commentary, 101–2; loudspeaker as narrative device, 90, 101–2, 104–6, 108, 117; partnership with TVA, 96–100; populist consumerism, 107–9; revival of, twentieth century, 114–17; Ritz Theatre opening, 100–101, *101*; script/characters, *107*, 110–13; special effects and lighting, 103–4
Prisoners of Myth (Hargrove), 16–17
progress, myth of American, 63, 72
Promised Land myth, 81–82
propaganda: and art, merged with, 6; imagery used in, 57–58; and "living newspapers," 105–6; pro-TVA theater, 90, 95, 97–98, 103; short films, 80; Soviet, 46
public works, 5, 12; global initiatives, 25–26, 58–59, 61, 63, 82–83; meaning of, 12, 27, 34, 40, 49; regional rehabilitation, 7–8, 105, 126
Public Works Administration (PWA), 12
Puget Power, 97–98

Rabinowitz, Paula, 57, 61, 84
racism: Black workers, 46–47; segregation, 99
Randolph, Mattie, 132
Rankin, John E., 99, 117
"Rape of the Appalachians, The" (Caudill), 21–22
Ray, Nicholas, 92
regional frameworks: efficacy of, 8–9; region/nation model vs. global lens, 9–10
regionalism, 52; critical practice, 8–9; frameworks of, 17–18, 189n60; New Deal planning, 19, 98–99; organizing principle of TVA, 18–19, 70; sectionalism, contrasted with, 69, 99
relocation, forced, 121, 146–48, 152–53, 163–64. *See also* displacement, sense of
Remick, Lee, 129
Report on Economic Conditions of the South (National Emergency Council), 22
Resettlement Administration (RA), 59
Rhône River Valley, France, 26
Rice, Elmer, 92–93
Rice, James, 55
Rice, Rufus "Uncle Rufe," 55
Riefenstahl, Leni, 62–63
Ring, Natalie J., 70, 104
Rising, The (Cole), 151
Riskin, Robert, 80
Ritz Theatre, New York City, 90, 94, 100–101, *101*
River, The (documentary film), 58, 121, 123, 167; address, modes of, 66–67; capitalism and cotton production, 67–72; economic/environmental exploitation, 70–71; on flooding, 72–78; graphic

maps used in, 75–76; impact of, 78; as poetic cinema, 64–66; reception and influence, 62–67; visual perspectives, 167
Road, The (McCarthy), 183–84
Robbins, Bruce, 10–11
Roholl, Marja, 80–81
Rollins, Peter, 65
Roosevelt, Franklin Delano: inaugural address (1933), 3; Muscle Shoals visit (1933), 24–25; Museum of Modern Art radio address (1939), 32–33, 38; TVA, promotion of, 3–5, 16
Roosevelt Year, The (Lorentz), 59
Rose, Jacqueline, 157–58
Rubenstein, Michael, 10–11, 12
Rubin, Louis, Jr., 150
rural electrification movement. *See* electric power
rural/urban divide, 4, 91, 102–3, 110–11, 112–13

Saal, Ilka, 91, 107–8
Salmi, Albert, 138
Sandburg, Carl, 66
Sand County Almanac, A (Leopold), 45
Sayre, J. Willis, 98
scale: of dams as cultural representations, 13, 16, 26; portrayed in cinema, 63–64; shifts in, 76; in southern studies, 9–10; and symbolism, 29, 30–31, 40
Schivelbusch, Wolfgang, 105, 109–10, 198n43
science and technology, faith in, 14, 159
Scott, Ian, 80
sectionalism, 18–19, 69, 99, 157, 162, 164
segregation, 140–41
Seinknecht, Emil, 35
Selu: Seeking the Corn-Mother's Wisdom (Awiakta), 146–47, 148
Selznick, Philip, 17
sense of place, 9, 132, 153, 163, 205n22
Sequoyah Birthplace Museum, 149
Serra, Luciano, 62
settler colonialism, 19, 20, 43, 82, 135, 146, 148, 152, 173
Shahn, Ben, 35

Shapiro, Edward, 157
sharecropping, 131, 141–42
Shelley, Percy Bysshe, 21
Sherwood, Robert, 80
Silenced Rivers (McCully), 13, 184
Simonson, Walter "Walt," 180–81
Smith, Adam, 12
Smith, Jon, 9
Smith, Neil, 10
Smith, Todd, 53
snail darters, 146, 148
soil conservation, 14, 52, 76–77
soil erosion, 4, 43–44, 58, 74–75, 83
Soloski, Alex, 115
South: critical conceptions of, 8–10; monolithic model of, 9, 132, 204n11; perception of, as national problem, 70, 75, 104–5; "postsouthern" as concept, 205n22; regional frameworks, 17–18; romanticization of, 162; southern literary studies, 153; southern modernism, 128; tourism and leisure, 161–63; uneven development, 70
Southern Agrarians, 9, 20, 108–9, 128–29, 132, 154, 157, 199n52; *I'll Take My Stand*, 162
southern Democrats, 99
Southern Highland Craft Guild, 53
Southern Regions of the United States (Odum), 17
South: Modern Southern Literature in its Cultural Setting (Rubin and Jacobs), 153
Stalin, Joseph, 26, 63, 64
Stanislavski, Constantin, 94
Star, Susan Leigh, 11
Steinbeck, John, 60
Steiner, Ralph, 123
Stern, Robert A. M., 29–31
Stevens, Walter, 51
Stewart, Jimmy, 29
"stigmatypes," 129–30
strip-mining, 22
"stripped classicism," 28–29
Sublett, Carl, 51

symmetry, 39, 43–44; symbolism of, 5
Szeman, Imre, 15

Taylor, Melanie Benson, 154
"technological sublime," 133, 144, 155, 168, 176, 177; American, 102, 106
Tellico Dam Project, 21, 145–49, 162, 181
temporal patterns: deep time in nature, 64; developmental time, 60–61; frameworks in fiction, 167–68; geologic time, 5, 44, 116, 158, 167; "infrastructural time," 60–61
Tennessee, The (Davidson), 20–21
Tennessee Valley: cultural region, 6–7, 17–19, 188n41; natural beauty, 36; poverty, longstanding, 3–4; public works model of regional rehabilitation, 7–8; settlement patterns, 67–68; uneven development, 4, 27, 79, 91, 104–5, 111
Tennessee Valley Authority (TVA): blackouts (2022), 181; counternarratives to, 6; creation of, 3–4; cultural context, 5–7, 20, 185n2; environmental impact, 12–13; establishment of, 3–5; global influence of, 7–8, 10, 58–59, 78–79, 87; historical context, 7–8; ideology and myth, 17–18; imagery and symbolism, 27; modernist style, 30–31; modernity, message of, 19; MoMA collaboration, 31–35; monumentality and symbolism, 5; and national recovery, 26–27; opposition to, Congressional, 15–16; opposition to, regional, 20–21; phases of, 17; promotion of, 15–16; public awareness, lack of, 181; regional goals, 4–5; regional planning, 98–99; relocation programs, 10; transition (1960s), 120; yardstick metaphor for, 15, 19, 87, 112–13
theater, pro-TVA, 88–100
Thomas, Jean, 113
Thomson, Virgil, 80
Thoreau, Henry David, 45
Timberlake (planned community), 145–46
Timberlake, Henry, 145–46
time. *See* temporal patterns

Time Variance Authority (*Loki*), 179–80
Tobacco Road (Caldwell), 130
tourism and leisure, 161–63
Treeborne (Johnson), 151
Triple-A Plowed Under (drama), 92
Truscello, Michael, 135, 163, 166, 172–73
Turner, Frederick Jackson, 68
TVA (documentary film), 33
TVA and the Dispossessed (McDonald and Muldowny), 151
"TVA Architecture and Design" (MoMA exhibition), 31–32, 33–35
TVA: Democracy on the March (Lilienthal), 18–19, 21, 33, 78–79, 117–18
"TVA Song, The," 113, 199n56
Twelve Southerners, 20–21, 45

"unimagined communities," 152–53
United States Information Service (USIS), 33
US Supreme Court, 117, 196n3; *Ashwander v. TVA*, 196n3

Valley and Its People: A Portrait of TVA, The, 41–48, 167
Valley of the Tennessee, The (documentary film), 58, 78–87; individualism as theme, 85–86; production history, 79–80
Vance, Rupert B., 17, 18
Van Fleet, Jo, 121, 130, 134
Van West, Carroll, 54
Venice Film Festival, 62
Vertov, Dziga, 63, 64–65, 77, 133
visibility/invisibility of infrastructure, 11–12
visual arts, TVA represented in, 24–56; imagery and symbolism, 27; Krutch photography, 35–37; monumentality portrayed in, 27–31, 49–56; murals, 51–54, 192n61; photobooks, 41–48. *See also* Museum of Modern Art (MoMA)
von Sternberg, Josef, 80

Wagner, Aubrey "Red," 145–46
Walden (Thoreau), 45

Wallace, Henry, 59
Wank, Ronald, 30, 34, 50, 190n27
Warden, John, 84
Warren, Brett, 89
Warren, Robert Penn, 150, 154–56, 162. See also *Flood: A Romance of Our Time* (Warren)
Watershed (Barr), 151
Watson, Morris, 93
Watts Barr Dam/facility, 34, 52, 145
Wealth of Nations, The (Smith), 12
Welty, Eudora, 153, 204n11
Werkbund, 30; conference (1965), 37–38
West, Don, 123
Wheeler Dam, 31, 34
Whisnant, David E., 20
Whitman, Walt, 66, 194n28
Wiggins, Marianne, 151
Wild River (film), 120–45, *143*, 158, 162, 164, 201n6; development models, 125–45; documentary techniques, 124–25; Faustian model and modernization, 139–45; Faustian model and romance in script, 136–39; Faustian model of development, 125–36; Indigeneity, erasure of, 135; nostalgia, 122–25; production history, 125; reception of, 201n12; screenplay and source material, 121–22; stance toward TVA, 122, 201n12
Wilkie, Wendell, 16
Williams, Guy, 97–98
Wilson, Edmund, 96
Wilson Dam, Alabama, 16, 25; neoclassical design, 28–29; Lilienthal's visit, 27–29, *28*
Workers' Theatre Movement, 94, 107
Works Progress Administration (WPA), 73, 88, 97, 114, 115
Wray, Matt, 129
Wright, Frank Lloyd, 40
Wyler, William, 81

Yaeger, Patricia, 10, 14–15, 142, 184
"yardstick" metaphor, 15, 19, 87, 112–13
You Have Seen Their Faces (Caldwell and Bourke-White), 41, 130

ABOUT THE AUTHOR

Photo by Jonah Holland, Office of Public Affairs, Mississippi State University

TED ATKINSON IS A PROFESSOR OF ENGLISH AT MISSISSIPPI STATE UNIVERSITY AND editor of *Mississippi Quarterly: The Journal of Southern Cultures*. Atkinson's areas of research and teaching interest include US southern studies, modern and contemporary US literature and culture, William Faulkner, and film studies. Atkinson's first book was *Faulkner and the Great Depression: Aesthetics, Ideology, and Cultural Politics*, published by the University of Georgia Press in 2006. He has published articles in *American Studies*, *Southern Quarterly*, *Journal of American Studies*, *Mississippi Quarterly* (before becoming editor), and *The Faulkner Journal* among others. Atkinson has contributed to several edited volumes, including *Reassessing the 1930s South*, *Keywords for Southern Studies*, *A Literary History of Mississippi*, *Queering the South on Screen*, and *The Routledge Companion to the Literature of the U.S. South*. Atkinson has several essays on Faulkner in edited volumes in the Faulkner and Yoknapatawpha series published by the University Press of Mississippi. Atkinson earned a bachelor's degree from the University of Mississippi, where he first developed an interest in southern studies; an MA in English from Mississippi College; and a PhD in English from Louisiana State University.

www.ingramcontent.com/pod-product-compliance
Lightning Source LLC
Chambersburg PA
CBHW022010220426
43663CB00007B/1035